MUSIC & MEANING

Music & Meaning

EDITED BY

JENEFER ROBINSON

CORNELL UNIVERSITY PRESS

ITHACA AND LONDON

Published with the help of the
Charles Phelps Taft Memorial Fund,
and the McMicken College of Arts and Sciences,
University of Cincinnati

The passage from "Peter Quince at the Clavier," in *Collected Poems* by
Wallace Stevens, is reprinted by permission of Alfred A. Knopf, Inc.
Copyright 1923 and renewed 1951 by Wallace Stevens.

The lines in the dedication are from Charles Kingsley, "A Farewell."

First published 1997 by Cornell University Press
First printing, Cornell Paperbacks, 1997

Printed in the United States of America

Cornell University Press strives to utilize environmentally responsible suppliers and
materials to the fullest extent possible in the publishing of its books. Such materials
include vegetable-based, low-VOC inks and acid-free papers that are also either
recycled, totally chlorine-free, or partly composed of nonwood fibers.

Library of Congress Cataloging-in-Publication Data

Music and meaning/edited by Jenefer Robinson.
p. cm.
Includes index.
Contents: Language and the interpretation of music/Leo Treitler—Listening with
imagination/Kendall Walton—Musical idiosyncrasy and perspectival listening/Kathleen Marie
Higgins—Music as drama/Fred Everett Maus—Mahler's Ninth symphony, second
movement/Anthony Newcomb—Shostakovich's Tenth symphony/Gregory Karl and Jenefer Robinson—Schubert's last sonata/Charles Fisk—Two types of metaphoric transference/Marion A. Guck —
Music and negative emotion/Jerrold Levinson—Why listen to sad music/Stephen Davies.
ISBN 0-8014-3299-5 (cloth: alk. paper)   ISBN 0-8014-8367-0 (pbk: alk. paper)
1. Music—Philosophy and aesthetics.   2. Symbolism in music.   3. Music and language.
4. Music and literature.   5. Music, Influence of.   6. Music—Psychology.   I. Robinson, Jenefer.
ML3845.M972   1997
781.197—DC21

96-50450

Cloth printing   10 9 8 7 6 5 4 3 2 1
Paperback printing   10 9 8 7 6 5 4 3 2 1

IN MEMORY OF MY MOTHER

WINIFRED CLARA ROBINSON

AND MY AUNT

EDITH ALICE DUTHIE

And so make life, death, and that vast for-ever
One grand, sweet song!

Contents

III
EXPERIENCING MUSIC EMOTIONALLY

Contributors

STEPHEN DAVIES is Associate Professor of Philosophy at the University of Auckland.

CHARLES FISK is Phyllis Henderson Carey Associate Professor of Music at Wellesley College.

MARION A. GUCK is Professor of Music Theory at the University of Michigan.

KATHLEEN MARIE HIGGINS is Professor of Philosophy at the University of Texas at Austin.

GREGORY KARL received his doctorate in musicology from the University of Cincinnati in 1993.

JERROLD LEVINSON is Professor of Philosophy at the University of Maryland.

FRED EVERETT MAUS is Associate Professor of Music at the University of Virginia.

ANTHONY NEWCOMB is Professor of Music and Dean of Humanities at the University of California at Berkeley.

JENEFER ROBINSON is Professor of Philosophy at the University of Cincinnati.

LEO TREITLER is Distinguished Professor of Music at the Graduate Center of the City University of New York.

KENDALL WALTON is James B. and Grace J. Nelson Professor of Philosophy at the University of Michigan.

Preface

Some years ago, while teaching aesthetics to a group of graduate
students in musicology, I began to realize that musicians and philosophers of music were asking similar questions about what and how music
means—and what is more, they were finding similar answers to these
questions. By and large, however, the two groups were working without knowing much about each other's endeavors. This realization led
me to collaborate on two papers with the musicologist Gregory Karl and
to organize a conference, "Music and Meaning," at the University of
Cincinnati, involving music theorists, musicologists, and philosophers of
music.

This book contains essays on musical meaning and expression by
musical scholars from philosophy, music theory, and musicology. It represents the culmination of these various interdisciplinary efforts. Some of
the articles were specially written for the Cincinnati conference and are
published here for the first time. Others have already become central to
the field. Altogether, they represent some of the best scholarly work being
done today on musical meaning and expression.

It has been a privilege to work with so many eminent thinkers, and I
thank them all for their contributions to this volume. I also thank the
Charles Phelps Taft Fund, the Department of Philosophy, and the
College–Conservatory of Music at the University of Cincinnati for support
of the 1993 conference, which provided the seeds for this book. I am very
grateful to Philip Alperson, Gregory Karl, John Martin, and Edward

Nowacki for their help in the preparation of the book. Finally, I also owe a debt of gratitude to Roger Haydon at Cornell University Press.

Some of the essays in this volume have already appeared elsewhere, and permission to reprint is gratefully acknowledged.

"Language and the Interpretation of Music," by Leo Treitler, is an expanded version of "What Obstacles Must Be Overcome, Just in Case We Wish to Speak of Meaning in the Musical Arts?" in *Meaning in the Visual Arts: Views from the Outside. A Centennial Commemoration of Erwin Panofsky (1892–1968)*, ed. Irving Lavin (Princeton: Princeton University Press, 1995), pp. 285–303. Copyright © 1995, by the Institute for Advanced Study.

"Listening with Imagination: Is Music Representational?" by Kendall Walton, is reprinted from *Journal of Aesthetics and Art Criticism* 52 (1994): 47–61.

"Music as Drama," by Fred Everett Maus, is reprinted with minor editorial changes from *Music Theory Spectrum* 10 (1988): 56–73. Copyright © 1988, by *Music Theory Spectrum*. Reprinted with permission.

"Shostakovich's Tenth Symphony and the Musical Expression of Cognitively Complex Emotions," by Gregory Karl and Jenefer Robinson, is reprinted from *Journal of Aesthetics and Art Criticism* 53 (1995): 401–15.

"Two Types of Metaphoric Transference," by Marion Guck, is reprinted with minor editorial changes from *Metaphor: A Musical Dimension*, Australian Studies in History, Philosophy, and Social Studies of Music, vol. 1, ed. Jamie C. Kassler (Paddington, N.S.W., Australia: Currency Press, 1991), pp. 1–12.

"Music and Negative Emotion," by Jerrold Levinson, is reprinted with minor editorial changes and additional footnotes from *Pacific Philosophical Quarterly* 63 (1982): 327–46.

"Why Listen to Sad Music if It Makes One Feel Sad?" by Stephen Davies, is adapted from *Musical Meaning and Expression* (Ithaca: Cornell University Press, 1994), pp. 307–19. Copyright © 1994 by Cornell University. Used by permission of the publisher, Cornell University Press.

This book is dedicated to the two women who first taught me to love and understand music.

JENEFER ROBINSON

Cincinnati, Ohio

MUSIC & MEANING

1

Introduction: New Ways of Thinking about Musical Meaning

JENEFER ROBINSON

Hanslick's Legacy

In 1854 Eduard Hanslick, who was later to become Professor of Music at the University of Vienna and the preeminent music theorist of the preeminent musical city in Europe, published a small volume called *Vom Musikalisch-Schönen (On the Musically Beautiful)*.[1] In that influential book Hanslick defended a formalist conception of instrumental music as "tönend bewegten Formen," tonally moving forms. "Pure" music—as opposed to song or opera—consists simply of structures of tones with no meaning or reference outside themselves. The beautiful in music consists in beautiful musical forms, especially melodies. We can *describe* music as fresh or graceful or melancholy, but this is to characterize qualities of the music itself, not to refer to anything fresh or graceful or melancholy in the world beyond the music, the so-called extramusical world. Hanslick's tract was directed particularly against the music of Richard Wagner, who in turn pilloried Hanslick as the foolish pedant, Beckmesser, in *Die Meistersinger*. In Wagnerian opera music and words are indissoluble; together they are capable of expressing the deepest thoughts and feelings of which human beings are capable; and it has even been argued that *Die Meistersinger* in particular celebrates the impor-

[1] Eduard Hanslick, *On the Musically Beautiful*, trans. Geoffrey Payzant (Indianapolis: Hackett, 1986).

tant role that music can play in promoting harmony in the larger *social world*.[2]

The battle between Hanslick and Wagner is justly famous, but it may stand as exemplary of two very different attitudes toward music that have vied for dominion in the history of Western music from Plato to the present day. Wagner is heir to the tradition of romantic composers and idealist philosophers that holds that music can be expressive of the profoundest human concerns. According to Hegel, Schopenhauer, and Nietzsche, music provides access to the nature of reality itself; romantic composers such as Berlioz and Schumann thought of themselves as expressing deep insight into human subjectivity. By contrast, Hanslick exemplifies an attitude toward music that stresses the musical work as an autonomous entity divorced from the extramusical world, a structure of forms that can be studied in an objective, quasi-scientific way.

In recent times, formalism has had distinctly the upper hand, alike in composition, music theory, and philosophy of music. In twentieth-century composition, the complex serialism of Schoenberg, Webern, and Boulez is based on rigidly rule-governed compositional methods, while Boulez and Babbitt have employed mathematical techniques in their precompositional planning. Music theory has been gobbled up by analysis, the systematic study of music's internal structural relationships, especially harmonic relationships. The dominant systems of analysis—such as Schenkerian theory, named for the influential theorist Heinrich Schenker,[3] and set theory—have emphasized structural hierarchies and mathematical models of various kinds. A recent example of such a system is Lehrdahl and Jackendoff's "generative theory" of tonal music, based on the hierarchies of generative grammar. In philosophy of music, too, under the influence of Hanslick, formalism has been very important. Hanslick's modern descendants include the philosophers Monroe Beardsley, Roger Scruton, and Malcolm Budd, as well as Peter Kivy, who has done perhaps more than anyone to formulate a contemporary philosophy of music. For Kivy music is a "decorative" art, valuable and significant for its intrinsic internal relationships rather than for any broader extramusical meaning it may have.[4]

Mathematical models are no longer so fashionable in composition, and analysis as it is practiced at present is also increasingly coming under fire.

---

[2] See Paul Robinson, *Opera and Ideas* (Ithaca: Cornell University Press, 1985), esp. p. 225.
[3] Schenkerian analysis is by no means a monolithic whole. I am thinking here preeminently of such analysts as Allen Forte.
[4] Kivy, however, does recognize the aesthetic importance of expressive qualities and indeed has written a book on the subject. See *Sound Sentiment* (Philadelphia: Temple University Press, 1989).

Over the past twenty years or so,[5] several important musicologists such as Leo Treitler, Anthony Newcomb, Joseph Kerman, and Edward T. Cone have become increasingly skeptical about the ability of analysis as currently practiced to explain all that is interesting about musical meaning. Without rejecting all forms of analysis, they have argued that music is not just structures of sound but can express feelings and thoughts that may be of profound human significance. They have also rejected timeless mathematical models of musical meaning in favor of closer attention to the historical context in which a piece is composed and listened to.

More recently the so-called New Musicologists, including Susan McClary and Lawrence Kramer, have stressed the important ideological messages that music can encode if it is approached as a cultural construct both reflecting and creating attitudes toward work, class, gender, sexuality, and other basic categories that organize our lives. McClary, for example, has given insightful feminist readings of music in which she lays bare the underlying assumptions about gender that are embodied in much tonal music. One example, from which McClary draws the title of her celebrated book, *Feminist Endings*, is the conventional description of decisive final cadences as masculine, and weak cadences as feminine.[6]

At the same time that these developments have been revolutionizing musicology and making some traditional music theorists feel embattled, among professional philosophers of art and aesthetics, formalism has also come under attack. Reacting against Kivy, Budd, and the Hanslick legacy, such philosophers as Kathleen Marie Higgins, Jerrold Levinson, and Kendall Walton have explored questions about musical meaning and expression, and have attempted to explain the value of music in terms of its connections with other aspects of human life.

This volume brings together well-known music theorists, musicologists, and philosophers of music who believe it is important to go beyond formalism and who seek to understand the meaning of music in broader terms. The two groups of scholars—music theorists and philosophers of music—typically publish in different academic journals, work in different departments of their institutions, and attend different national conferences, yet they are engaged in similar ways with similar problems. There are some differences in approach between the two groups: on the whole music theorists and musicologists tend to emphasize the interpretation of particular pieces of music, paying attention to issues of musical expression and significance as a way to understand those pieces, whereas

[5] I date the movement from the publication of Edward T. Cone's *The Composer's Voice* (Berkeley and Los Angeles: University of California Press, 1974).

[6] Susan McClary, *Feminine Endings* (Minneapolis: University of Minnesota Press, 1991).

philosophers of music tend to be more concerned with general questions about the nature of musical meaning and expression. Yet these differences are differences in emphasis only. Throughout this book we find the same themes and the same questions recurring in the essays, regardless of the various disciplines of their authors.

The Meanings of Music

The most fundamental questions broached in this book are: Can music, without the help of words (as in song, opera, or program music), signify aspects of human life and experience "beyond" the music? And if so, how? For pure formalists—whether music theorists or philosophers—the meaning of a piece of instrumental music is explained simply as its musical structure, and musical structure is defined solely in terms of theme, rhythm, and harmony. Anything that is not part of this purely musical structure is dismissed as extramusical association, irrelevant to understanding or appreciating music. Yet maybe these themes, rhythms, and harmonies and their interrelationships not only are interesting and beautiful in themselves, as the formalists insist, but also signify something other than themselves. If so, then the question is how.

Our paradigms for systems of meaning are languages, but without specially introduced conventions—such as stipulate the meaning of national anthems and leitmotifs—musical phrases and chords do not normally have conventional meanings as words and sentences in a language do. Pictures represent things and so can be said to signify them, but again, without special stipulations, such as is given by a title, music cannot normally represent particular people, scenes, and events as pictures do.[7] So how does music signify anything in the extramusical world?

The first three essays in this collection address these fundamental questions from three different perspectives. In "Language and the Interpretation of Music," Leo Treitler defends the view that music includes not just formal, syntactic qualities and relations, such as its tempo or its tonal plan, but also expressive qualities such as foreboding and melancholy. Treitler criticizes semiotic theories of musical meaning according to which such expressive qualities are somehow "outside" the music and "signified" by it. If music signifies, it does not do so in a transparent way, so that all our interest is directed to what is signified rather than to the signifier itself:

[7] For more on musical representation, see Peter Kivy, *Sound and Semblance*, 2d ed. (Ithaca: Cornell University Press, 1991), and Jenefer Robinson, "Representation in Music and Painting," in *What Is Music?* 2d ed., ed. Philip Alperson (University Park: Pennsylvania State University Press, 1994).

"the sign is not absorbed by the signifying process, it is not transparent to the signified." Rather, the qualities expressed or exemplified by music are *in* the music itself. For example, the slow movement of Beethoven's Piano Sonata Op. 10, no. 3, is marked *Largo e mesto* (Broad—slow and dignified—and mournful), and the mournfulness is just as much a part of the music as the tempo. The experience of the mournfulness is not mediated by thoughts of some *other* objects out in the world that are mournful.

Treitler then argues that expressive qualities such as foreboding or mournfulness belong to music quite literally rather than figuratively. He points out that many terms descriptive of music, such as "dark" register, "unstable" harmonies, and even "high" and "low" pitches, started out as metaphors but are now applied literally to music. To call a piece of music mournful or gloomy is no more metaphorical than saying that a piece of news is mournful or gloomy: the piece literally has a mournful or gloomy character. As Treitler puts it: "I experience the mournfulness and the gloom directly, as much so as the more literally possessed properties into which I can analyze them." The mournfulness is an *emergent* quality, dependent on constellations of details of the musical surface although not reducible to these details, and it belongs as literally to the music as the details out of which it is constructed. Treitler draws a parallel between saying that music has expressive qualities only metaphorically rather than literally and attributing expression to the extramusical rather than the purely musical domain. He claims that there is no clear boundary between the literal and the metaphorical and, similarly, no clear distinction between the purely musical and the extramusical. The distinction is "a creature of the project of redefining music undertaken around 1800 by those whose aim was to elevate the status of music that was independent of language, mimesis, and functions related to the institutions of church and state authority."

In claiming that music literally has expressive qualities, Treitler is not making a claim that all formalists would reject. Peter Kivy, for example, has been called an "enhanced formalist," because he recognizes the structural importance of expressive qualities in music in addition to more purely formal qualities. But toward the end of his essay, Treitler takes a step away from even enhanced formalism, when he defends what he calls the "narrative dimension" of music and says that music is sometimes "capable of metaphorlike effects." As an example he cites Franz Schubert's Trio in E♭ major, D. 929. The second movement begins with a funereal theme in C minor accompanied by a "trudging figure," which alternates with a "soaring" E♭-major theme that "seems as though it might be capable of lifting the movement out of the hopelessness of the C-minor music," although in the end it always "slumps back" into it: "The whole movement has the aspect of circular, obsessive thinking." The finale is a lengthy rondo, modulating through many different keys "in an endless patter of mindless energy." But toward the middle of the movement, the trudging figure returns in the violin and piano, while the cello plays the funereal theme very quietly. Treitler comments: "Suddenly it is as though this is what all that patter had been intended to suppress."

Among the many other themes that Treitler touches on in his essay is the question of whether the narrative dimension in music is better thought of as the narration of a story or as a drama. In a playful discussion of Bartok's *Mikrokosmos*, volume 6, no. 142, "Mese a Kis Legyroll," he points out that neither way of talking quite captures what this music is so elegantly able to accomplish.

In "Listening with Imagination: Is Music Representational?" Kendall Walton discusses ways in which the imagination functions in the understanding of musical meaning. The view that Walton defends in this essay is an extension and application of the general theory of representation in the arts, which he develops in his book *Mimesis as Make-Believe: On the Foundations of the Representational Arts*.[8] For Walton a representation is something whose function it is to be a prop in an imaginative game, or what he calls a game of make-believe. A prop is something that generates "fictional truths" in a game of make-believe—that is, it prescribes what is to be imagined in that game. When I read in a novel, "Once upon a time there was a young woman who was reading a letter," the novel is a prop in a game of make-believe: it generates the "fictional truth" that there was a young woman reading a letter, and this means that it prescribes that I imagine there was a young woman reading a letter. By contrast, Fragonard's painting *The Letter* is a prop in a game of *visual* make-believe: my looking at the picture makes it "fictionally true" that I am looking at a young woman reading a letter; that is, the picture prescribes that I imagine that in looking at the picture I am looking at a young woman reading a letter.

Walton wants to distinguish between the world of the work and the world of the game of make-believe that I play with a work when I look at a painting or read a novel. A representation generates a set of "fictional truths" that define a "fictional world." But if I am looking at Fragonard's painting, and imagining that in looking at it I am looking at a young woman, then in addition to the fictional truths generated by the representation there are also fictional truths generated by my contemplating

[8] Kendall Walton, *Mimesis as Make-Believe: On the Foundations of the Representational Arts* (Cambridge, Mass.: Harvard University Press, 1990).

the painting, for example, the fictional truth that I am looking at a young woman. This fictional truth is not part of the work-world, since I do not exist in the work-world; it is just part of the world of the game I am playing with the work.

One odd consequence of Walton's theory is that many paintings that most of us would want to call abstract turn out to be representational. That is because many abstract paintings require us to engage in much the same sort of imaginings that we do when faced with depictions. For example, any abstract painting that requires us to imagine we are seeing one color behind or in front of another is, on Walton's view, representational because it mandates this kind of imagining. Such paintings, which Walton calls representational but nonfigurative, therefore have a work-world just as much as Fragonard's straightforwardly figurative painting of a young woman.

In "Listening with Imagination," Walton discusses whether music can ever be said to be representational and, in particular, whether music ever has a work-world. He begins by pointing out that music certainly "induces imaginings," often about features of the music itself. Just as a nonfigurative painting may mandate that we imagine the blue oblong to be behind the yellow circle, so a piece of music may mandate that we imagine an intermittently sounding pedal tone to be sounding continuously. Walton also seems to accept a kind of human agency in music: the music prescribes that we imagine "exuberant or agitated or bold behavior." Similarly, although pure instrumental music does not prescribe that we imagine a particular person's acting in some way, it does seem to prescribe that we imagine instances of actions, of being late, of dallying, of moving on to something new, and so on. To this extent, then, music can perhaps have a work-world.

There are reasons, however, for denying that instrumental music usually has a work-world independent of the games people play with it. Walton sees the representational elements in music as fragmentary rather than uniting into a "world." Moreover, we do not have the same kind of "perceptual access" to musical fictional worlds as we do to the fictional worlds of pictures: we do not, fictionally, hear Christ's ascending into heaven in a piece of music, as we might, fictionally, see him ascending into heaven in a picture.

Walton suggests that very often music gets us to imagine that we ourselves are feeling something: the sounds induce us to "imagine introspecting or simply experiencing" exuberance, tension, determination, anguish, or wistfulness. When this happens, I am playing a game of make-believe with the musical work: it is "the listener's auditory experiences that, like feelings, cannot exist apart from being experienced, that make it fictional that there are feelings." But by the same token, there need be no work-world in the music: the music itself does not generate the fictional truth that I am feeling wistful; it merely supplies me with the personal auditory experiences that generate this fictional truth. It follows that in this respect music is not representational even in Walton's extended sense of this term. It is, however, expressive. Indeed, what Walton has articulated in this paper is essentially a new theory of musical expression.

Kathleen Marie Higgins addresses the question of musical meaning in a very different way. In "Musical Idiosyncrasy and Perspectival Listening," she attacks the Hanslickian idea that musical understanding is nothing but analysis, the quasi-scientific study of a structure or syntax timelessly embodied in a score. She argues that the Western tradition of art music as autonomous works to be studied in isolation from any particular listening experience and detached from any broader human significance endorses an impoverished concept of what music is. By contrast, in many other societies music is at the heart of life, playing important and diverse social and religious roles.[9] Whereas in our society music has lost its connections with everyday life, in more primitive societies music can help people map their place in time and space, aid in medicine, and advise them how to live their lives. Moreover, aspects of music in other cultures may be important in ways that are not conducive to study by Western analytic techniques, such as textual and timbral qualities. Higgins cites a number of examples from ethnomusicology, including "lift-up-over-sounding," a textural ideal in music from the Kaluli people of Papua, New Guinea.

What is more, even within the Western musical tradition some of the most rewarding and informed responses to particular pieces are idiosyncratic responses that are denigrated on the "scientific" model of analysis. Higgins argues that "musicians and other knowledgeable listeners form something like personal relationships with particular works of music," because such listeners are actively trying to relate the music to their broader experience, including their social experiences of music-making. Because people's experiences differ, what they hear in the music will be different, and how they relate it to broader life experiences will also be different. Higgins comments on differences that arise from different performance backgrounds, such as the difference between the often solitary music-making of the classical pianist with the experience of playing in a rock band. In general, she argues, idiosyncrasy in musical interpretation

[9] This is a theme Higgins pursues further in her book *The Music of Our Lives* (Philadelphia: Temple University Press, 1991). For the idea that the current dominance of the concept of a musical "work" is itself a historical phenomenon, see Lydia Goehr, *The Imaginary Museum of Musical Works* (Oxford: Oxford University Press, 1992).

is something to be celebrated rather than condemned. Furthermore, we should think of the score not as the work itself but rather as a useful tool to help us arrive at our individual interpretations of a piece.

Music as Story-Telling: The Literary Analogy

The essays in the second section of this book all explore the idea that music has a plot or narrative and that its meaning can be explained by analogy with the plot of a story or play. Each essay, while pursuing theoretical questions, also gives a detailed account of a particular piece, or part of a piece, of music to illustrate the theoretical claims being defended.

In his groundbreaking book *The Composer's Voice*, Edward T. Cone argues that Berlioz viewed his *Symphonie fantastique* as expressing the reactions of a persona to the sequence of events outlined in the program for the symphony. Like the narrator of a story, this persona expresses his reactions through the "characters" that appear in the symphony, in particular, the instruments or groups of instruments that are individualized as "agents." Cone generalizes this "lesson from Berlioz" to all instrumental music: "In every case there is a musical persona that is the experiencing subject of the entire composition, in whose thought the play, or narrative, or reverie takes place—whose inner life the music communicates by means of symbolic gesture."[10] An agent need not be an instrument or a group of instruments; it can be "any recognizably continuous or distinctively articulated component of the texture: a line, a succession of chords, an ostinato, a pervasive timbre."[11] An analysis of the formal development of motives, harmony, and rhythms will then necessarily be at one and the same time an account of the psychological development of the "characters" and the narrative "persona." Cone argues that "in music, as in any art, formal and expressive concepts are not separable but represent two ways of understanding the same phenomena."[12]

Anthony Newcomb took up Cone's idea in his 1984 essay "Sound and Feeling." Newcomb argued there that the only difference between expressive interpretation and formal analysis is that the former goes beyond the latter "in pointing out, through metaphor, relationships between the structures of the artwork and those of other aspects of experience."[13] In such essays as "Once More 'Between Absolute and Program Music': Schumann's Second Symphony" Newcomb has given insightful examples

[10] Edward T. Cone, *The Composer's Voice*, p. 94.
[11] Ibid., p. 95.
[12] Ibid., p. 112.
[13] Anthony Newcomb, "Sound and Feeling," *Critical Inquiry* 10 (1984): 637.

of the kind of criticism he advocates. In the Schumann article he also develops the useful idea of a "plot archetype": "The conception of music as composed novel, as a psychologically true course of ideas, was and is an important avenue to the understanding of much nineteenth-century music; . . . thus we may find at the basis of some symphonies an evolving pattern of mental states, much as the Russian formalists and the structuralists find one of several plot archetypes as the basis of novels and tales."[14]

Thus Schumann's Second Symphony has the same plot archetype as Beethoven's Fifth: "suffering leading to healing or redemption."[15] It is no accident that Cone and Newcomb are students of late eighteenth- and nineteenth-century music, for Beethoven, Berlioz, and Schumann are but three of the composers of that era who—sometimes, at least—thought of their instrumental music as in some sense telling a psychological story.

The idea of music having a plot is taken a step further in Fred Everett Maus's seminal article "Music as Drama," which opens the second section of this book.[16] For Maus music is a drama with interacting agents, and its structure is not just a structure of harmonies, rhythms, and themes but a dramatic structure whose unity is like the unity of a story. In Maus's striking phrase, "The structure of music is its plot."

Maus is interested in the relationship between traditional musical analysis and descriptions of music in more anthropomorphic, dramatic terms, as actions and reactions by musical agents. Even if music is no longer conceived as pure form, analysis still seems to be an important discipline; but what role can it play in a music criticism that conceives of musical structure as dramatic structure? Maus wants to combat the idea that theory and analysis constitute an autonomous discipline that studies musical structure in abstraction from its human significance or meaning. In his view, musical structure cannot be described exclusively in music-theoretic terms. He wants to get away from a picture in which musical structure is studied by analysis and is independent of wider questions of meaning and expression, which are then left to be dealt with by a "fuzzy" music criticism, existing alongside analysis but untouched by it. He also wants to broaden the notion of the "meanings" with which criticism deals; especially among philosophers of music, Maus finds too much emphasis on emotion or "affect," whereas in his view music has significance that includes but goes beyond the realm of feeling.

[14] Anthony Newcomb, "Once More 'Between Absolute and Program Music': Schumann's Second Symphony," *19th-Century Music* 7 (1984): 234.
[15] Ibid., p. 237.
[16] Fred Everett Maus, "Music as Drama," first published in *Music Theory Spectrum* 10 (1988). See also his "Music as Narrative," *Indiana Theory Review* 11 (1991).

Maus's strategy is to undertake an analysis of the first seventeen measures of Beethoven's Quartet Op. 95 and then examine the language and content of that analysis. What he finds is that he initially describes the piece as a succession of dramatic actions, "an abrupt, inconclusive outburst," a "second outburst in response," and then "a response to the first two reactions." The description of these actions is anthropomorphic: the first outburst is called "clumsy and incomplete," the second outburst "abrupt and coarse," and the final response "calmer and more careful." Even more important, these actions are explained in the same sort of way as human actions; the analysis cites "reasons consisting of psychological states, explaining the events of the piece just as actions are explained." For example, in calling the second outburst a "reasoned response," Maus attributes a motivation to the outburst: it "intends to respond" to the first outburst.

Maus points out that both the dramatic or anthropomorphic and the music-theoretical descriptions play vital roles in the analysis, and that the two kinds of description interact. The explanation for why the first outburst Maus identifies is characterized anthropomorphically as "clumsy" is given in music-theoretic terms: it is because of peculiarities in the relation between the pulse and the pitch structure. Frequently, music-theoretic descriptions describe the actions in the music in such a way as to explain their motivation, just as we explain human actions by reference to their motivations. For example, the second gesture Maus identifies is describable as a "response" to the first because it is an unsuccessful attempt to clarify the first gesture; it reworks the rhythm and pitch material to make it simpler and less ambiguous (although at the end of it there is still some harmonic unclarity). Maus comments: "Many features of the second outburst are explained by ascribing an intention to respond to the first outburst and beliefs about the precise points of unclarity in the opening gesture." For example, a belief about the vagueness and ambiguity of the opening harmony and a desire "to replace the sound of the opening with something clearer" together give the motivation for the second outburst.

One of Maus's important achievements is to come up with a new model for understanding the relation between traditional "analysis" and more humanistic modes of music criticism. In his view, the theoretical language describes the dramatic actions in such a way as to explain their character and the intention with which they are performed: in the Beethoven analysis the music-theoretic language brings out aspects of the piece "that are pertinent in describing and evaluating the events as actions."

To whom or what should we attribute these thoughts, actions, and motivations? Maus insists that musical agents are "indeterminate"; music is a kind of drama that lacks determinate characters. In "Action and Agency in Mahler's Ninth Symphony, Second Movement," Anthony Newcomb takes up this question: If music is or represents actions and events, who is acting? Newcomb explores this question by reference to the second movement of Mahler's Ninth Symphony,[17] the musical "plot archetype" of which he sees, in general terms, as a struggle between rustic innocence and urban glitter, in which rustic innocence is too weak, too ill-focused, too brutalized to resist the attraction of "entertainment, and the racy life." Newcomb stresses that the psychological meaning of a complex piece such as this derives not just from the expressive qualities of individual musical gestures or particular "slices" of music but, more important, from the "succession, interrelation, and transformation of these slices in the course of an entire piece." Moreover, Newcomb is careful to emphasize that not every element in a musical work is part of some agent or narrative element. As he puts it, "In music, as in the other arts, . . . aspects of agency are not continuously displayed, nor are aspects of narration. Both are only intermittently operative."

Newcomb agrees with Maus that musical agencies in instrumental music are generally indeterminate: we have to decide on a case-by-case basis how many agents there are and how they interact. Like Cone, Newcomb thinks that a musical agent can be identified as a striking or characterful musical idea of any sort. When a new motive or instrument or tempo or rhythm appears, how we interpret it will depend not only on its own character but on how it interacts with previously identified musical agents.

Newcomb illustrates the problem by reference to three dances that appear in the opening section of the second movement of Mahler's Ninth Symphony: first, a moderate-tempo ländler, Dance A; then a faster waltz, Dance B; and finally, a slow ländler, Dance C. Newcomb identifies Dance A as rustic, clumsy, coarse, ungainly, and lacking staying power: there is "an interruptive or petering-out impression in the phrases." Dance B is a waltz and evokes a very different, harmonically more sophisticated world from that of the rustic Dance A. It "rushes, so to speak, onto the stage" with great energy and eventually swallows up Dance A. Dance B is clearly a different force from Dance A, but is it a different character or merely a different force within a single protagonist? Dance A and Dance B do share certain attributes, suggesting they are one and the same agent, but they have very different characters, suggesting different agents or conflicting forces within a single agent.

[17] Newcomb has given a analysis of this movement in *Music and Text: Critical Inquiries*, ed. Anthony Scher (Cambridge: Cambridge University Press, 1992), pp. 118–36.

How agencies are individuated in a particular case depends on one's overall interpretation of the piece; and, of course, it is in the nature of the hermeneutic circle that the overall interpretation will in turn depend on how one construes agency. In his Mahler example, Newcomb argues that the "most fruitful" interpretation is that Mahler is depicting a conflict between two aspects of the same protagonist, the clumsy, rustic, innocent side and the side that yearns for glamour and sophistication. Significantly, this conflict also reflects a larger conflict between the innocent, rural world and the slick, sophisticated, urban world: indeed, Newcomb says the two interpretations can co-exist in the mind of the listener.

The entrance of Dance C brings a new stage in the unfolding psychological drama. This slow ländler has a relaxed, pastoral style; its theme refers back to a theme from the first movement, which there symbolized Arcadian innocence, and it also incorporates part of Dance A. Significantly, Dance B returns and sweeps away Dance C. As Newcomb tells the "story" of the movement to this point, there is a single chief protagonist in the music who is "psychologically highly complex and conflicted." Newcomb interprets this musical agency as experiencing nostalgia for an innocent rustic past but as incapable of resisting the temptation of the glittering, sophisticated urban world.

An important feature of Newcomb's interpretation is that it explains how in instrumental music without any accompanying explicit program or other verbal hints, musical agents can develop psychologically in very complex ways and can express complex inner states, especially emotional states. Thus Newcomb attributes to his chief protagonist the cognitively complex emotional state of nostalgia, on the basis of features of nostalgia that he detects within the music itself: for example, the motivic reference of Dance C to a past Arcadian innocence, represented by the same motive in the first movement; the yearning for this past innocent state, embodied in the "willful stopping of the runaway process of Dance B and the slow, effortful climb to Dance C"; and the "wistfulness" of the drooping lines of the whole section, together with "the relative lack of energy in the rhythmic activity, and, most strikingly, in its inability to reach closure."

The idea that complex emotional states can be conveyed by instrumental music without the help of words is taken up and developed in "Shostakovich's Tenth Symphony and the Musical Expression of Cognitively Complex Emotions," by Gregory Karl and Jenefer Robinson. This essay is the product of a collaboration between a philosopher concerned with general questions about the nature and capabilities of musical expression and a musicologist concerned with making dramatic sense out of a particular problematic piece of music. The theoretical point claimed is that, in direct contradiction to one of Hanslick's most fundamental points, "pure" instrumental music can express emotions with a complex cognitive content, and furthermore that it can do so by suggesting the cognitive content itself. The interpretative point is that a passage in the third movement of Shostakovich's Tenth Symphony expresses the cognitively complex psychological state of hopefulness. Like Newcomb, the authors stress the importance of the overall structure of the entire piece in their interpretation of one portion of it.

One of the main motivations for dramatic or narrative interpretations of music is that purely formal analyses often fail to account for striking passages in dramatic instrumental works, especially when these passages contain anomalous elements. Very often these elements are best explained by reference to a psychological "story" that the music tells, always assuming, of course, that such an interpretation is consistent with the composer's conception of the work. In Shostakovich's Tenth Symphony, the "aberrant" element is a horn call, appearing in the third movement out of nowhere and insisting on being heard, despite being unrelated to any earlier material and despite its apparent refusal to adapt to any of the surrounding music. The authors claim that interpreting the structure of the piece as an integrated formal-expressive structure rather than merely a formal structure helps to explain this seemingly anomalous element as part of an expression of hopefulness.

Like Cone and Newcomb, Karl and Robinson believe that "some music can be interpreted as an unfolding of the psychological experience of [a] musical persona over time," and in this particular case a specific passage is interpreted as an expression of the persona's hope for a brighter future, despite being confronted with menaces from the past. The authors outline the most important elements in the cognitive content of hopefulness, and they show how the music is able to convey these cognitive states by musical means. For example, part of the cognitive content of the persona's hopefulness is a wish for and attempt to bring about a future that is conceived of as pleasanter than the present grim state of affairs. This is conveyed musically by the steadfastness of the horn call in keeping to the same pitches regardless of what is going on in the accompaniment, by the way it insists on its own tonal center in the face of resistance until it is rewarded by the work's first unclouded passage, and finally by the way the contours of this passage are gradually and with great effort transformed into the principal theme of the finale, a maniacally cheerful theme in which the tension of the preceding movements finds a temporary release. The authors argue that their expressive interpretation is fully integrated with a "purely formal" analysis of the piece: the two cannot be prized apart.

In his moving essay "What Schubert's Last Sonata Might Hold," Charles Fisk offers a detailed interpretation of the first movement of the B♭-major Sonata, D. 960, that is at once technical analysis and expressive interpretation. Just as Robinson and Karl were led to explore the Shostakovich symphony as a psychological drama in order to explain the significance of the horn call, so Fisk is led on a voyage of discovery by his puzzlement about the trill on G♭ that comes at the end of the first phrase of the sonata.

Fisk begins his essay by giving a harmonic, rhythmic, and motivic analysis of the first movement and the role of the trill, but he goes on to claim that "in order to experience the music with any involvement, most listeners make use of their faculties for emotional engagement and for the configuration of actions in ways that cannot be separated from the supposedly pure perception of the parameters that musical analyses address." For Fisk the first movement of the Schubert sonata is the complex tale of an "outsider," identified harmonically with G♭, who wishes to sing in harmony with the main group, identified with the home key of B♭, but who is excluded from membership in it, although members of the group reach out to him from time to time. The outsider eventually finds a way to be integrated into the group, but only after periods of reflection on past experience, of pressing anxiously through unfamiliar territory, of searching for his way, and of a moment of epiphany or revelation. Fisk remarks that the idea of an outsider appears in several other Schubert works, and he speculates that Schubert might have identified "alienated aspects of himself" with these outsiders and perhaps "took solace, at least unconsciously, in their eventual musical integration."

Fisk's harmonic, rhythmic, and motivic analysis of the piece is designed to show that the "network of musical events to which the trill belongs . . . [culminates] in the famous D-minor passage at the end of the development" when the trill returns in a way that suggests integration with the home key. After a frenetic passage of continuous modulation, which Fisk characterizes as struggling through a "wilderness," the key of D minor arrives unexpectedly, and we experience it as "lost, cut off from any tonal mooring, neither close to home nor recognizably far from it." There are reminiscences here of motives, keys, and rhythms from the past. It is a time of stillness, of "hushed expectancy" that leads to the "revelatory" moment when the dominant of B♭ major takes the place of D minor, suggesting "a reversal of the tonally conferred roles of insider and outsider" and giving the outsider at long last some chance of access to the group.

Fisk acknowledges that in one sense the story he has told is "little more than a naively poetic description of what happens in the music" and in another it is "completely personal, a projection of states of mind from my own experience, albeit ones I believe I share with many others, into Schubert's music." Significantly, Fisk himself is not only a theorist but a performer, a professional pianist, and he is seeking an understanding of the piece not just as a listener but as a performer who needs to know how to play the trill and how to dramatize its relationship with the rest of the movement. Like Higgins, he thinks of his interpretation of the piece as a "reading," one that complies with the harmonic, rhythmic, and motivic details of the piece but that makes no claim to be the one and only correct account of the piece. It is only what Schubert's last sonata *might* hold.

In "Two Types of Metaphoric Transference," Marion A. Guck examines how metaphorical language functions in humanistic music criticism. Like Treitler, Guck is interested in the language we use to describe or interpret music and how the metaphors we apply to music reflect the layers of meaning that lie within the music itself. Like Treitler, she notes that much of even the technical vocabulary applied to music, such as "moving lines," or "rising and falling" melodies, is rooted in metaphors although it has now become, in her phrase, "music-literal."

In her study of Chopin's Prelude in B minor, Op. 28, no. 6, Guck notes that the metaphor of the "arch" plays a number of different roles. First, the shape of the melodic line can be characterized in terms of the arch metaphor: the musical phrases literally ascend and descend. Like Walton, Guck emphasizes that understanding the melodic line involves not only perception but imagination: "I imagine the Prelude as two-measure arching melodies nested within phrase-length arches in turn nested within a single-piece arch."

Second, the arching melodies can be heard in terms of tension and effort and decrease of tension and effort, as in the arching movement involved in throwing a ball. Now the arch metaphor is being applied to the (metaphorically) swelling and subsiding dynamic movement of the piece. Finally, we can also hear the arch movement as a movement in human psychological states, as "expressing rising moods in opposition to exhausted, falling moods." The increase and decrease in tension is now heard to be an increase and decrease in "emotional tension."

For Guck the arch shape unifies the piece both formally and dramatically: "The piece's arch is a narrative curve," by which she means "the presentation of a situation that, through some exploration, development, or complication, rises to a confrontation, culmination, or climax," which in turn "initiates the untangling, resolution, or simplification that leads to closure."

Guck believes there are two kinds of metaphor. Some are "comparative" metaphors in which directly perceivable features of one thing (such as an arch) are correlated with directly perceivable features of another (such as a rising and falling melodic line or a rising and falling movement, as in throwing a ball). More interesting, however, are "ascriptive" metaphors in which the analogies are less precise and more evocative, requiring "an imaginative leap to conjoin the image and the music," as in the arch as a metaphor of psychological states. Both kinds of metaphor, however, deepen our understanding of music by drawing attention to its humanly significant qualities.

Experiencing Music Emotionally

Hanslick thought the value of music resided unproblematically in its beautiful forms, its harmonies, rhythms, and especially its melodies; but, as we shall see throughout this book, there are other important aspects of music that Hanslick persistently undervalues. Despite Hanslick's strictures, it seems as if music can be expressive of other aspects of human life, especially human emotion and action. If music can tell psychological stories in the way described by Fisk, Karl and Robinson, and Newcomb, then it is reasonable to suppose that part of the value of music lies in these stories and how they are told. People may well respond emotionally to music in ways they find rewarding because they hear in the music stories that move them.

Many listeners have the experience of sharing the feelings that seem to be expressed by a piece of music: nostalgic music makes listeners feel nostalgic, cheerful music cheers them up, languorous music makes them feel languorous, and so on. In other words, the listener mirrors the feelings expressed by the music. We might think of Fisk, who reports that in listening to Schubert's last sonata he empathizes with the outsider whom he identifies with particular expressive elements in the music.[18] The problem is that if listeners mirror the negative emotions they hear in music, then we seem to be landed with a paradox; indeed it is one version of a very old paradox, known as the "paradox of tragedy," which can fairly be said to have originated with Aristotle. The paradox of tragedy is

---

[18] Not everyone agrees that this happens. Peter Kivy has argued forcefully that although we should recognize the emotions expressed by a piece of music (if any), we never actually feel those emotions. Sad music may delight me, move me, or bore me, depending on how good it is, but it will not actually sadden me unless I am saddened by some fault in the music or some failing by the composer. See Peter Kivy, *Music Alone* (Ithaca: Cornell University Press, 1990), esp. chap. 8, "How Music Moves."

that people apparently take great delight in watching and hearing about people in hideously unhappy situations and undergoing terrible suffering. Oedipus unwittingly kills his father and marries his mother, and when he discovers what he has done, he punishes himself by putting out his own eyes. Yet for centuries people have delighted in the tale of Oedipus. The musical version of the paradox is this: If people actually feel sad when they listen to sad music, why do they go on doing it? All they have to do is leave the room or flip the switch, and the music would vanish, along with the pain it causes. Yet people continue to listen, apparently complacently, to the most anguished and wrenching strains. This is the problem addressed by the last two essays in this collection. There must be some value to experiencing the sadness in sad music, or otherwise people would not do it; but what value can it have?

Jerrold Levinson aims to give a "comprehensive answer" to this question in his essay, "Music and Negative Emotion." He identifies eight separate "rewards" that accrue from listening to sad music and thereby coming to feel sad. First, he acknowledges Nelson Goodman's point that sometimes an emotional response may help us understand the qualities in the music that produce the response; and second, he agrees with Aristotle that sometimes an emotional response has a beneficial cathartic effect on the listener. Most of the rewards he identifies, however, depend on his detailed account of what goes on psychologically when we feel negative emotions in response to music—not just sadness but other, more complex emotions, such as tragic resolve, unrequited passion, and angry despair.

On Levinson's account, when we experience negative emotions in ordinary life, the emotion has a cognitive component—a "belief, attitude, desire, or evaluation, focused on and identifying the object of the emotion"—as well as an "affective" component, a state of "inner feeling" involving a phenomenological aspect (a "certain quality" of inner feeling) and a sensational aspect (the sensation of bodily changes). But when I feel sad as a result of listening to sad music, while I still experience the affective aspects of sadness, the cognitive aspect of the emotion is "etiolated" (and so, as a result, are its usual behavioral consequences). I am not sad about anything in particular, nor do I have any beliefs, desires, or attitudes about any particular object. Nevertheless, in order for my emotion to count as being sadness, there must be a cognitive component to my experience. Levinson suggests that when we focus intensively and sympathetically on a piece of music in a relatively familiar style and recognize the emotions expressed by the musical gestures, we may come to identify and empathize with the music or, better, "with the person whom we imagine owns the emotions or emotional gestures we hear in the music." As Fisk suggests, we "adopt these emotions as our own" and "end up feeling as, in imagination, the music does." When I feel sadness empathetically in response to sad music, I am thinking about the general idea of sadness, "imagining that the music is either itself a sad individual or else the 'audible expression' of somebody's sadness," and I am imagining that this sadness is my own. There is still a cognitive dimension to this emotion, but it has an indeterminate focus: I imagine that there is something I am sad about and that I believe some situation or other to be unfortunate, but there is nothing in *particular* I am sad about, nor is there any *particular* situation that I believe to be unfortunate. In summary, empathetic emotional responses to music typically comprise "physiological and affective components of the emotion that is embodied in the music, the idea or thought of this emotion, and the imagination, through identification with the music, of oneself as actually experiencing this emotion, though without the usual determinateness of focus." Like Walton, although in a slightly different way, Levinson thinks that our emotional experience of music is partly an imaginative experience.

According to Levinson, there are a number of rewards for listening to sad music in the empathetic way that he envisages. Because the feeling of sadness we experience when listening to sad music lacks a full-fledged cognitive component and is independent of one's actual life situation, we can savor and enjoy the feeling for itself; we can scrutinize it and come to understand it better; and we can exercise or "tone up" our feeling capacities in preparation for actual life situations. There are further rewards for imagining one is in a full-fledged emotional state of sadness, when one's sadness is really cognitively truncated: we may derive a sense of mastery and control over the emotions we empathetically feel, as they develop purposively through a lengthy piece or passage of music; we may enjoy the sense of our expressive power as we identify with powerfully expressive music; and sometimes when the feelings we experience are feelings actually experienced by the composer, we may enjoy a sense of emotional communion with the composer.

Stephen Davies agrees with Levinson that some listeners are moved by music "to feel emotions that mirror the expressive character of the music," but he is unimpressed with Levinson's eight reasons why we value the experience of sad music. As the paradox of negative emotional responses to music is generally conceived, he says, there are two horns to the dilemma.[19] Suppose that in listening to sad music I become sad. On the one hand, if I enjoy the sadness (as Levinson seems to suggest), it can't really be sadness, for sadness is by its very nature not enjoyable; but if,

---

[19] Stephen Davies's views on musical expression are found in *Musical Meaning and Expression* (Ithaca: Cornell University Press, 1994). His essay here is an adaptation of the concluding section of chap. 6 of that book.

on the other hand, sadness really is not enjoyable, then I ought not seek out works that make me feel sad. Davies explores various solutions, including Levinson's, which are based on blunting one horn or the other of this dilemma, but he concludes that this is not the right way to proceed. Instead, we should reject the question as it is commonly asked. The important and interesting question is not "Why listen to music that makes one sad?" but rather "Why listen to music?" There is no special problem associated with listening to sad music; given that listening to music is a worthwhile experience, we will naturally want to listen to the full range of music, including sad music.

In general, "much music presents a content such that the deeper one's understanding, the more enjoyable is the experience, and we value as great those works providing such enjoyment." Works dealing with negative emotions are just as much worth understanding as those dealing with positive emotions. Furthermore, our emotional response to a piece of music may be integral to our understanding of that piece. In that case feeling the sadness may be necessary to acquiring the understanding. If it is then objected that on this view understanding art sometimes requires suffering yet is supposed to be enjoyable, Davies replies that understanding is in itself enjoyable, regardless of whether a particular piece of knowledge makes us feel happy or sad. Listening to music is a cognitive activity, and if it involves some suffering, that is not unusual. Many activities that humans find generally rewarding have their unpleasant aspects: "At least some of the pleasure life can give comes from one's attempting with a degree of success to deal with one's situation and circumstances—controlling what can be controlled, accepting with grace and equanimity the unavoidable. If the appreciation of art is especially important in this process, it is . . . because it is a celebration of the ways people engage with each other and the world in giving significance to their existence."

I

THE MEANINGS OF MUSIC

2

Language and the Interpretation of Music

LEO TREITLER

Talk about music has turned again to its possibilities as a conveyor of meaning.[1] As past restraints on such talk have always stemmed from one form or another of a belief about music's ineffability, the removal of those restraints entails renewed accommodations between music and language. The nature of such accommodations is the subject I want to address here, with attention to two main aspects: first, assumptions about the nature of language communication which we take as the standards for assertions about what and how music can and cannot mean; and second, the correspondences that are drawn between music and language. Unexamined habits and assumptions and undefended dogmas about both aspects abound in the discourse on this subject.

For the philosophers who contributed to this volume and for the readers who are familiar with their writings on music, the preceding paragraph may be surprising, for questions about meaning have engaged

[1] As an indication, note that the following books dealing directly with the subject of musical meaning were published just in the last year: Stephen Davies, *Musical Meaning and Expression* (Ithaca: Cornell University Press, 1995); Charles Rosen, *The Frontiers of Meaning* (New York: Hill and Wang, 1995); Michael Krausz, ed., *The Interpretation of Music* (Oxford: Clarendon Press, 1994); Philip Alperson, *What Is Music?* (University Park: Pennsylvania State University Press, 1987; reprinted with updated bibliography, 1994); Anthony Pople, ed., *Theory, Analysis, and Meaning in Music* (Cambridge: Cambridge University Press, 1995); Eero Tarasti, *A Theory of Musical Semiotics* (Bloomington: Indiana University Press, 1994); and Robert Hatten, *Musical Meaning in Beethoven* (Bloomington: Indiana University Press, 1995).

"What's it all about, Alfie?"

Figure 2.1. Cartoon by Woodman, copyright © 1992 by the *New Yorker Magazine* Inc.

music philosophers without interruption. I write as a musicologist, and when I read a new story by Gabriel García Marquez in the *New Yorker*, I was stopped by this sentence: "Inside the lights burned in the middle of the day and the string quartet was playing a piece by Mozart, full of foreboding."[2] The formal discourse of my field, operating under no-matter-what scruples, under regimes modern or postmodern, always manages to keep out such characterizations of music as irrelevant and meaningless. When I read it, my mind was instantly sucked into a fantasy in which Marquez is reading the story aloud and has just come to that sentence himself. A squad of young men and women rush up to him, outfitted in black leather boots, breeches, and vests. Their hair is close-cropped or slicked back. Their leader hands Marquez a summons. I shall pick up this story again later on.

Figure 2.1, a cartoon from an earlier issue of the *New Yorker*[3] can serve as an icon for my subject. A bewildering musical situation; but what is the "it" of the caption—the music that is being played? The situation as a whole? Life?[4] Who wants to know? Why? Who or what is that figure at the keyboard? What are they all doing there? Where?

---

[2] Gabriel García Marquez, "Bon Voyage, Mr. President," *New Yorker*, 13 September 1993, pp. 100–111.
[3] Drawing by Bill Woodman, *New Yorker*, 3 February 1992.
[4] The caption has reference, first, to the last line of the 1965 film *Alfie* by Lewis Gilbert (based on a play by Bill Naughton). The title character is a sort of Cockney Don Giovanni who addresses the audience in a running commentary as he dashes through delightful, bewildering, and finally disturbing engagements with women. In the end he looks at the viewer and asks "What's it all about?" This is taken up in the song "Alfie" by Burt Bacharach with words by Hal David. The first lines are, "What's it all about, Alfie? Is it just for the moment we live? What's it all about when you sort it out, Alfie?" Perhaps the

In its atmosphere of mystery, enigma, otherworldliness, and icy cold-
ness, there are hints of the atmosphere of some of the most influential
answers that have been given to the question about musical meaning—
identified sometimes as transcendentalist, sometimes as formalist.[5] As far
apart as those two thinking styles now seem—one metaphysical, the other
positivist—they were once (in the early nineteenth century) two sides of
the same efforts to rescue wordless music from the threat of being empty
and meaningless. Like the scenario of the cartoon, music is said to be
otherworldly and inscrutable. Like the cartoon itself, music is said both
to demand exegesis and to defy it. In the very posing of the question
of meaning there is implication of its pointlessness, of the impossibility

---

penguins are all singing this song? I am much obliged to Stephan Lindeman of the Rutgers
University Department of Music for directing me to the film and song.
[5] See Lydia Goehr, "'Music Has No Meaning to Speak of': On the Politics of Musical
Interpretation," in *The Interpretation of Music*, ed. Krausz, pp. 177–92. I should say how I
understand the term "Formalism." First, I mean it to be descriptive and not accusatory.
The term denotes an attitude whose present emphases I do not share, but not one that I
take to be self-evidently false or wicked, as in recent writing where formalism is regarded
as an obstacle to musical understanding. The word stands for a serious attitude that has
been held by musicians and musical scholars during a particular historical period (from
the early nineteenth century to the present) and under particular systems of belief.
Reduced to its simplest terms the attitude of formalism is that the contents of music are
nothing other than notes—either sounded or written—and their patterns, and that understanding music, i.e., apprehending its meaning, is understanding those elements and
patterns. Although this attitude is often represented as the opposite of romantic transcendentalist attitudes about music, the two are really quite continuous, one with the other.
Heinrich Schenker, for whom formalism offers a sufficient account of the wonders of music
that provoked transcendentalist *beliefs*, cited this formulation of Arthur Schopenhauer's
transcendentalist doctrine in the introduction to book 1 of his *Kontrapunkt*: "The composer
reveals the innermost essence of the world and expresses the most profound wisdom in a
language which his rational faculty does not understand." Schenker continued, "If we but
supplement such vague opinions with the organic, the unique-absolute qualities of the
tonal world, we have nothing less of wonder and mystery! But we understand all the better
why music, resting in its special tonal processes and released, by virtue of its inborn world
of motivic association, from any need to establish connection with the external world, man-
ifests that character which has been observed but little understood by philosophers and
aestheticians. . . . [But] Schopenhauer's conclusion, that 'music represents the innermost
core preceding all creativity, or the heart of things . . .' finally fails because of lack of clarity.
Music is not 'the heart of things'; on the contrary, music has little or nothing to do with
'things.' Tones mean nothing but themselves, they are as living beings with their own social
laws." In other words the transcendentalist Schopenhauer was simply not transcendentalist enough for the formalist Schenker. (Schenker's text is taken from *Counterpoint: A
Translation of Kontrapunkt*, book 1, trans. John Rothgeb and Jürgen Thym [New York:
Schirmer Books, 1987], pp. 15–16). What separated the transcendentalist and formalist attitudes, I believe, was the interpretation of formalism through the rules of positivist episte-
mology, largely through the American institution of music analysis. See Marion Guck,
"Rehabilitating the Incorrigible," in *Theory, Analysis, and Meaning in Music*, ed. Pople, pp.
57–76.

of finding answers. Music, uniquely among the arts, is considered ineffable. Cunning theories have been erected in defense of this negative conclusion, which, as I mean to suggest here, has been somewhat exaggerated.

Alfie could have followed the advice of Robert Schumann in thinking about an answer: "The best way to talk about music is to be quiet about it!"[6] This comes in an article entitled "Chopin's Piano Concertos" published in the *Neue Zeitschrift für Musik* (Schumann's journal of music criticism) in 1836. But what did Schumann mean in saying that? Was it music's oft-mentioned "ineffability" that led him to the remark, or the vagueness of language?

Schumann did not follow his own advice to remain silent. The critical essay in which he offered it is signed "Florestan," one of his alter egos. The essay continues in Schumann's own voice: "If things were ordered according to that lunatic Florestan, one could call the above a review—and let it stand as an obituary for this periodical."

But Schumann was not all at odds with his lunatic. He went on to say, "We, ourselves, may regard our silence as the ultimate homage . . . , due partly to the hesitancy one feels when confronted with a phenomenon one would prefer to approach through the senses." The ambivalence is a romantic characteristic. People liked talking about the difficulty or impossibility of talking about music, as much as they liked talking about music. We have inherited that quirk.

Felix Mendelssohn, in a famous letter of 1842, turned things around in a stunning way, reminding us that attitudes were by no means uniform in his day. He replied thus to Marc-André Souchay, who had written Mendelssohn about the meanings of some of his "Songs Without Words":

> There is so much talk about music, and yet so little is said. For my part, I believe that words do not suffice for such a purpose. . . . People often complain that music is too ambiguous; that what they should think when they hear it is so unclear, whereas everyone understands words. With me it is exactly the reverse, and not only with regard to an entire speech, but also with individual words. These, too, seem to me so ambiguous, so vague, so easily misunderstood in comparison to genuine music. . . . The thoughts which are expressed to me by music that I love are not too indefinite to be put into words, but on the contrary, too definite. . . . The same words never mean the same things to different people. Only the song can say the same thing, can arouse the same feelings in one person as in another, a feeling

---

[6] "Chopin's Piano Concertos" (1836), in *The Musical World of Robert Schumann*, trans., ed., and annotated by Henry Pleasants (New York: St. Martin's Press, 1965), pp. 112–13.

which is not expressed, however, by the same words. . . . Words have many
meanings, but music we could both understand correctly. Will you allow
this to serve as an answer to your question? At all events, it is the only one
I can give, although these, too, are nothing, after all, but ambiguous words![7]

The letter is often cited for its assertion about the preciseness of music's
expression, but it is for its far more radical assertion about the opposite
effect of language communication that I cite it here. It is not music's ineffability that makes for the difficulty of talk about musical meaning, says
Mendelssohn, but the ambiguities, vagueness, and inconsistencies that
are inherent in the practice of language communication about music,
and about anything else. I believe that Mendelssohn has here touched
the heart of the problem of musical meaning, and the source of much
disagreement and confusion.[8]

A century earlier the music pedagogue Daniel Gottlob Türk had
written, in his *School of Clavier Playing*, that "certain subtleties of expression cannot really be described, they must be heard."[9] It could not be said

---

[7] The full text of both Souchay's and Mendelssohn's letters are given in English translation in Oliver Strunk, *Source Readings in Music History*, rev. ed., Leo Treitler, general ed.
(New York: Norton, forthcoming).

[8] Mendelssohn's insight here anticipates the pragmatic perspective on language use that
is owing to Ludwig Wittgenstein, expressed, for example, in this passage: "We are incapable of circumscribing clearly the concepts that we use, not because we do not know their
true definition, but because they have no true 'definition.' The presumption that they must
have such a definition would be like the presumption that children playing ball do so
strictly according to rules" (Ludwig Wittgenstein, *Das Blaue Buch*, ed. R. Rhees, in L.
Wittgenstein, *Schriften*, vol. 5 [Frankfurt: Suhrkamp, 1970], p. 49). Carl Dahlhaus seems to
dispute Mendelssohn about this fundamental matter, with a viewpoint that must also be
considered. He writes, "The feelings that music possesses with the determinacy extolled
by Mendelssohn prove to be not impulses existing outside and without music and whose
sounding portrayal is musical, but rather qualities that are feelings at all only as they are
expressed by music. That they cannot be translated into language—that language does not
reach them—accordingly means simply that they can be what they are only in musically
expressive form; it in no way means that language remains behind music in the characterization of real feelings because it is poorer and more undifferentiated. Music is not the
more specific representation of impulses that are also comprehensible linguistically, but
instead the different expression of different feelings" ("Fragmente zur musikalischen
Hermeneutik," in *Beiträge zur musikalischen Hermeneutik: Studien zur Musikgeschichte des 19.
Jahrhunderts* 43 [Regensburg: G. Bosse, 1975]: 159–72; trans. Karen Painter as "Fragments
of a Musical Hermeneutics," *Current Musicology* 50 (1992): 5–20 [the passage cited is on p.
8]). Despite the apparent disagreement, the two attitudes have in common the consequence
that qualities or characters that are commonly labeled "extramusical" are precisely the
opposite; they can *only* be musical (see n. 23 and the surrounding argument). And that, in
turn, renders the common assertion that music can have expressive qualities only in a
metaphorical sense rather meaningless, as I shall argue further on.

[9] Daniel Gottlob Türk, *Klavierschule, oder Anweisung zum Klavierspielen für Lehrer und
Lehrende* (Leipzig and Halle, 1789), trans. Raymond H. Haggh as *School of Clavier Playing*
(Lincoln: University of Nebraska Press, 1982), p. 337.

more bluntly: language cannot match music's subtlety and preciseness of expression.

Mendelssohn's skepticism about the assumption that language expressions have a precise and stable reference from one speaker to another would throw suspicion as well on rigorous theories of musical meaning that depend on that assumption, and leave us to make formulations that are sketches of our understanding in the effort to convey our apprehensions to one another. We would be obliged to recognize such sketches for what they are and to practice tolerance in place of the customary dogmatism. And we would be well advised to try pragmatic descriptions of our use of language in talking about music in place of prescriptive theorizing. We should give serious attention to the writings of those who are skilled in the imaginative and creative use of language—that is, writers of poetry and fiction—whose use of language is often more subtle and versatile than those who are skilled in theorizing, and who may be more concerned with representing through language their experience of music.

I rather share Mendelssohn's skepticism, and I believe in the consequences that flow from it. If I therefore turn now to what is perhaps the most explicit and musically concrete effort to formulate a theory of musical meaning with a claim to rigor that has been put forward in recent years by a musical scholar it is in order to show how, even through the posture of rigor, and even where the explicit aim is to demonstrate how musical meaning works, the tools of language have been so blunted by a combination of rhetorical and doctrinal motives, that language has been drained of the potency and versatility that can be the positive side of the ambiguity that Türk and Mendelssohn identified.[10]

I have culled from Kofi Agawu's *Playing with Signs: A Semiotic Interpretation of Classic Music* a basic vocabulary of the main predicates through which its author seeks to identify the modalities of musical meaning: denoting, embodying, expressing, representing, symbolizing—all ways of linking the concrete musical event to something other than itself, ways in which music is supposed to correspond to other things. My purpose is to see whether it is possible to recognize what is to be understood by them, and especially how they are differentiated from one another—in short, whether it is possible to recognize what conception about the modalities of musical meaning underlies the use of language. Emphases in the following citations are mine.

"Measures 72–76 present a concentrated passage of descending fifths, *symbolizing* one high point of the learned style" (p. 107); and "The alla

---

[10] The book is Kofi Agawu, *Playing with Signs: A Semiotic Interpretation of Classic Music* (Princeton: Princeton University Press, 1991).

breve *denotes* learned style" (p. 90): "symbolizing" and "denoting" are treated as synonyms. That seems fair enough, since to denote something is to be a sign or symbol for it; 🎼 denotes the sound A440 according to prevailing tuning standards. Any sign that we would agree upon, regardless of its own shape, size, or color, would do the same job. Less easy to see is that those passages could be said to be signs for a style— pointing to it—rather than *embodying, exemplifying,* or *being in* that style. There are important differences that make for the difficulty. First, once we have been led by the sign 🎼 to the sound A440 we lose interest in the sign. But we do not lose interest in the passage of descending fifths or the *alla breve* passage once we have been led by them to focus on the concept "learned style." We experience them as part of the music, and we would be more accustomed to saying that they embody, exemplify, or are in learned style. By the same token we would be less willing to accept such passages as arbitrary conventions that could be replaced by any others. We would be likely to insist that there are reasons within the character of those passages for their being earmarks of a style we call "learned." And just as they identify "learned style" for us, the phrase "learned style" characterizes them; it sums up the properties for which it is a label. "Symbolizing" and "denoting" lack the reciprocity of "embodying" or "exemplifying." I shall return later to this important point and its consequences. If the author really means to say that those passages denote or symbolize "learned style"—and I believe he does—it can only be because he is unfolding a conception of music as a play of signs that signify things beyond themselves.[11] That is a radical idea, and one that has a fair amount of currency just now. I have taken so much trouble over this analysis in order to bring that out, not merely to engage in semantic quibbling.

The following passage demonstrates this distancing even more clearly: "*Sturm und Drang denotes* instability" (p. 87). Now, we usually say either that "instability"—for example, the instability of a series of diminished seventh chords or of a syncopated passage—is a property or character of such passages that is capable of being directly experienced or felt by the listener, or that it is what the listener experiences upon hearing the passage. To say that instability is "denoted" by the characteristic style *Sturm und Drang* (which we must presumably first recognize before we can think "instability") is to go out of one's way to deny that instability can be an experienced property of music. Consequently it empties the word itself of its suggestiveness, acquired through use, of such feeling or

[11] But just exactly how he means that is made uncertain by the fact that he regards the word "style," as applied to music, to be a metaphor—which is to say that music does not literally have or embody style, or is not in a style. Then what those passages denote is itself shadowy. See the discussion of metaphor in what follows.

feature. For it says that in identifying "instability" we simply recognize that the music has met certain conventional conditions for the use of that term, conditions that may, again, be quite arbitrary. We could just as well say "omega" as "instability." This is to say something very special indeed about the experience of music and about the language in which we try to describe it. It is understandable, again, from the vantage point of a postmodern attitude toward music as an indifferent play of signs.

Language is used here to hold music at arm's length from the listener but also from meanings that may be attributed to it—to make musical meaning indirect and conceptual and to locate it outside of music. Words are asked to identify not music's properties or the experience of those properties but abstractions that music *signifies*. That is the doctrinal tendency to which I refer, a tendency to address the question of meaning in music via the semiotic transaction of signifying, hence a tendency to regard "interpreting" as being virtually synonymous with "decoding." A sign of that, so to speak, is the tendency to speak of interpretations of music as "readings." And even though it is most explicit in the semiotic line of interpretive theory with which Agawu identifies his work, it is equally at play in some current hermeneutic and feminist theories and interpretations.

It is a use of signs that I came to appreciate especially well from the recent experience of seeing a young woman walking up Fifth Avenue in New York, dressed in the tattered layers of a homeless person. I reacted at first with the numbing feeling of sorrow and guilt that is part of the affect of every New Yorker with a home and an income. But that feeling was cut short when I noticed the confident, sashaying stride with which she walked, and her well-cared-for look from the neck upward. Those signs brought awareness that she must have had the outfit at a high price from some fashionable couturier, to wear as her radical statement of solidarity with the homeless. The clothes are signifiers.

Another, more arcane use of the word "denote" takes us a step still further into abstraction (the following will require some patience): "Introversive semiosis[12] [as when a first-movement theme is cited in the last movement of the same work] denotes internal intramusical reference . . . while extroversive semiosis [e.g., a fanfare] denotes external, extramusical, referential connection" (p. 132). How are the roles of subject and object in each pair determined? Could the members of each pair be reversed, for

---

[12] "Semiosis" has been defined as "a process in which signs function as vehicles, interpretants, and interpreters [interpretants and interpreters would both be things or persons that interpret]." See "Semiotics," in *The Johns Hopkins Guide to Literary Theory and Criticism*, ed. Michael Groden and Martin Kreiswirth (Baltimore: Johns Hopkins University Press, 1994), p. 659.

example, "internal intramusical reference denotes introversive
If so (and I see nothing in the way of the reversal), the equ
amounts to a translation from the familiar Latin-based "reference" to the
unfamiliar Greek-based "semiosis." Such translations tend in any case to
have an alienating, distancing effect that influences understanding, like
the rendering of Freud's terms in his mother tongue, "das Ich," "'das
Überich," and "das Es" (a literal translation would be the "I," the "super-
I," and the "it") in the English versions of his works with the Latin-based
words "ego," "super-ego," and "id." But then, too, the purport of those
sentences would not be reduced if "denote" were replaced each time by
"is equivalent to," or simply by "is." This substitution would, however,
remove the confusion—indeed incoherence—that is created by asserting
that a signifying process ("semiosis") "denotes" (i.e., signifies) a kind of
reference (which is a way of signifying). The whole passage seems to be
about language, skating on the surface of some idea about music as a signifying process. But it makes no contribution to the question about how
music signifies.

Now to the use of the word "represents": "Measure 32 *represents* some
sort of beginning" (p. 106). As "beginnings, middles, and endings" are
also said to be "symbolized" (p. 118), then "representing" joins the synonyms "symbolizing-denoting." There is talk of "representations that
Beethoven makes toward sonata form" (p. 118) and of "representations
toward the tonic" (p. 124). But "beginnings," "middles," "ends," "sonata
form," and "tonics" are properties about which we usually say "this *is* the
beginning" or "this is (on or in) the tonic," or "this is in sonata form"
(qualified as much as you like), but not "this is a representation" of those
things. What phantoms would those things be, anyway, if music is only a
representation of them?

The farthest extreme is reached in the uses of the word "express." Dictionary definitions usually begin with the idea of bringing out, stating,
showing, or giving manifest form to attitudes, feelings, characteristics, or
beliefs that are held or embodied, before moving to the very different
sense of signifying something by certain characters or figures (as in "mathematical expression"). Wittgenstein likened musical expression to the
expression on a person's face, and in order to make sense of this it is useful
to think of Peter Kivy's distinction between "expression" and "being
expressive of."[13] Put this second way, it seems to be closer to what we
mean in speaking of music as expressive, for it is noncommittal with
respect to the fundamental question whether music holds, or contains,

[13] Ludwig Wittgenstein, *Culture and Value*, trans. Peter Winch (Chicago: University of
Chicago Press), p. 40; and Peter Kivy, *Sound Sentiment* (Philadelphia: Temple University
Press, 1989), pp. 12–17.

what is expressed. In any case, in ordinary usage the term would seem to be resistant to exploitation for any such distancing function as the other terms undergo. But "expression" is straightaway defined by the author as "extroversive semiosis" (i.e., signification of external, extramusical objects, e.g., a cuckoo). It is converted to a term of reference in preparation for the exposition of a theory of musical expression that depends entirely on codes for external reference.[14]

With this conversion of "expression" to a term of reference there remains no real differentiation among these terms; they are all interchangeable, and all come down to "signify."

I wonder whether this strong tendency to regard music as a play of signs might arise out of a wish to compensate for the condition of music, as it is so often characterized (or a wish to dispute the characterization), that it lacks semantic content, that it bears no denotative relation to an object. Whether or not that is so, it has quite radical implications for the way we would address music, were we to follow it consistently, implications that would certainly run counter to the reasons that most of us have for listening to music. I shall try to bring this out first through citation of a work of fiction, then through a simple philosophical analysis.

In Italo Calvino's story "A King Listens," a narrating voice in the second person reflects to the monarch, who has stolen the throne and sealed his predecessor into a dungeon deep in his fortress, how his life has been given over to two purposes only: self-indulgence and the retention of his power. Calvino turns to music to convey how, paradoxically, this self-preoccupation has destroyed the king's sense of self along with the cultural life of his city.

> Among the sounds of the city you recognize every now and then a chord, a sequence of notes, a tune: blasts of fanfare, chanting of processions, choruses of schoolchildren, funeral marches, revolutionary songs intoned by a parade of demonstrators, anthems in your honor sung by the troops who break up the demonstration, trying to drown out the voices of your opponents, dance tunes that the loudspeaker of a nightclub plays at top volume to convince everyone that the city continues its happy life, dirges of women mourning someone killed in the riots. This is the music you hear; but can it be called music? From every shard of sound you continue to

[14] V. A. Howard, in "On Musical Expression," *British Journal of Aesthetics* 11 (1971), considers the theory that music "expresses" by signifying something else and shows the errors of reasoning and unwarranted assumptions that it entails. It comes down to a confusion between denotation and exemplification. See pp. 271–73 and 275, and p. 35 here.

gather signals, information, clues, as if in this city all those who play or sing or put on disks wanted only to transmit precise, unequivocal messages to you. Since you mounted the throne, it is not music you listen to, but only the confirmation of how music is used: in the rites of high society, or to entertain the populace, to safeguard traditions, culture, fashion. Now you ask yourself what listening used to mean to you, when you listened to music for the sole pleasure of penetrating the design of the notes.[15]

The philosophical analysis begins with an insight that strikes at the heart of the problem: "It is probably more true of music than of any other art that the sign (if we conceive it as such) is not transparent—that is, the sign does not disappear in favor of its function as pointing to the signified."[16]

The context of this remark, which goes by rather too quickly, is a discussion of the way that signs and the things signified are connected through the action of reference, which the author aims to clarify by way of drawing a distinction between two main types of reference-relations, as they apply to music: denotation and exemplification. The distinction turns on the direction of the flow of reference between the sign and its referent, and by implication on the question which of the two stands out more in the receiver's attention to the whole process—the sign or the thing signified.

The terminology and the question can be highlighted through a simple example, to begin with: a cinema marquee with its text as sign for the film(s) that is (are) being shown inside the theater. The reference usually flows from the marquee to the film, from the sign to the signified. The marquee refers to the film; that is its purpose. Although it is possible to think of the film referring to the marquee, it would be quite unusual to take the pair in that way (not, however, for someone writing a dissertation about cinema marquees). After we have seen the film and left the cinema, it is the film that will usually occupy our residual attention, the film that we will discuss on our way home. In this sense the sign is transparent to the signified. It is totally absorbed in its signifying function. It is this process that Anthony Newcomb calls "denotation," following Nelson Goodman,[17] and our example is an extreme case of it.

If we think next of the appreciation of a figurative work of visual art—such as Michelangelo's sculpture *Pietà*—in these terms, we are certainly involved in following a denotative flow of reference from the sculpture to

[15] Italo Calvino, *Under the Jaguar Sun*, trans. William Weaver (New York: Harcourt Brace Jovanovich, 1988), pp. 51–52.
[16] Anthony Newcomb, "Sound and Feeling," *Critical Inquiry* 10 (June 1984): 614–43.
[17] Nelson Goodman, *Languages of Art*, 2d ed. (Indianapolis: Hackett, 1981), pp. 45–52.

what it signifies: a lifeless male figure identifiable as Jesus, draped across the lap of a mourning female figure identifiable as Mary. But appreciation of the work involves us in reflecting back onto the sculpted figures what tradition and experience, and our own reflection and feelings, bring us about the meaning of Jesus' death and Mary's mourning, and about devotion, sacrifice, death, and mourning in general. Such meaning and feelings are *exemplified* by the work, and the reference between sign and signified flows in both directions. We do not lose interest in the sign once our attention has been drawn to the signified; the sign is not absorbed by the signifying process, it is not transparent to the signified. We would be more likely to say that the artwork in this case is an amalgam of sign and signified.

Here is the first couplet of Shakespeare's Sonnet 27:

> *Weary* with *toil*, I *haste* me to my *bed*
> The dear *repose* for *limbs* with *travel tir'd*;

There is a flow of reference from each italicized word to a condition, action, or object that it signifies. But the mood that is evoked by the words signifying the speaker's state, and the action that follows from it, both of which we know from our own experience, refer back to the words themselves, and especially to the pacing of the prosody. By convention the syllables of sonnets move in iambs. But the poet has contrived to block such movement until the comma in the first line, after which, as though acting out the word "haste," the prosody can swing into the iambic rhythm. The second line recites in a regular iambic pentameter. Not only does the poem denote through the signifiers of its words a state of being and a consequent action, it also exemplifies both through that rhythmic device. The reference flows in both directions.

Can we imagine music that, when considered as signs, is transparent to the things it signifies? There is a film in the Sherlock Holmes series from the 1930s called *Dressed to Kill* (it is not based on an Arthur Conan Doyle story). For a particular gang of thieves and the detectives trying to identify them, the variants in the way a series of music boxes play the same tune constitute an encoded message about the location of a huge fortune. None of the characters display the slightest interest in the music for itself, and there is no way that grasping the information that it denotes enriches the experience of it for them. But this is an extreme, and an unreal case. Perhaps one would even question whether the performances by those music boxes constitute music at all, any more than does a Morse code transmission.

But everyone knows of music that sends coded messages without ceasing to be music. In act 2, scene 1, of Alban Berg's *Lulu*, the love scene between Alwa and Lulu, Alwa sings "Mignon, ich liebe dich" (mm. 335–36). At the word "liebe" the strings are exposed sustaining the Tristan chord in its original position. Lulu's reply is "Ich habe deine Mutter vergiftet." In Tristan interpretations a symbolic identity of the chord with the love potion is a common theme, and Berg has here taken the further step of interpreting love potion as poison, *Liebestod*. There is irony in this, and perhaps even cynicism. The music signifies, unquestionably, but it is not absorbed in signifying. Reference flows from this complex signified back to the music, which, rather than vanishing once it has done its job of signifying, is richer as a result of the reference from the signified to it. This sort of thing is characteristic of Berg's music—and not only his operas. Of course, its great earlier practitioner was Wagner, but he was not the first, either.

In the second-act finale of Mozart's *Le Nozze di Figaro* the gardener Antonio reports to the Count that he has seen someone jump from the window of the Countess's chamber. He suspects correctly that it was Cherubino. But Figaro, trying to save Cherubino's skin, pretends it was he. Antonio produces evidence that it was Cherubino: the document certifying the latter's commission in the army, which Antonio found at the place where Cherubino landed (m. 609). Figaro casts about for a way of explaining why he would have had the document in his possession, and as he does so the orchestra modulates steadily, as though groping for a resolution. And just as Figaro finds his explanation under prompting from Susanna and the Countess (the document lacked an official seal), the orchestra finds its harmonic clearing (a cadence on the dominant of B♭ major, m. 671). The flow of reference in both directions is apparent here. The orchestral music, giving off a purely musical sense of searching for a way out, enliven's Figaro's search, and we transport the feeling of this man caught in a lie, desperate to find a way out—a feeling we surely all know from childhood—back to the music. In doing so we invest the feeling that the music gives off with that concrete content of human action and feeling. It is the two-way flow that creates the humor.

The passages from Berg and Mozart show that music, even at its most specifically denotative, is never reducible to a play of signs. The pseudo—Sherlock Holmes case shows that when music has an exclusively denotative function, a function as nothing but a play of signs, it is at least questionable whether we would consider it music at all.

The conclusion is that music is not transparent, and arraying the semiotic vocabulary to have all musical signs pointing to the conceptual signified somewhere outside the music is at odds with our experience. If music signifies, its sounds do not fade for us once its work of signifying is done. This observation is profound, for the contradiction that it reveals

Example 2.1. Beethoven, Piano Sonata in D, Op. 10, no. 3, beginning of second movement

is a risk everywhere in the current zeal to regard music as cultural, social, or political practice—a zeal that is understandable, to be sure, in view of the long neglect of those aspects. But the tendency of the moment is toward the replacement of music with interpretation.[18]

The difference between explaining musical expression as a matter of denotation and of exemplification is important, but not as great a difference in the long run as it seems at first. If we think of Beethoven's marking for the slow movement of his Piano Sonata Op. 10, no. 3, *Largo e mesto*, for example, both as an instruction for performance and as an identification of its character, then on the first view the focus would be on the "mournfulness" that the music signifies, whereas on the second it would be on the music and its mournful character, which the performer is asked to bring out; the music would be said to exemplify mournfulness (see example 2.1). It is the notion of musical expression as exemplification that I want to pursue now.

Goodman makes a further distinction. He allows that "sadness" is a property that a painting can possess and exemplify, but he observes that paintings are insentient objects that cannot literally feel sad. If a painting possesses and exemplifies the property of sadness, which does not come naturally to it, it has it by acquisition or borrowing—the sort of borrowing that is commonly identified as metaphorical transfer. This he contrasts with properties that paintings can literally possess and exemplify, such as yellowness. Hence expression in art is for him a matter of *"metaphorical* exemplification." (Of course, volumes have been written about "metaphor," but a simple dictionary definition can be a helpful point of departure. The *Random House Dictionary of the English Language*[19] defines "metaphor" as "A figure of speech in which a term or phrase is applied

---

[18] It is interesting, at this moment, to return to Susan Sontag's once-famous essay of 1961, "Against Interpretation," in her book *Against Interpretation and Other Essays* (New York: Delta, 1961).

[19] *Random House Dictionary of the English Language*, 2d. ed. unabridged (New York: Random House, 1987).

to something to which it is not literally applicable in order to suggest a resemblance, as in 'A mighty fortress is our God.'")

Goodman's line of reasoning and the distinction to which it leads may be carried over exactly to my Beethoven example. It would thus be congruent with the widespread view that music can be "picturesque" or "expressive" (e.g., "mournful") only in a metaphorical sense. On most accounts of metaphor, that means it is *not* either picturesque or expressive in the literal sense, and we just transfer temporarily the expressive or picturesque property from something that *literally* possesses it to music. But this is a deceptive explanatory route. It may seem to be a technically correct explanation by definition and to be satisfactory in that sense, but it will hardly assuage our desire to understand our response to that piece, and Beethoven's instruction to perform it, as mournful.

There are numerous problems. If mournfulness—to follow our example—is a borrowed property, its source must be human feelings, for human feelings are the only place where mournfulness can "literally" reside. To speak of music being mournful would be a kind of anthropomorphizing. Even a human face can, by the same token, be mournful only through metaphorical transfer, since it is not the face that is sentient but the mind or soul whose state is given visible expression by it. But then what would it really mean to say that the mournful property of Beethoven's sonata movement has been borrowed from human feelings? Does it mean that the music becomes in some nonliteral sense sentient? How would that sense be described? Would the description of the expression on a person's face as mournful imply that the face itself becomes sentient? If a painting cannot be literally sad because it is insentient, then what of the expressions "It was a sad day for America when John F. Kennedy was assassinated" or "The negotiations over the baseball strike have had a sad outcome"? Anyone making those remarks would certainly mean them literally. What would be the point of insisting that they are, strictly speaking, metaphorical because days and negotiations are not sentient? There is clearly something wrong about the reasoning here, and at the root of it is Goodman's misleading and irrelevant initial step—arguing that paintings, being insentient, cannot be literally sad. If we characterize a painting or a day or the outcome of a negotiation as sad, or another day as gloomy, or a piece of music as gloomy, we do not mean that they experience those feelings, we mean that they have that character. And underlying that meaning is the conviction that they *can* have that character. If we respond to a piece of music as being mournful, we are responding to musical properties that the piece possesses, without qualifications, and with experience and sufficient knowledge of musical principles we can say just what those properties are. Then—keeping in mind

Mendelssohn's caveats about language—it is perhaps better to say that it is the *word* "mournful" rather than the property of mournfulness that has been borrowed from another domain and fitted, however imperfectly, to those musical properties. That seems at least to be truer to experience. In identifying a figure in language as a metaphor we recognize the foreignness of the metaphorical image or idea to the prevailing domain—a mathematical proof characterized as a mousetrap, for example; mousetraps are foreign to the domain of mathematics. If I experience Beethoven's sonata movement as mournful, I do not experience that quality as something foreign to the prevailing character, quality, or sense of the music; on the contrary I experience it as being of the essence of the piece, and I can even imagine presenting that piece as an exemplification of mournfulness—a more fine-tuned one than, say, the howling of a dog. The effect of metaphor is no part of the experience for me.

Elsewhere in his exposition Goodman provides his own highly imaginative characterization of metaphor that is at the same time an exemplification of its effect: "A metaphor is an affair between a predicate with a past and an object that yields while protesting." The force and the beauty of this metaphor is at once in the subtlety with which the foreign domain is insinuated, in the cognitive jolt that comes from the juxtaposition of the contexts of semiotic analysis and sexuality, and in the sharpness with which it delivers at the same time the definition that is its literal meaning. Such juxtaposition of incommensurates is always to the point of metaphor, if it has any point. It is something that we appreciate for its own sake about metaphor, beyond the precision of its semantic value. But the character of music—for example, the mournfulness of Beethoven's sonata movement—does not necessarily depend on any such effect.

All told, it is hard to see what the theory that music can possess its affective properties only metaphorically really means, and what it really accomplishes beyond a rather low-level act of classification that is not of much value to music criticism.[20] That mournfulness has been regarded by

---

[20] Nor to philosophy. Stephen Davies, in his book *Musical Meaning and Expression*, writes, first, that "the focus lies now on the idea that it is descriptions of music that are metaphoric (rather than on the far from clear notion that the music possesses some of its properties metaphorically)" (p. 114). But even if it is descriptions that are metaphoric, in order to understand the point of them we must be able to paraphrase them, to say what is "the sense contained in the metaphor." If we cannot—and Davies intimates that the kind of description of music that is mainly characterized as metaphorical usually cannot be paraphrased—then "to say that the description is metaphoric, and to say no more, is to stop short of giving the analysis required" (ibid.), which is "an explanation of why we describe artworks in terms usually confined to the description of sentient creatures (more specifically, persons)" (ibid.). As for Goodman's explanation, he writes, "Just what 'metaphorical exemplification' amounts to in musical expression is so obscure that the account is deprived of explanatory power" (p. 125).

practitioners of music as a musical quality—certainly since the sixteenth century—is clear from the simple fact of the appearance of the word "mesto" in pedagogical writing about music[21] and as performance indication right into the present century.[22] It is hard to imagine composers, performers, and teachers for whom such terms have currency being much affected by the admonition that it is all metaphorical.[23]

When I experience Beethoven's sonata movement as mournful I am not anthropomorphizing any more than when I experience the day on which I write this text as gloomy. In neither instance do I find it difficult to analyze the predicated property into its constituent causal factors, in case I should find it necessary or desirable to do so: in the first instance the tempo, the dark register, and voicing, the tendency to move to the subdominant harmony, the insistent reiteration of the chromatic dyad $C\sharp$–D within D–$C\sharp$–D and F–$C\sharp$–D (see example 2.1);[24] in the second the gray sky, the mist and rain, the grotesque bare trees with only the lifeless brown leaves of oaks hanging on. But I do not find it necessary, for I experience the mournfulness and the gloom directly, as much so as the more literally possessed properties into which I can analyze them.

If we say, "What a gloomy day this is," and someone says "but only in a metaphorical sense," that would mean "it is not literally a gloomy day because it cannot be; it is only a—somehow—gloomylike day." But that was not our intention. Our intention was to say, "What a gloomy day this is." The interjection that this is metaphorical is nonsensical. It turns the expression into a dialogue that one might hear in an absurdist play. And in case someone wishes to offer the correction that it is not the music or

---

[21] For example, in Gioseffo Zarlino's *Istitutioni harmoniche* of 1558 (trans. G. A. Marco and C. V. Palisca as *The Art of Counterpoint* [New Haven: Yale University Press, 1968]), book 3, chaps. 10 and 31; and Türk's *Klavierschule*.

[22] I cite an instance of Béla Bartók's use of the designation further on.

[23] Donald Francis Tovey spoke metaphorically about music when he found "a tragic irony" and the sound of "a distant happiness" in the conversation among the winds about the main theme of the first movement of Beethoven's Ninth Symphony in m. 469. And I, in turn, have just spoken metaphorically of "the conversation among the winds about the main theme." To speak metaphorically about music is not necessarily to imply a belief in the theory that music possesses its qualitative properties metaphorically. In these instances, efforts have been made to find language suitable for catching the quality of purely musical gestures, and metaphor answers very well to that need. Of course, what will count as metaphorical language will depend on what one will allow as "literally musical" properties. The location of the dividing line is always arbitrary. I have deliberately chosen language here that I think most would agree to be quite distant from it. I shall cite some extreme judgments in the opposite direction in what follows.

[24] See my "Contributions on Beethoven, Pianoforte Sonata op. 10 no. 3: Largo e Mesto," in the roundtable discussion "Style Analysis," *International Musicological Society: Report of the Eleventh Congress, Copenhagen 1972*, ed. Henrik Glahn, Soren Sorensen, and Peter Ryom (Copenhagen: Wilhelm Hansen, 1975), pp. 80–82. Ideally the reader would play all the examples at the keyboard or listen to them in recordings.

the day that is mournful or gloomy but I who is made to feel mournful or gloomy, I shall remind him or her that if I were suffering under either of those states and were to walk into a bright yellow kitchen I could easily recognize the cheerfulness of the yellow without being cheered up by it. To insist that the labels "mournful" and "gloomy" can mean only that the music and the day have those properties through metaphorical transfer is to make a point of it that the experience of the music as one or the day as the other is mediated by thoughts of objects that are literally mournful or gloomy—otherwise why bother to say it?—and that is what I doubt. But when I hear someone speak of a mathematical proof as a mousetrap, my thinking about the proof is mediated by the image of a mousetrap. That is what makes the metaphor work.

I said "dark register and voicing." I must have meant, literally, "low and dense voicing." But wait—there cannot be anything *literally* low or dense about a musical sound, either, any more than there can be dark voicing. I seem to be stepping in quicksand here. "High" and "low" are acquired properties of music that we treat as literal properties without any hesitation. I believe they were acquired with the invention of musical notation in Western Europe in the ninth century. We assume too much when we make an easy assessment about "literal" meanings. But when we speak of dark musical sounds, I believe we mean the experience of darkness as a peculiarly musical, sonic quality that can also be enhanced by tempo, rhythm, voice-leading, and harmonic relations, an experience not mediated by thoughts of things that are literally dark, like Rembrandt's painting *The Night Watch* prior to its cleaning, or a moonless night. Perhaps we recognize in those darknesses some overlapping fringe of affective quality. But on the whole I am not certain that when we say "dark" of a musical work, a contralto's voice, a painting, a night, or the mood of a lover, we are really talking about the same quality. The fact that we use the same word for those predicates does not give self-evident assurance of that.[25] Think again of Mendelssohn's letter on language. It is this sort of consideration that leads me to wonder what it would even mean to say that the quality of darkness is transferred from *The Night Watch* or a moonless night to Beethoven's sonata movement, that is, what it really means to say that the character of that movement can be dark only in a metaphorical sense.

I am questioning here the sense of two practices in talk about musical meaning as metaphorical: (1) assuming a clear distinction between

---

[25] Frank Sibley writes, "The warmth or chill of music is only audible; it is not the warmth or chill felt in bath water or seen in smiles" ("Making Music Our Own," in Krausz, *The Interpretation of Music*, p. 175). See also Dahlhaus, "Fragmente zur musikalischen Hermeneutik."

"metaphorical" and "literal" meaning in general, that is, in language usage; and (2) singling out music among meaning-bearing systems as being incapable of anything but metaphorical meaning, and being unsusceptible to description in anything but metaphorical terms, so far as its meaning, expression, or character is concerned. I aim my questioning less to the correctness of the propositions implicit in these practices than to the sense of the practices themselves: what is their point? What do they accomplish?

The musical analogue of the duality of metaphorical and literal meaning is the duality of the musical and the extramusical, which underlies the theory that music has its qualitative properties through metaphorical transfer. It would be implicit, for example, in any adaptation to music of Goodman's distinction between literal and acquired properties—literal properties would be those that are strictly musical; acquired ones would be extramusical. But just as the boundary between metaphorical and literal meaning in language communication cannot be drawn, so the boundary in the duality of the musical and the extramusical cannot be located. A consequence, whether intended or not, is the implication that virtually all descriptive language about music is metaphorical. That is the burden of the remark in Eduard Hanslick's *On the Musically Beautiful* (1854), that "all the fanciful portrayals, characterizations, circumscriptions of a musical work are either figurative or perverse. What in every other art is still description is in music already metaphor."[26] And it is acted out in Agawu's book, which I cite again because as an extreme case it brings out what is implicit in the general practice all the more clearly. Agawu draws the line between the musical and the extramusical very close to the edge.

The words "style," "grammar," "syntax," and "language," are all identified as metaphors when applied to music, because they all have their origins in the domain of language.[27] If we think historically about the first of those terms, "style" originated as a word for a writing instrument, then was adapted for manners of writing, thence for rhetorical styles, thence for description and classification in all domains. Perhaps it delivered a metaphorical kick each time it entered service in a new domain. But that is not sufficient cause to make a point of identifying it forever as a metaphor in each of those domains. Its history provides a fine illustration of the way that language is, through its history, fundamentally metaphorical, not exceptionally so. To insist on pronouncing, four

---

[26] Eduard Hanslick, *Vom Musikalisch-Schönen: ein Beitrag zur Revision der Ästhetik der Tonkunst*, trans. Geoffrey Payzant as *On the Musically Beautiful: A Contribution Towards the Revision of the Aesthetics of Music* (Indianapolis: Hackett, 1986), p. 30.
[27] Agawu, *Playing with Signs*, p. 9.

centuries after the currency of *stile concitato*, that "style" functions today as a descriptive category only through the figure of metaphor—that music cannot "literally" embody style—is to raise the questions what, if any, literal, nonmetaphoric descriptive language is left to music and how one is to recognize the boundary between the musical and the extramusical.[28]

The following descriptive phrases are characterized as metaphoric: "movement to and from points of metric stability" (p. 117) and "the shift from instability to stability and back again" (p. 130). The words "movement," "shift," and "stability," and its opposite, "instability," would be found as well in descriptions of poems and sculptures (e.g., ballerina figures by Degas), where I do not believe trouble would be taken to identify them as metaphorical.

It seems odd in any case to insist on this identification, more than eleven hundred years after the poet Notker of St. Gall wrote of the "motus cantilenae"—exactly our sense of melodic movement—and the music pedagogue Aurelian of Reôme displayed a melodic conception with movement at its core. His principal words for melody or melodic passages all imply movement: modulation, inflection, and "accent," the latter understood as rising ("acute") or falling ("grave") motion. Such terms as these, which may have had metaphorical function at one time but have given up that function for participation in the non-metaphorical vocabulary, are sometimes called "dead metaphors." But as Stephen Davies remarks, "Dead metaphors no more remain metaphors than false friends remain friends."[29] Strictly speaking, "musical movement" is in the same category of predicates about music as is Marquez's predicate, "full of foreboding," about the Mozart string quartet. Neither is literally, objectively, confirmably predicable of music. In my fantasy, Marquez demands of the magistrate, "Tell me, then, what it is that I may safely say about the Mozart quartet," and the magistrate, finding herself unable to provide a clear answer, is obliged to release him.

If there is nonmetaphorical descriptive language for music, it would presumably refer strictly to the domain of the musical, set apart from the

---

[28] The eighteenth-century philosopher Thomas Reid wrote, "In harmony, the very names of concord and discord are metaphorical, and suppose some analogy between the relations of sound, to which they are figuratively applied, and the relations of minds and affections, which they originally and properly signify (quoted in Peter Kivy, *Music Alone: Philosophical Reflections on the Purely Musical Experience* [Ithaca: Cornell University Press, 1990], p. 46). What music borrowed from interpersonal relations it repaid in kind, with the words consonance and dissonance.

[29] Davies, *Musical Meaning and Expression*, p. 164.

domain of the extramusical, as the domain of essentially uninterpreted tones and tone complexes or patterns—"music itself," as Heinrich Schenker put it early in this century, in which "tones mean nothing but themselves."[30]

I have tried to offer glimpses of the difficulty of defining such a domain and of differentiating it from the domain of the extramusical in practice. But is the alternative to watching the domain of "music itself," of "literally musical properties," shrink virtually to nothingness to allow it to expand almost without limits? That would lead to another misleading inquiry. If we are to clear the way for the consideration of musical meaning, I think it more important to be aware of that duality as a player in a certain history in which it has met a certain need, than it is to try through painstaking verbal formulation to draw the fine line between its members. That is what I meant in suggesting how revealing it is that music has been so singled out for all this metaphor-labeling. The idea of a musical domain that is so narrowly and exclusively defined as Schenker defined it belongs to the dualistic conception from the beginning. In fact it should be considered to have given rise to the duality in the first place. The duality of the musical and the extramusical was a creature of the project of redefining music undertaken around 1800 by those whose aim was to elevate the status of music that was independent of language, mimesis, and functions related to the institutions of church and state authority. The distinction, as an opposition, was created with the declaration that high-valued music could be free of nonmusic.[31]

Schenker's conception of "music itself" is already apparent in writings of the early decades of the nineteenth century. Johann Friedrich Herbart, for example, stated the position that has come to be associated with Hanslick, but four decades earlier in 1813: "In music . . . the elements are

---

[30] Heinrich Schenker, *Counterpoint: A Translation of "Kontrapunkt,"* trans. John Rothgeb and Jürgen Thym (New York: Schirmer Books, 1987), p. 16.

[31] The account of this history must not be oversimplified by representing it as an orthogenic development. Even as music was declared to be independent of language, a language-based music concept survived from the earliest history of Western musical practice and has been thought to influence the practice and theory of instrumental music in the late eighteenth and nineteenth centuries. This is so in two respects: the modeling of the phrase structure of instrumental music—essentially melodic phrase structure—on the phrase structure of language; and a conception of musical form based on rhetoric. With respect to the first see Wye Jameson Allenbrook's essay " 'Ear-Tickling Nonsense': A New Context for Musical Expression in Mozart's 'Haydn' Quartets," *St. John's Review* 38 (1988): 1–24. With respect to the second see Elaine R. Sisman, *Haydn and the Classical Variation* (Cambridge, Mass.: Harvard University Press, 1993).

tones, or really relations of tones, and the objectively beautiful arises from their combination."[32]

Herbart is also the first, as far as I know, to assert that the tones do not need to be heard, they need only to be read in order to apprehend the objectively beautiful in music. The score is regarded as a safe haven for the purely musical work.

Whether intentionally or otherwise, the insistence upon labeling as "metaphorical" any qualitative properties that are found in music has the effect of reasserting the absolute authority of Herbart's dictum over music. But because no explanation has been offered of how such qualities can be metaphorical, the insertion of the term "metaphor" into the discourse in this way has no explanatory value and does not in any way qualify Herbart's dictum.

The alternative is to take a remark like Marquez's at face value, accepting "foreboding" as a verbal descriptive approximation for a property that music can have, if anything can have it, and that we can experience in an unmediated way, analyzing that property, if we like, in terms of the finest details of the musical materials and processes that are its component elements—not unlike the label "'drohendes Gefahr" that Arnold Schoenberg provided for the first part of his "Begleitungsmusik zu eine Lichtspielscene," Op. 34. That is, after all, what the achievements of a century of practice in musical analysis have prepared us to do.[33]

Otherwise, if the property that Marquez identified as "foreboding" is acquired through metaphorical transfer, what would it be transferred from—painting, poetry, film, or tragedy, all of which have it literally, whereas music cannot? There is something not right about the distinction.

Monroe Beardsley writes, "Some terms seem to apply literally to all processes, musical, physical and mental, e.g. fast, slow, accelerating, smooth, sudden; some apply literally to mental processes and metaphorically to music, e.g. tense, relaxed,"[34] with the implication, again, that music cannot be literally "tense" or "relaxed." Why not? Tension and

---

[32] See Edward Lippman, *A History of Musical Aesthetics* (Lincoln: University of Nebraska Press, 1992), pp. 291–319. In Payzant's translation of the 6th ed. of *Vom Musikalisch-Schönen* (1881) Hanslick wrote "So far as I know, the first person to have attacked the feeling-theory in musical aesthetics is Herbart" (p. 85).

[33] This is said against the misguided notion abroad that musical analysis and musical hermeneutics are at odds with one another, that the advancement of the latter requires the rejection of the former. That idea has been mistakenly attributed to me. See Lawrence Kramer, "Haydn's Chaos, Schenker's Order; or, Hermeneutics and Musical Analysis: Can they Mix?" *19th-Century Music* 16 (1992): 3–17; Scott Burnham, "The Criticism of Analysis and the Analysis of Criticism; Criticizing Criticism, Analyzing Analysis," ibid., pp. 70–79; and Leo Treitler, "Comment and Chronicle," ibid., vol. 17 (1993): 103–5.

[34] Monroe Beardsley, *Aesthetics: Problems in the Philosophy of Criticism* (New York: Harcourt, Brace and World, 1958), p. 328.

relaxation have been regarded as properties of music at least since Plato spoke of the "intense Lydian harmonies" and of "certain Ionian and Lydian ones that are called relaxed" (*Republic*, book 1). This morning I heard a radio critic characterize country music as "intense and relaxed at the same time." Music is capable of exemplifying those qualities as well as anything, as pianists in movie houses knew in the era of silent film.

What interest would Plato, the radio critic, and movie-house pianists have in Beardsley's reminder that music cannot literally exemplify those qualities, only metaphorically so? Or, even worse, that it can literally exemplify them but only metaphorically possess them? If it were not for Plato's presence in this company we could speak of a divide between philosophers on one side—to whom Beardsley's distinctions matter—and composers, performers, and critics on the other—to whom they do not. Such a divide has been in the air at least since Schopenhauer's criticism of composers and critics "who try 'pathologically' to pull music down into the phenomenal world by subordinating it to the sentimental expression of an ordinary person's individual emotions, interests, and concerns."[35] And it is embodied in the writings of Eduard Hanslick, whose reduction of descriptive language to the status of metaphor—when arguing for a scientific aesthetics—we have already noted, but whose own music criticism displays no scruples about metaphor at all.[36] But of what value to either side is a distinction between the philosopher's way of understanding music and the musician's and critic's way?

As for Marquez, his aperçu is intuitive. He is one of those "talented laymen" of whom Erwin Panofsky wrote, in whom the faculty of synthetic intuition in the interpretation of art may be better developed than in erudite scholars.[37]

The most gifted of such laymen, as far as music is concerned, was surely Marcel Proust. I introduce here a few passages from *Swann's Way* that seem to me to represent in an extraordinarily sensitive way the registers through which music is presented to us and through which we re-present it in order to display how this virtuoso of language moves from directly

---

[35] Quoted from Lydia Goehr, "Schopenhauer and the Musicians: An Inquiry into the Sounds of Silence and the Limits of Philosophizing About Music," in *Schopenhauer, Philosophy, and the Arts*, ed. Dale Jacquette (Cambridge: Cambridge University Press, 1996).

[36] See Peter Kivy, "What I've Always Wanted to Know About Hanslick," in *The Fine Art of Repetition: Essays in the Philosophy of Music* (Cambridge: Cambridge University Press, 1993).

[37] "To grasp those principles we need a faculty comparable to that of a diagnostician—a faculty which I cannot describe better than by the rather discredited term 'synthetic intuition,' and which may be better developed in a talented layman than in an erudite scholar." Erwin Panofsky, "Iconography and Iconology: An Introduction to the Study of Renaissance Art," in *Meaning in the Visual Arts: Papers in and on Art History* (New York: Doubleday Anchor, 1955), p. 38.

perceived qualities, gradually through conscious interaction with impressions, feelings, and outward associations (of which there are strikingly few in the passage), to reflection—even musical analysis—synthesis, and recollection.

> The year before . . . he had heard a piece of music played on the piano and violin . . . and it had been a source of keen pleasure when, below the delicate line of the violin part, slender but robust, compact and commanding, he had suddenly become aware of the mass of the piano part beginning to emerge in a sort of liquid rippling of sound, multiform but indivisible, smooth yet restless, like the deep blue tumult of the sea, silvered and charmed into a minor key by the moonlight. But then . . . suddenly enraptured, he had tried to grasp the phrase or the harmony . . . that had just been played and that had opened and expanded his soul, as the fragrance of certain roses, wafted upon the moist air of evening, has the power of dilating one's nostrils. . . . Scarcely had the exquisite sensation which Swann had experienced died away, before his memory had furnished him with a transcript, sketchy, it is true, and provisional, which he had been able to glance at while the piece continued, so that, when the same impression suddenly returned, it was no longer impossible to grasp. He could picture to himself its extent, its symmetrical arrangement, its notation, its expressive value; he had before him something that was no longer pure music, but rather design, architecture, thought, and which allowed the actual music to be recalled.[38]

Shall we simply regard such writing as belonging in another world, irrelevant to our theoretical discussions of musical meaning and expression? We would do better to accept its authority and learn from it of the multiplicity of ways in which we must approach the interpretation of music if we are to approximate our experience of it, even if that cannot yield the formulations of a consistent theory.[39]

We prize metaphor, not only for its ability to impart meaning in a particularly telling way, but even more—at its best, at least—for the way in which its incongruities affect the intellect (Goodman's metaphor for metaphor), the emotions (Shakespeare's line "How sweet the moonlight sleeps upon this bank" [*The Merchant of Venice*]), the senses (Proust's

---

[38] Marcel Proust, *In Search of Lost Time*, vol. 1: *Swann's Way*, trans. C. K. Scott Moncrieff and Terence Kilmartin, rev. D. J. Enright (New York: Modern Library, 1992), pp. 294, 295–96.
[39] Samuel Beckett wrote that "a book could be written on the significance of music in the work of Proust" (*Proust*, 1931), and Jean-Jacques Nattiez has done it (*Proust as Musician*). But in my reading of it the book is too single-mindedly devoted to extracting just such a consistent theory from Proust.

Example 2.2. Schubert, Piano Trio in E♭, D. 929, beginning of second movement, mm. 1–6

metaphor for the impact of the piano sound: "the liquid rippling of the piano sound . . . silvered and charmed into a minor key by the moonlight"). Metaphor inhabits a realm where imagination, not logic, rules. Donald Davidson begins his essay "What Metaphors Mean" metaphorically: "Metaphor is the dreamwork of language."[40]

Music is capable of metaphorlike effects, entirely within its own idiom. The second movement of Franz Schubert's Trio in E♭ major, D. 929, *Andante con moto*, begins with a long discursive theme in C minor, accompanied by a trudging figure that, even though played a touch too fast (we learn why only in the finale), registers as the tattoo of a funeral march— repeated chords, accent on the fourth beat followed by dotted rhythm, and occasionally drumroll-like trills, all conventional gestures that could be heard throughout the nineteenth century in music recognizable as funereal (see example 2.2).

That theme, made more to be repeated than developed, alternates with a soaring, more modular E♭-major theme that undergoes a vigorous, affirmative development; it seems as though it might be capable of lifting the movement out of the hopelessness of the C-minor music but in the end always slumps back into it. The movement has the aspect of circular, obsessive thinking (see example 2.3).

The finale, *Allegro moderato*, is one of those endless rondos of Schubert's that seem to modulate through more keys than there are, this one going on in an endless patter of mindless energy (see example 2.4).

Toward the middle of the movement the piano's right hand converts its simple triplets to a hemiola rhythm, the violin in pizzicato chords and the left hand of the piano take up the tattoo from the second movement, and,

[40] Donald Davidson, "What Metaphors Mean, " in *Inquiries into Truth and Interpretation* (New York: Oxford University Press, 1984), pp. 246–64.

Example 2.3. Schubert, Piano Trio in E♭, D. 929, second movement, mm. 41–44

Example 2.4. Schubert, Piano Trio in E♭, D. 929, beginning of finale, mm. 1–9

as if out of the depths of the unconscious, the cello steps forward to play the morose theme *sotto voce*. Suddenly it is as though this is what all that patter had been intended to suppress (see example 2.5). (The reason for the faster-than-funeral-march tempo of the second movement now appears: it is that the cello must be able to recall the theme in the finale at something approaching its original tempo, but without changing the tempo of the finale.) The music gains meaning by bringing together recognizably disjunct or even incompatible realms, producing as powerful a metaphoric effect as any that I can think of in language. Metaphor is as normal a source of meaning for music in its own domain as it is in language in *its* domain. Often what we call motivic work or thematic transformation is musical metaphor; but not always. Musical metaphor works directly within the musical domain, not indirectly through signifying processes that refer to "extramusical domains." Music inhabits the mental realm in which metaphor communicates. We are used to hearing that the

Example 2.5. Schubert, Piano Trio in E♭, D. 929, finale, mm. 277–85

expressive effect of music is metaphorical. It is worth considering that the expressive effect of metaphor is musical.

Schubert recalls the first theme of the second movement a second time near the end of the finale, in fact he makes an end to the piece through that return. By the simple move of opening the third phase of the theme—which until now had always looped back to the beginning—into the major mode (changing G♭ to G♮; see example 2.6), he emancipates the piece from the sense of entrapment with which the second movement had closed—a sense that is reinforced by a single failed attempt at escape near the end (see example 2.7)—and from which the scherzo and finale had seemed simply to walk—or skip—away.

What I am responding to here is a narrative dimension in the piece, and I say this in the face of serious questions that have lately been raised about the interpretation of music as narrative. Comparing music with literary narratives, critics of such an idea call attention to certain differences: the absence of a narrating voice in instrumental music, the inability of music to speak in the past tense, the location of the narrative in the description rather than the music, the inconsistencies about agency in musical "nar-

Example 2.6. Schubert, Piano Trio in E♭, D. 929, finale, mm. 721–25

Example 2.7. Schubert, Piano Trio in E♭, D. 929, second movement, mm. 196–202

rative"—narrative accounts of music follow, now musical elements such as keys and themes, now persons, such as the listener as he or she moves through the piece or the composer as he or she composes it. There can be no question about these differences, which are all owing to the differences between music and language. But that has not deflected composers and critics from their interest in something like a narrative dimension in music.[41]

Carolyn Abbate has made the strongest representations against such interpretations.[42] She reminds us of the distinction articulated by Plato

[41] For something of an overview of the range of approaches to this topic, see *Indiana Theory Review* 12 (1991), special issue on narrative, ed. Richard Littlefield.

[42] Carolyn Abbate, *Unsung Voices: Opera and Musical Narrative in the Nineteenth Century* (Princeton: Princeton University Press, 1992).

(in the third book of the *Republic*) and Aristotle (the *Poetics*) between the diagetic (epic or narrative) and mimetic (dramatic) modes of representation in poetry (pp. 53–56), and she asserts that music is more like the latter than the former, more like enactment than narrative. But we should also remember that theorists from Plato to Goethe point out that in practice the two modes are frequently combined.[43] It makes sense to identify them separately in classificatory exposition as ideal types, but that does not carry the stipulation that every passage must be clearly identifiable as either one or the other. More useful here is Abbate's own declaration earlier on that music is "radically unlike language, that the *trope* of music as a language needs to be resisted" (p. 18; I must return to this last phrase) and that "we cannot accept analogies between music and language as easily forged and straightforward" (p. 19). It is not self-evident that the distinction between narrative and drama is transposable to (instrumental) music. There is no reason to assume that, as a point of departure, and in general, critics who speak of musical narrativity do so not in the light of such an assumption but rather with reference to properties that music shares with both narrative and drama.[44] We need to operate here with the kind of suppleness of language use that allows us to speak, for example, of certain events in a narrative as "dramatic." In any case if music is to be described on the basis of any such system, it seems particularly odd to choose an ancient system that had no place for lyric. The current discussions about narrative are all about music of the eighteenth and nineteenth centuries—a time when lyric had a place in such classifications along with narrative and drama, and when the descriptive mode entered prominently into musical composition—whatever one may think about the dramatic and the narrative.[45]

Abbate declares that music is mimetic, and then identifies all the properties of the diagetic mode of poetic presentation that it cannot, in consequence, have. Chief among these, for her, seems to be that music has no past tense—it "traps the listener in present experience and the beat of passing time"—whereas narrative is by definition "a tale told later, by one who escaped to the outside of the tale" (p. 53). The reader need only turn back to the narrative passage cited earlier from Italo Calvino's story to be

[43] E.g., Plato (*Republic* 3.393): "Then in this case [when the epic poet speaks in the voice of another] the narrative of the poet may be said to proceed by imitation?"

[44] Fred Everett Maus, who writes perspicaciously about these matters, has written separately about music as narrative (*Indiana Theory Review* 12 [1991]) and music as drama (*Music Theory Spectrum* 10 [1988]: 54–74; reprinted in this volume on pp. 105–30).

[45] See Karol Berger, "*Diegesis* and *Mimesis*: The Poetic Modes and the Matter of Artistic Presentation," *Journal of Musicology* 12 (1994), for a fuller and far less dogmatic exposition of these matters.

reminded that tense cannot be counted on as a criterion for deciding what is and is not narrative.

As another reminder, I note that throughout this discussion I have followed the convention—literally inaccurate—of narrating with verbs in the present tense an event that is in the past—Abbate expressing the views that I am just now considering.

The grammatical categories of "present" and "past tense" contribute to the way events in literature strike us in relation to our—many-faceted and many-layered—time consciousness, but they do not by any means alone determine that experience. The consistent use of past tense in the following narrative from the beginning of book 22 of Homer's *The Odyssey*—a veritable model of diagetic presentation—does not prevent the poet's vivid language from causing its events to strike us as present. The story carries us along as we follow its telling, reflect, and anticipate:

> [Odysseus] drew to his fist the cruel head of an arrow for Antinous just as the young man leaned to lift his beautiful drinking cup, embossed, two-handled, golden: the cup was in his fingers: the wine was even at his lips: and did he dream of death? How could he? In the revelry amid his throng of friends who would imagine a single foe . . . could dare to bring death's pain on him and darkness on his eyes? Odysseus' arrow hit him under the chin and punched up to the feathers through his throat. Backward and down he went, letting the winecup fall from his shocked hand. Like pipes his nostrils jetted crimson runnels, a river of mortal red, and one last kick upset his table knocking the bread and meat to soak in dusty blood. Now as they craned to see their champion where he lay the suitors jostled in uproar down the hall, everyone on his feet.

If we are going to compare music with narrative literature, we must take care to compare their performance (the reading of narrative literature is a kind of performance) or their contents, *not* the performance of one with the contents of the other. If it is said that music "traps the listener in present experience and the beat of passing time," then that refers to its performance, and it is just as true of the performance of literary narrative. With both we want to know what happens next, and interruptions of any kind in the performance will create tension. It is just as true of both that when the performance is over we can both replay it in our minds and create nontemporal portraits of the totality of it.[46]

---

[46] This has been demonstrated in a masterful way by Edward T. Cone in "Three Ways of Reading a Detective Story—Or a Brahms Intermezzo," in his collection of essays, *Music: A View from Delft*, ed. Robert P. Morgan (Chicago: University of Chicago Press, 1989).

The difference that Abbate has tried to identify with her misplaced emphasis on tense is in the elements that are unfolded in the two arts: events or utterances preserved in language, and tone configurations. Musical unfoldings can refer to their own pasts and futures, that is, to past and future moments in their unfoldings (through memory and implications, respectively). So can literary unfoldings. Sometimes literary unfoldings can seem very like music in that respect (I think especially of Samuel Beckett's work, e.g. "Krapp's Last Tape"). There is not much point in comparing the two in terms of the morphological property of tense in the elements that are unfolded, since the elements of musical unfolding lack that morphological property altogether. But that is no new discovery, and it is hardly relevant to the consideration of narrativity in music.

That music is not verbal language is the burden of Jean-Jacques Nattiez's critique as well.[47] Music cannot *be* narrative, he writes, and adds, at various points, the qualifiers "strictly speaking," "in itself," "in the strict sense of the word," "properly speaking." The *idea* of a musical narrative is therefore a metaphor (how such an idea might function as a metaphor remains, here, too, unexplained).

Taken by itself the tautology that music is not language has little meaning and is of little value. The question whether music is a language of any sort would be better treated as a historical question than as an empirical or logical one, and addressed by way of the questions "What purposes have been served by considering music through comparison with language or by eschewing such comparison?" and "What have the consequences been?" They have been of various kinds—theoretical, critical, but also political. Music historians cannot afford to say that "the trope of music as language needs to be resisted."[48] The best line in Nattiez's paper is this: "There is no smoke without fire."

Béla Bartók's *Mikrokosmos* comprises 153 "progressive piano pieces" in six volumes. They are published with titles in Hungarian, French, German, and English. Bartók provided only the Hungarian titles; the translations were made by his friend Tibor Serly. Bartók named no. 142 in volume 6 "Mese a Kis Legyroll," "A Story about a Little Fly." The published French title is "Ce que la mouche raconte," or "What the Fly

---

[47] Jean-Jacques Nattiez, "Can One Speak of Narrativity in Music?" *Journal of the Royal Musical Association* 115 (1990): 240–57.

[48] Fritz Reckow's article "Tonsprache," in *Handwörterbuch der musikalischen Terminologie* (Wiesbaden, 1979), pp. 1–6, gives an overview of the conceptual and historical aspects of what he calls "the global parallelization of language and music." His unpublished Habilitationsschrift (Freiburg University, 1977), "'Sprachähnlichkeit' der Musik als terminologisches Problem," treats the subject at length.

Recounts." Note the difference: Bartók's title presents the piece (or the score or the performance) as the story. Who is the narrator? Perhaps Bartók, perhaps the performer, perhaps the listener. In the French, the fly may be the narrator, but it may be that what we hear is the contents of the fly's story, with Bartók as the ghost writer. Perhaps the present tense—"raconte"—favors the fly as narrator. The published German and English titles seem to nail that down: "Aus dem Tagebuch einer Fliege" and "From the Diary of a Fly." As the fly tells it. None of the titles presents the piece as an enactment, for example, "A Day in the Life of a Fly," although that might be the more precise way of characterizing my experience of it. But it would not be entirely satisfactory, either, for there is no element in the music that is clearly identifiable as the fly, to whom it all happens, nor are the musical events clearly identifiable as imitations of the fly's actions. Perhaps we could think of it as something like a film in which the camera is the eye of the character.

There are some relevant signs in the published score. At a certain point there is an increase in tempo, indicated by a metronome marking and the word *Agitato* above the system. Between the two staves at that point are the words *molto agitato e lamentoso*. The moment is easily recognizable in performance. Also above the system at that point are the Hungarian words "Jaj, pokhalo!!" with two exclamation points, in quotation marks. "Pokhalo" is a spider web. The words in Italian are the composer's, those in Hungarian are spoken by the fly, directly or as quoted by someone. Ten measures later, above the system, are the words *con gioia, leggero*. Now *lamentoso* and *con gioia* belong to that category of composers' instructions, half prescription, half description or commentary, like Beethoven's *Largo e mesto*. In Bartók's case, those words seem to suggest commentary by the composer as narrator.

In any case, in presenting the piece as a story rather than an enactment Bartók was committing no greater impropriety than that committed by painters and art critics or historians who speak, as they often do, of "narrative painting." This exemplifies again that insufficiency of language to say precisely what it is that music does that Mendelssohn put his finger on. The right word would be between "narrative" and "enactment." But just how important—or possible—is it to find the right word? Will those black-leathered critics turn from Marquez to Bartók and hand him a summons as well, for falsely representing a piece of music as a story as though he were passing a three-dollar bill? In our ordinary exchanges of language we take the words that are uttered by our fellow interlocutors as clues to what they have in mind to convey to us, not as fixed and invariable coinage.

But perhaps it was no impropriety at all. Hayden White writes of the "cognitive contents" of musical works.[49] Reacting to the way the harmonic progress of the first movement of Beethoven's Seventh Symphony is prefigured in its introduction—as a "prolepsis" (recall Marquez's "foreboding," but notice the difference in stance between "prolepsis" and "foreboding"), he calls that a "narrational" relationship. The awareness of such categories, he suggests—others are "actions," "events," "conflicts," "development over time," "crisis," "climax," "denouement"—is a kind of tacit preknowledge, like the knowledge of a mother tongue. The point of the comparison is that a mother tongue is the language we speak and understand most directly, in the least mediated way, because we begin to learn it from the beginning of our consciousness. And that is when we begin to learn those categories of experience, which are to us intrinsic qualities. We know them in a nondiscursive as well as discursive way. This is the "structural reciprocity" between the temporality of human existence and Narrativity to which Paul Ricoeur refers when he writes, "I take temporality to be that structure of existence that reaches language in Narrativity and narrativity to be the language structure that has temporality as its ultimate referent."[50] In like manner narrativity in music is that structure that has temporality as its ultimate referent.

Mikrokosmos no. 144 is entitled "Minor Seconds, Major Sevenths." Nevertheless, I experience it, just as much as the "Fly" piece, which might have been called "Overlapping Whole-Tone Segments," in terms of the same sorts of "narrativizing" categories, but not at the expense of attending to the minor seconds and major sevenths, which are controlled in a very beautiful way. It is marked *Molto adagio, mesto*, by the way.

Neither the narrative nor the formalist title alone can reveal what either piece is all about. There are other titles in the *Mikrokosmos* that suggest sonorities ("Bagpipe"), genres ("Peasant Dance"), styles ("From the Island of Bali"), actions ("Wrestling"), affects ("Merry Andrew"); different emphases, but none tells what the piece is all about, and none excludes the other categories. One could associate a different aesthetic or historiographic theory with almost every category. But the lesson I draw from *Mikrokosmos* is that these aspects do not compete but coexist in music, and they ought not to compete in the interpretation of music. Music is protean and its meanings span the range of human action and experience. Whether he knew it or not, Bartók, in composing this multidimensional

[49] Hayden White, *Music and Text: Critical Inquiries*, ed. Peter Paul Scher (Cambridge: Cambridge University Press, 1992), pp. 293–95.

[50] Paul Ricoeur, "Narrative Time," in *On Narrative*, ed. W. J. T. Mitchell (Chicago: University of Chicago Press, 1980), pp. 165–86.

work, exemplified an old sense of the word "mikrokosmos" that we find expressed in the *Proportionale musices* (1473–74) of Johannes Tinctoris: "If so much harmony is found in celestial and terrestrial things . . . why should we believe man himself to be bereft of it? . . . God created man according to the plan of the larger world, called by the Greeks 'Kosmos' . . . and made him similar to the world but of lesser quantity, whence he is called 'Mikrokosmos,' or 'small world.'"[51]

[51] Johannes Tinctoris, *Proportionale musices*, trans. Gary Tomlinson, in Oliver Strunk, *Source Readings in Music History*.

3

Listening with Imagination: Is Music Representational?

KENDALL WALTON

P lato characterized the music of the flute and lyre as mimetic, assimilating it to painting and poetry. This attitude contrasts starkly with the modern tendency to distinguish music sharply from the representational arts. Eduard Hanslick and others insist that music is just sound or sound structure, that its interest lies in the notes themselves, not in stories that they tell or anything that they "mean." Peter Kivy calls music an art of "pure sonic design."[1] There is, to be sure, explicit program music. And music sometimes combines with words or images to form a representational whole, as in song, opera, film, and dance. But some will set aside the combinations as impure instances of music, mixtures of music with other things. And purists dismiss program music as of little intrinsic interest or even as only marginal examples of music. Music itself, "pure," "absolute" instrumental music such as Bach's Brandenburg Concertos, Brahms's symphonies, and Anton Webern's Five Pieces for Orchestra, appears to be quite a different animal from the standard "mimetic" or representational arts, such as (figurative) painting and literature.

This is a revision of the third of three Carl G. Hempel Lectures given at Princeton University in May 1991. It develops a suggestion I broached in "What Is Abstract about the Art of Music?" (*Journal of Aesthetics and Art Criticism* 46 [Spring 1988]: 359–60) and mentioned in *Mimesis as Make-Believe: On the Foundations of the Representational Arts* (Cambridge, Mass.: Harvard University Press, 1991), pp. 335–36. I am indebted to Karol Berger, David Hills, Marion Guck, Anthony Newcomb, and Alicyn Warren for helpful discussions and comments.
[1] Peter Kivy, "Is Music an Art?" *Journal of Philosophy* 88 (October 1991): 553.

Given the strength of purist intuitions, it is disconcerting to discover how quickly qualms arise. Distinguishing "absolute" music from program music is not nearly as easy as one might expect. There is no sharp line between explicit and subtle program music, or between subtle program music and music that is as unprogrammatic as it gets, and one can be puzzled about the location even of fuzzy lines. When music—what taken by itself would seem to be "absolute" music—teams up with words or images, the music often makes definite *representational* contributions to the whole, rather than merely accompanying other representational elements. Opera orchestras and film sound tracks frequently serve to "describe" the characters and the action, reinforcing or supplementing or qualifying the words or images. Mere titles often suffice to make music patently representational; indeed I cannot imagine music that an appropriate title could not render representational. Music stands ready to take on an explicit representational function at the slightest provocation.

If music can be nudged so easily into obvious representationality, can we be confident that without the nudge it is not representational at all? Most if not all music is *expressive* in one way or another, and its expressiveness surely has a lot to do with its susceptibility to being made explicitly representational. To be expressive is to bear a significant relation to human emotions or feelings or whatever it is that is expressed. Why doesn't this itself amount to possessing extramusical "meanings," and why shouldn't expressiveness count as a species of representation?[2] What is to stop us from saying that exuberant or anguished music represents exuberance or anguish, or instances thereof?

One possible answer is that music is expressive by virtue of its capacity to elicit feelings in listeners, and that possessing this capacity doesn't amount to representation. Arousal theories of expression have not been popular recently. Theorists typically prefer to locate the feelings expressed in the music rather than in the appreciator, and so must face the question why the feelings in the music, those the music expresses, aren't represented. Is exuberance "in" the music in the way that a train is "in" a picture of a train? Arousal theories have obvious difficulties, but there is more to them than is usually acknowledged.

Further considerations that I will adduce shortly do more than raise qualms; they put the burden of proof squarely on those who would resist Plato's assimilation of music to poetry and painting. They may not, however, cure the inclination to resist, or rid us of the initial intuition that

---

[2] This possibility alone shows Kivy's peremptory declaration in "Is Music an Art?" that music is not representational to be seriously premature.

there is a gaping chasm of some sort between (absolute)
hand and painting and literature on the other. I prefer t
resentation in such a way that virtually all music qualifi
not be satisfied until we can accommodate and exp
inclinations.

No sophisticated theory of representation will be nececu to see why
music can reasonably count as representational, however unattractive that
conclusion might appear initially. The hard part will be recapturing a
sense of music's purity, understanding how fundamentally music differs
from the paradigmatically representational arts, whether or not we count
it as representational.

Imagination in Musical Experience

Literary and pictorial representations establish *fictional worlds*. There
is the world of a story and the world of a picture. Does music have
fictional worlds? We might be tempted to speak of the "world of the
music" when we listen to a Brandenburg Concerto, for instance, but this
may be a world of a very different sort. Story worlds contain (fictional)
ghosts and goblins, or murderers and detectives, or jealous lovers, or
tragic heroes. There are people in the world of Brueghel's *The Peasant
Dance* and unicorns in that of the *Unicorn Tapestries*. But if a Brandenburg
Concerto has a "world," it may seem to be one that contains nothing but
notes, harmonies, melodies, rhythmic motives, developments, and so
on—the material of the music itself—not fictional characters and fictional
events represented by the music. (This needn't mean that the world is not
a fictional one.) One can always construct a world of the usual sort for a
piece of music. One can, if one wants to, make up programs for the Brandenburg Concertos, tell stories to go with them—stories about ghosts and
goblins or murderers and detectives, or whatever one allows the music
to suggest. But such stories seem irrelevant at best to an understanding
of the music, and they are more likely to hinder than to enhance
appreciation.

So speak purist intuitions. But let's look further. Fictional worlds are
imaginary worlds. Visual and literary representations establish fictional
worlds by virtue of their role in our imaginative lives. *The Garden of Earthly
Delights* gets us to imagine monsters and freaks. On reading Franz Kafka's
story "A Hunger Artist," one imagines a man who fasts for the delight of
spectators. It is by prescribing such imaginings that these works establish
their fictional worlds. The propositions we are to imagine are those that
are "true in the fictional world," or *fictional*. Pictures and stories are rep-

resentational by virtue of the fact that they call for such imaginings.[3] Music also induces imaginings. If we look carefully, especially if we are willing to look under the surface, we stand to find more than a little imagining in our experience of music, even of fugues and sonatas, and many of our imaginings would seem to be called for by the music. Why doesn't the content of these imaginings constitute fictional worlds, the worlds of the music? And doesn't this make the music representational, as literature and painting are?

In what ways does music engage our imaginations? A large and diverse range of cases needs to be considered, although what is to be said about many of them will depend on how broadly one construes the notion of imagining. Imagining as I understand it can be spontaneous, nondeliberate, a passive experience rather than something one does. Dreaming is one kind of imagining. I also favor understanding imagining in a way that allows for implicit or unacknowledged or nonconscious or subliminal imaginings; one may imagine something without noticing that one does. To insist that a person imagines only if the thought of what is imagined occurs to her would be far too restrictive. (This doesn't mean that it will be easy to ascertain whether a person does engage in a given imagining, when the thought does not occur to her.)

Some imaginings that listeners plausibly engage in are about elements of the music itself, about tones and harmonies and melodies. Beethoven's String Quartet Op. 59, no. 3, opens with a diminished seventh chord, giving the impression that what we hear first is not its beginning, that it started before we heard it. Perhaps we imagine that it did. On hearing the arpeggiated Prelude to Bach's G-major Cello Suite, perhaps we imagine the intermittently sounding pedal tone to be sounding continuously. (Heinrich Schenker speaks of imagining in cases like this.[4]) We may imagine events of a piece to be causally related in various ways. We speak of one musical idea or event growing out of another, of one interrupting or interfering with another, of one preparing the way for another. In many instances we probably imagine that there is a nomological connection of some sort between events without imagining what specifically is the cause of what. This is enough to explain our "expectation" that a tonic harmony will succeed a dominant seventh, for instance, even if, having heard the piece many times before, we know that the cadence is

---

[3] This is the central feature of the account of representation I develop in *Mimesis as Make-Believe*.

[4] Heinrich Schenker, *Counterpoint: A Translation of Kontrapunkt*, trans. John Rothgeb and Jürgen Thym (New York: Schirmer Books, 1987), vol. 2, book 2, chap. 2, §2, pp. 56–59.

deceptive.[5] We imagine (subliminally, anyway) that causal principles are operating by virtue of which the occurrence of the dominant seventh makes it likely that a tonic will follow, and on hearing the dominant we imaginatively expect the tonic, whether or not we actually expect it.[6] If, or to the extent that, these various imaginings are prescribed, we have fictionality.

In our examples so far, the "characters" in the fictions are elements of the music. It is fictional that the initial diminished seventh chord of Beethoven's Op. 59, no. 3, was preceded by sounds we did not hear, that the pedal tones of the Bach Prelude sound continuously, that certain musical events are nomologically connected in such a way that the occurrence of some makes the occurrence of certain others likely. But the world of the music is a *fictional* one, not just part of the real world, even if it is populated by immigrants from the real world; they behave, in the musical world, in ways they do not in the real one. (Fictional worlds contain plenty of real world immigrants. There are novels, stories, yarns about Julius Caesar, Napoleon, Richard Nixon, the Civil War, etc.)

Music, in the cases I have described, is like nonfigurative paintings that present fictional worlds populated by features of the paintings themselves, as when it is fictional that one rectangular shape lies in front of another.[7] If, as I recommend, we count such nonfigurative paintings as representational, much music will qualify as well. This result need not distress musical purists. They may be willing to call music representational in a sense that applies also to paintings of Piet Mondrian and Kasimir Malevich and Frank Stella, provided that they can still find a way to distinguish both sharply enough from literature and figurative painting. This may not be easy, however, especially in the case of music. It is not easy to deny that music often has fictional worlds containing characters that are not themselves features of the music, as we shall see.

There is a lot of mimicry in music. Instrumental music sometimes mimics vocal music. Keyboard instruments, percussive though they are, sometimes play *cantabile*.[8] Vocal music occasionally mimics instrumental music. Dance rhythms are used in pieces that are not dances. Stravinsky

[5] See Leonard Meyer, *Emotion and Meaning in Music* (Chicago: University of Chicago Press, 1956).
[6] See Edward T. Cone, "Three Ways of Reading a Detective Story—Or a Brahms Intermezzo," in *Music: A View from Delft*, ed. Robert P. Morgan (Chicago: University of Chicago Press, 1989), p. 87.
[7] Cf. Walton, *Mimesis as Make-Believe*, §1.8. I follow Richard Wollheim in understanding representationality in a way that covers much nonfigurative painting.
[8] "The left hand begins to sing like a cello." David Lewin, "Auf dem Flusse: Image and Background in a Schubert Song," *19th-Century Music* 6, no. 1 (1982): 53.

mimics a baroque musical style in his *Pulcinella* Suite, and so does Ernst Bloch in his Concerto Grosso. Mere similarities do not necessarily induce imagining or constitute make-believe. But it is surely not out of the question that one is to imagine the melodic line of the *Adagio cantabile* movement of Beethoven's "Pathetique" Sonata as being sung, and that it is best played in such a way as to encourage this imagining.[9] Here, as in the previous examples, the actual sounds of the music belong to its fictional world, but so does a (fictive) person. It is fictional that a person is singing them.

This is one of many cases in which one has a sense of performers' actions by which they produced the sounds or of composers' thoughts as they wrote the score. We may not care what the performer or composer actually did or thought or what feelings she might actually have been expressing thereby. The impression the music gives of having been produced in a certain manner or as being the expression of certain feelings or emotions may be what we are interested in.[10] Joseph Kerman suggests several such characteristics in the *Heiliger Dankgesang* of Beethoven's String Quartet Op. 132.

> The mystic aura is furthered by the unnaturally slow tempo and the scoring or, rather, by what seems to be an unnaturally slow tempo on account of the scoring. The image is orchestral: forty strings could sustain the hymn at this speed with comfort, but four can bear it only with a sense of strain, tenuousness, and a certain gaucherie. This Beethoven certainly wanted. . . . Again one thinks of the Great Fugue, another work in which the instruments are made to outdo themselves, and in which their unhappy striving is incorporated into the essential aesthetic.[11]

I take the notation "run amok" in the score of William Kraft's *Momentum* (1966) to be advice that the performer make the music sound as though he has run amok.

[9] The slow section of the third movement of Beethoven's A♭-major Piano Sonata, Op. 110, is titled "Recitativo" and obviously mimics a vocal recitative. (Alicyn Warren pointed out this example to me.)

[10] The notion of composers' *personas* comes under this heading. See Edward T. Cone, "Persona, Protagonist, and Characters," in Cone, *The Composer's Voice* (Berkeley and Los Angeles: University of California Press, 1974), pp. 25–26; Jerrold Levinson, "Hope in the Hebrides," in Levinson, *Music, Art, and Metaphysics* (Ithaca: Cornell University Press, 1990); Fred Everett Maus, "Music as Drama," in this volume; and Bruce Vermazen, "Expression as Expression," *Pacific Philosophical Quarterly* 67 (1986). Also my "Style and the Products and Processes of Art," in *The Concept of Style*, 2d ed., ed. Berel Lang (Ithaca: Cornell University Press, 1987), pp. 72–103.

[11] Joseph Kerman, *The Beethoven Quartets* (New York: Norton, 1966), p. 256.

It is not a large step to regarding music that gives an impression of the composer's or performer's actions or feelings or thoughts to be *representing* itself as the product of a composer's or performer's acting or feeling or thinking in certain ways, to be mandating that listeners imagine this to be so.

Expressive music, some say, is music that suggests or portrays or somehow recalls expressive human behavior, behavior by means of which human beings express exuberance or anguish or gaiety or agitation or serenity or anger or timidity or boldness or aggressiveness.[12] This will include music that represents itself as resulting from such expressive behavior, but there is no reason to suppose that music cannot simply portray expressive behavior without portraying itself as the product of such behavior. In any case, there can be no doubt that some kinds of expressive music are expressive by virtue of connections with human behavior. There is little strain in thinking of some musical passages as representing, as inducing us to imagine, exuberant or agitated or bold behavior. Vocal music portrays expressive verbal behavior, including not just the utterance of certain words but the manner of their utterance, a tone of voice. The expressive quality of an utterance, the tone of voice, remains in much instrumental music even without the words. Some music has more or less obvious connections with nonverbal behavior, with physical movement. This is evident in the case of marches and dances, but listeners' tendencies to tap their feet or move in response to rhythmic features of other music as well suggests that they understand music of many kinds to have some important connection with agitated or calm or determined or lackadaisical behavior.

Where there is behavior there is a behaver. If music represents an instance of behaving calmly or nervously or with determination, it represents, at least indirectly, someone so behaving. So the fictional world contains human beings, anonymous fictive agents, whether or not the sounds themselves are characters in it.

The prevalence and variety of imaginings in our experience of music, including many of the examples I have mentioned and others as well, is reflected in the prevalence and variety of metaphors we use to describe it. We call passages of music exuberant, agitated, serene, timid, calm, determined, nervous. We speak of rising and falling melodies, of wistful melodies and hurried rhythms, of motion and rest, of leaps, skips, and

---

[12] See, e.g., Stephen Davies, "The Expression of Emotion in Music," *Mind* 89 (1980); R. K. Elliott, "Aesthetic Theory and the Experience of Art," in H. Osborne, *Aesthetics* (Oxford: Oxford University Press, 1972); Peter Kivy, *The Corded Shell: Reflections on Musical Expression* (Princeton: Princeton University Press, 1980); Levinson, "Hope in the Hebrides"; and Vermazen, "Expression as Expression."

stepwise progression, of statements and answering phrases,[13] tension and release, resignation and resolve, struggle, uncertainty, and arrival. Music can be impetuous, powerful, delicate, sprightly, witty, majestic, tender, arrogant, peevish, spirited, yearning, chilly.[14] I do not think that metaphorical descriptions always indicate imaginative experiences (even subliminal ones) on the part of listeners, but in many instances they do. We imagine agitation or nervousness, conflict and resolution. Sometimes we imagine (something's) rising or descending. (Or we can easily get ourselves to imagine thus as we listen to the music; an awareness of this possibility may color our hearing even when we don't actually engage in the imagining.) The metaphors purists are least able to avoid, those of tension and release, motion and rest, seem to me to involve imagination. To appreciate music one must feel tension and release; one must allow oneself to imagine motion and rest.[15]

What we have noticed so far seems suspiciously like the beginnings of story fragments in music, the beginnings of programs. I conclude this collection of examples with one that is a little less fragmentary. Consider the opening of the adagio movement of Mozart's A-major Piano Concerto, K. 488 (example 3.1).[16] The last half of bar 7 is in the dominant, heading for the tonic, F♯ minor. But it doesn't get there for a while—not until the cadence in bars 11 and 12. Instead, the dominant goes first to a D-major triad (the submediant), in bar 8. This is a deceptive cadence, an instance of Meyer's thwarted expectation, but a very special one. The left hand does go immediately to the tonic, on the first beat of bar 8. The right hand gets there too, but not until the second beat. And by then the bass has moved down to D. That gives us—accidentally, as it were—the D-major triad instead of the tonic. The D-major triad is understood later as the dominant of a Neapolitan sixth, which resolves eventually to the dominant and then to the tonic.

The upper voice is *late* coming to the A in bar 8. There are precedents for this tardiness earlier in the passage. The upper voice was late getting to the A (and F♯) at the beginning of bar 3; in bar 4 it participates in a sus-

[13] Lewin speaks of "the mimesis of a giant question mark" ("Auf dem Flusse," p. 54).

[14] These last examples are Hanslick's (*On the Musically Beautiful*, trans. Geoffrey Payzant [Indianapolis: Hackett, 1986], pp. 9, 10, 32).

[15] For a discussion of the ways in which metaphors do and do not involve imagination and make-believe, see my "Metaphor and Prop-Oriented Make-Believe," *European Journal of Philosophy* 1, no. 1 (1993).

[16] I am indebted to Marion Guck for introducing me to this passage and pointing out many of its interesting features. She discusses it in "Taking Notice: A Response to Kendall Walton," *Journal of Musicology* 11, no. 1 (Winter 1993): 45–51.

Example 3.1. Mozart, Piano Concerto in A, K. 488, second movement, mm. 1–12

pension; in bar 6 it is late getting to the C♯. In the first two cases the bass waits "patiently" for the soprano to arrive. But in the second phrase, the bass can't wait. It is locked into a (near) sequence, which allows no delay. In bar 6, as in bar 8, the bass has moved on, changing the harmony, by the time the soprano arrives.

One could tell a story to go with this: a character, call her Dalia, is going to catch a train. She has a habit of being late. And in bar 7 she dallies—she's off chasing butterflies. She dallies so long that she misses the train (the bass), which is on a fixed schedule and can't wait. But missing the train sets up a fortuitous meeting (D major), perhaps with a member of the opposite sex, which leads to unexpected new adventures (G major).

This is silly—like musical renditions of thunderstorms or locomotives or feline serenades. The music certainly doesn't tell this story. We aren't supposed to think of the story as we listen. And it is likely to be distracting. But the lateness of the upper voice, and its dallying quality, the rigidity of the bass's progression, the fortuitousness or accidentalness of the D-major triad, the movement to something new, are in the music. To miss these is, arguably, to fail fully to understand or appreciate the music. And talking about the train, the butterfly chase, and so on is one way of bringing out the lateness, the dallying, the fortuitousness.[17] Some of this, at least, is a matter of imagining. We imagine something's being late, probably without imagining what sort of thing it is. And we imagine a fortuitous or accidental occurrence. (The imaginings needn't involve saying to oneself that something is late, fortuitous, etc.) If the music told the story, it would certainly be representational. But why shouldn't it count as representational anyway, as representing instances of lateness, fortuitousness, and so on, even if its fictional world is very incomplete and indefinite? (It would be inadequate to think of it as merely indicating or expressing the property of lateness; it portrays a particular [fictitious] instance of something's being late, even if nothing much can be said about what it is that is late. Listeners imagine something's being late on a particular occasion; they do not merely contemplate the quality of lateness.)

Some deceptive cadences consist in a clunking, unprepared for progression from V to vi, and give the impression of the composer playing a trick on us; we can hear him saying afterward, "Ha, ha! I fooled you!" But in the Mozart example, my sense is rather that things just happen in the natural course of events to turn out as they do; the vi chord results from occurrences earlier in the passage, including the top voice's dallying and the bass's rigid schedule. I don't think I would have this sense if I weren't engaged actively, if subliminally, in imaginings like those I have described.

Does the dallying cause or explain the lateness? Try a less dallying melodic line in bar 7 (example 3.2). If the lateness now seems to you less expected, less inevitable, more in need of explanation than it did in the original, this is evidence that in Mozart's version you implicitly imagined dallying, and that you imagined it to be responsible for the lateness. ("How could she have missed the train? She was right there when it arrived!")

There is room for disagreement, concerning some of the above examples, about whether normal or appropriate musical experiences involve imagining or make-believe in the ways I have described. But it is clear that we cannot simply dismiss out of hand the idea of musical works' having fictional worlds. It looks as though they may have worlds teeming with life, just under the surface at least—like swamp water seen through a

---

[17] Susanne Langer calls a program for pure music a crutch (*Philosophy in a New Key*, 3d ed. [Cambridge, Mass.: Harvard University Press, 1942], pp. 242–43). Crutches are sometimes helpful and sometimes get in the way. This one does no harm *as long as* the make-believe the story introduces is understood to be "prop-oriented" in the sense I explicate in "Metaphor and Prop-Oriented Make-Believe."

Example 3.2. Mozart, Piano Concerto in A, K. 488, second movement, *alternative to* mm. 7–8

microscope. If we follow through on our purist inclinations to reject stories or images or meanings attached to music as unmusical, if not childish or silly, we must begin to wonder how much of what we love about music will be left. Yet if we accept pervasive make-believe in music, the question of how to account for the evident contrast between ("absolute") music, and literary and pictorial representations becomes pressing. Our experiences of music seem shot through with imaginings, yet I, at least, continue to resist the idea that Bach's Brandenburg Concertos and Brahms's symphonies have fictional worlds, as *Crime and Punishment* and *Hamlet* do.

Differences

If musical works do have worlds, and if they involve very much of the make-believe I have suggested they might, they are zoos—full of life, but discrete bits of life, each in its own separate cage—not a working ecological system. It is not easy to make sense of the fictional world of a fugue or a sonata as a coherent whole, to see what the various diverse bits of make-believe have to do with one another. It will be fictional that there are instances of upward and downward movement, statements and answers, causes and effects, singing, unperceived sounds, determined or aggressive or timid behavior; all these fictional truths jumbled together with few coherent links among them. There will rarely be a plot line for the listener to follow, even as brief a one as I managed to find in—or impose on—the Mozart passage.

Musical worlds will be radically indeterminate with respect to the identity and individuation of agents.[18] Is it fictional that the agent who behaves aggressively in one phrase is the same one who behaves placidly in the next? Do we imagine that a single person behaves first aggressively and then placidly, or that different agents engage in the aggressive and the

---

[18] See Maus, "Music as Drama."

placid behavior? In an answering musical phrase, is the "character" giving the answer different from the one who made the "statement" or asked the "question," or does the original fictive speaker reply to herself? Sometimes we may have some sense of how to answer such questions; often we will not.[19]

It may seem that the various bits of make-believe do not even belong to the same fictional world, that the musical work has multiple worlds. But there is no good way of deciding where one world stops and another begins.

If we think of a musical work as a prop in a game of make-believe, the picture seems to be that of a succession of momentary skit fragments, unrelated to one another. This picture contrasts starkly with the profound sense we often have of the unity and coherence of musical works, the sense that their parts belong together, that one phrase leads naturally to the next, and that any surprising sequences ultimately seem to have been justified.[20] Perhaps the unity is to be explained in purely musical terms, even if the elements that are unified include ones with significant representational roles.[21] Compare a wallpaper design containing depictions of objects of many different sorts—a truck here, a dinosaur there, an ice cream cone over there—with no very salient connections among them. We may be expected to notice various individual depictions but not to think about how they are related within the fictional world or perhaps even to think of them as part of the same fictional world. The overall pattern may still be a highly unified one, however, even if its unity does not consist in a unified fictional world. The depictions may all be in the same representational style, and the overall design may be formally coherent. Likewise, perhaps, with music. Musical coherence may consist more in coherence of sound patterns than in unity of representational content. There may still be representational content, of course, and it may be important.

If the elements of fictionality in a musical work do not cohere well and the work's unity is based on something else, some may be inclined to deny

[19] Uncertainty about identity and individuation may be no accident in an aural representational art. Hearing, in real life, is typically less important than sight in the acquisition of knowledge *de re*, knowledge about particular things. On hearing the thunder of a team of galloping horses, I may have little notion which clops are made by the same horse and which by different ones. But I can do much better, when I see the horses, in identifying which seen bits of horse belong to the same horse and which do not.

[20] Anthony Newcomb emphasized to me the difference between a high degree of *connectedness* among the parts of a whole, and the whole having a coherent or intelligible *shape*; some theme-and-variation movements possess the former and lack the latter. My remarks in this paragraph apply to both of these varieties of unity.

[21] See Peter Kivy, "A New Music Criticism?" *Monist* 63 (1990): 260–67, and "Auditor's Emotions: Contention, Concession and Compromise," *Journal of Aesthetics and Art Criticism* 51, no. 1 (1993): 9–11. I owe the wallpaper example to David Hills.

that these elements constitute a fictional *world*. If instead of telling the Dalia story the Mozart passage presents more or less disassociated instances of things' being late, something's being on a fixed schedule, a fortuitous incident, and a change to something new, it may seem artificial to attribute all this to a single fictional world and presumptuous to speak of multiple fictional worlds. Even if a listener does imagine certain connections among the incidents, these imaginings may strike one as optional, as not mandated especially by the music itself, and so not contributing to a fictional world of the musical work. (They may belong to the world of the listener's imagination, however.)

There is a more important reason to hesitate attributing fictional worlds to musical works, even while recognizing the rich imaginative component in listeners' experiences that I have described. Explaining it will require further stage setting.

Paintings and novels are what I call props in games of make-believe, having much in common with dolls and hobby horses. All these props provoke imaginings. The child playing with a doll imagines a baby, as the spectator of a picture of a dragon imagines a dragon. The imaginings children engage in when they participate in make-believe are not just about babies and horses, however; the children imagine about themselves as well. A child imagines (himself or herself) putting a baby to bed, or riding a horse. The child belongs to the world of make-believe; it is fictional, in that world, that he or she puts a baby to bed or rides a horse. Spectators of pictures and readers of stories also imagine about themselves. On viewing a picture of a dragon, I imagine (myself) seeing a dragon. On reading "A Hunger Artist" I imagine being told (by the narrator) about a professional faster, or at least I imagine knowing about such a person. The appreciator does not belong to the world of the *story* or the world of the *picture*. But the appreciator uses the picture or story in a game of make-believe that has its own world, one to which the appreciator does belong. In the world of the picture, the work world, there is only a dragon. But in the world of the viewer's game with the picture, he sees a dragon.

(Absolute) music and the paradigmatically representational arts induce in appreciators significantly different imaginings about themselves. One difference is evident in the ways in which music and painting portray space. Pictures represent spatial properties of things. So, arguably, does music—when melodies rise and fall, when there is movement from one key to another, arrivals and departures, dense textures, open fifths, and so on, or at least in some such instances. (It is less clear in music than in painting what sorts of things fictionally possess the spatial properties.) But musical space, unlike pictorial space, is usually presented in a perspectiveless manner. It is fictional in my game with a painting that I have a spatial perspective in the fictional world, that *I* bear certain spatial relations to the objects in the painting. Fictionally I see a mountain towering above me; I imagine seeing it from below. Or fictionally I see a ship in the distance sailing toward me. The make-believe spatiality of music seems not to give rise to similar imaginings *de se*. When a rising melody makes it fictional that something rises, do I imagine something rising up toward me from below, or something above me rising away from me? At what pitch am I? When there is movement from one key to another, where fictionally am I in relation to it? Am I to imagine movement toward or away from me, or from my left to my right, or what? Answers are hard to come by. Listeners seem not to have spatial perspectives, even when musical worlds are spatial. The music appears to have its own separate space, one unrelated to the listener's space.

Occasional exceptions underscore this point dramatically. The middle section of Debussy's nocturne "Fetes" mimics a band approaching the listener—getting louder and louder. We imagine the musicians approaching *us*. We have a spatial position in the fictional world of our game relative to them, a spatial perspective. The contrast with more usual musical portrayals of space is striking. (It is curious that crescendos and diminuendos do not very often give the impression of something drawing closer to us or getting farther away, but they don't.) Looking ahead, I should mention another possibility: that *I* am what moves, that I feel as though I am rising, or imagine myself rising, when I hear a melody as rising, and that the listener has the impression of moving from one place to another when the music moves from one key to another.

The independence of musical space from us is linked to a more general respect in which fictional worlds of musical works, if there are such, appear often to be isolated from us. The experience of perceiving pictures is, at the most basic level, an experience of imagining seeing; on looking at a picture of a tree one imagines seeing a tree—from a certain angle and distance.[22] But the experience of listening to music, even obviously representational music, does not in general involve imagining hearing (or imagining perceiving of any kind). When music represents sounds—sounds of trains, babbling brooks, bird calls—listeners imagine hearing these sounds. But much representational music does not represent sounds at all. A rising melody portraying the ascension of a saint into heaven doesn't portray the *sound* of the ascension; I have no idea what a saint's ascent to heaven sounds like. Music probably does not portray sounds

---

[22] Sometimes the distance can be specified only approximately, and sometimes the angle is ambiguous, e.g., in some Cubist works.

when it portrays nonvocal behavioral expressions of emotion (aggressive rhythms). Tension and release in music, resignation and resolve, motion and rest are likely not to involve representations of sounds. When no sounds are portrayed, listeners do not imagine hearing things, as they listen to the music. They do not have the kind of perceptual access to the fictional world that spectators have to the world of paintings. One imagines instances of tension and release, but one probably does not imagine perceiving them. So one does not imagine having a particular perspective on them.

Things have taken a strange turn. We seem headed toward a conception of music that I find very unattractive, one very contrary to my experience of music. I have emphasized the importance of participation in our games of make-believe with paintings and novels, the importance of imagining doing and experiencing things in connection with what is represented, for example, imagining seeing things. What we seem headed toward is a conception of music involving much less participation, much less imagining *de se*, than there is in painting and literature. It may be fictional in our games that we know about instances of tension and relaxation, and perhaps about behavioral expressions of such states; we may imagine knowing about them. But we don't imagine perceiving them. This is a little like our response to descriptions, in a literary work, of characters doing various things and experiencing various feelings and emotions. But many literary works have narrators, and it is fictional that the narrator tells us about the characters. Even this is lacking in music. The listener doesn't imagine being told about someone's being tense or relaxed or euphoric or agitated. It would seem to be indeterminate (in many instances) how fictionally we know. We imagine knowing about them without, it seems, imagining anything concerning how we came to know. We don't imagine having a particular perspective on the fictional world.

To say there is not much participation is to say that there is not much of a game world, a world to which we ourselves belong. We would seem then to be distanced from the events of the work world, the fictional struggles and agitations and tension and release being most prominently a part of a world to which we do not belong.

My experience of music is not at all like this. My impression is the opposite of being distanced from the world of the music (if we can call it a world). I feel intimate with the music—more intimate, even, than I feel with the world of a painting. The world of a painting (as opposed to the world of my game with the painting) is *out there*, something I observe from an external perspective. But it is as though I am inside the music, or it is inside me. Instead of having an objective, aperspectival relation to the musical world, I seem to relate to it in a most personal and subjective manner.

Some will say that, yes, I am intimate with the music, with the auditory phenomena, but not with a fictional world that it creates. I am sympathetic, but things are not this easy. My intimacy is not just with sounds; it is with tension and relaxation in the music, with exuberance and wistfulness and aggressiveness and uncertainty and resolution. I share the purists' skepticism as to whether these add up to a fictional world like that of a picture or a novel, but we have to admit that they are part of the stuff that such fictional worlds are made of. (And we should wonder how involvement with mere sounds could be gripping in anything like the way involvement with monsters and dragons, innocent damsels, evil villains, and tragic heroes—even fictional ones—can be. Why should we care what happens to a four-note motive consisting of three eighth notes on a given pitch followed by a half note a third below? We do not follow the fortunes of musical motives in quite the way we follow the fortunes of Romeo and Juliet or Anna Karenina, wishing them well or ill and worrying about what might happen to them.)

I mentioned the idea that it is by portraying vocal or other behavioral expressions of feelings that music portrays the feelings. This is how feelings are, most obviously, presented in theater and painting. Schopenhauer and others have claimed that music gets at feelings more directly.[23] If music does bypass behavior and portray feelings directly, the listener will in one sense be closer to the portrayed feelings. She will not have to go through the portrayal of the behavior in order to ascertain what feelings are portrayed. But this does not provide for the intimacy that I think I have with the feelings portrayed in music. We don't experience this intimacy when we read descriptions in a literary work of characters' emotional states (rather than of their behavior). Consider a novel that tells us straight out that a character experiences a warm sense of security.[24] The contrast between the relevant words of the novel and a musical passage expressive of a warm sense of security—in Brahms, for instance—could hardly be greater.

[23] Schopenhauer objects strenuously to musical imitations of "phenomena of the world of perception." *The World as Will and Representation*, vol. 1, trans. E. F. J. Payne (New York: Dover, 1969), p. 264. See also pp. 257, 259–60, 262–64.

[24] Many literary works indicate characters' feelings by means of a narrator's description of their feelings. The following portrayal of a character's warm sense of security seems not to be indirect even in this way: "Chance circumstance which facilitated [Pancho's] intentions: the approach of a ferocious-looking stray dog who frightened Fanny and gave rise to an unmistakable show of courage on the part of Pancho, which awakened in Fanny a warm sense of security" (Mañuel Puig, *Heartbreak Tango*, trans. Suzanne Jill Levine [New York: Random House, 1969], p. 85).

Imaginative Feeling

Let's try something different. I suggest that music sometimes gets us to imagine feeling or experiencing exuberance or tension ourselves—or relaxation or determination or confidence or anguish or wistfulness. This accords with the idea that music sometimes portrays anguish, not by portraying behavioral expressions of anguish but more directly, and also with the thought that our (fictional) access to what is portrayed is not perceptual—we imagine introspecting or simply experiencing the feelings rather than perceiving someone's expressing them. And it goes a long way toward explaining the intimacy I said I felt with the anguish in the music. On reading that a character in a novel experiences a warm sense of security, one will imagine knowing about an instance of a warm sense of security, someone else's; but one probably will not imagine feeling warmly secure oneself.[25]

More needs to be said. Listeners are intimate with the feelings the music expresses—with exuberance or anguish, for instance—if they imagine experiencing exuberance or anguish. But this doesn't explain their intimacy with the music, with the *music's* exuberance or anguish. Musical experiences are not just experiences caused by music; they are experiences *of* music.[26] We don't merely hear the music and enjoy certain experiences as a result of hearing it. One possibility is that music stimulates imaginings that are in part imaginings about the sounds themselves. This is almost right but not quite. Listeners' imaginings are, in many instances, about their experience of hearing the sounds rather than about the sounds themselves.

The point here is analogous to one concerning pictures. A picture of a dragon induces the spectator to imagine seeing a dragon. But a vivid verbal description in a story about a dragon might do this much. The picture induces the spectator also to imagine of her actual visual experience of the picture that it is her visual experience of a dragon. One's seeing of the picture is not just a stimulus but part of the content of one's imaginative experience. Not only does anguished or agitated or exuberant music induce one to imagine feeling anguished or agitated or exuberant; it also induces one to imagine of one's auditory experience that *it* is an experience of anguish or agitation or exuberance.

R. K. Elliott, in a perceptive and suggestive essay, describes what he calls experiencing music *from within*—experiencing it "as if it were our

---

[25] Not anyway when reading something like the Puig passage in the preceding footnote. In other cases one might empathize with a character's feeling of warm security, imagining feeling this way oneself. I will discuss such instances shortly.

[26] See Malcolm Budd, *Music and the Emotions* (New York: Routledge, 1985), p. 123.

own expression" and feeling the expressed emotion "nonprimordially."[27] Elliott's characterization of this experience is sketchy, but it clearly has much in common with the experience I have described. He has the listener enjoying something akin to an experience of the emotion expressed, not just (somehow) observing the emotion in the music. Arousal theories, which in their crudest and least plausible form say that music expressive of exuberance or grief is simply music that makes listeners exuberant or stricken with grief, at least recognize that to appreciate expressive music is to *feel* something. Neither Elliott nor I think the appreciator, in general, simply and straightforwardly experiences the emotion the music expresses. Malcolm Budd encourages Elliott in my direction by suggesting that feeling an emotion nonprimordially be explained in terms of make-believe.[28] (Elliott himself speaks of "imaginatively enriched perception.") But in other respects Budd develops Elliott's account in ways I do not find plausible (at least some of which Elliott need not accept)—before finally dismissing it. "To experience music [either from within or from without] as if it were the expression of emotion it would be necessary . . . to imagine someone giving voice to the sounds of the music and in doing so to express his emotion," Budd says. "If I experience [a piece of music] M from within then I make-believe that I feel [an emotion] E and that I am expressing my E in the sounds of M: these sounds are issuing from me as a consequence of my feeling E and they bear the imprint of E."[29] Budd rightly observes that we do not very often hear expressive music in *this* way. The kind of experience I have described doesn't involve imagining oneself producing the sounds of the music, or imagining the emotion to be expressed in sound emitting behavior at all.[30] One needn't imagine expressive behavior of any kind, nor anything at all about the sounds one hears. One imagines experiencing the emotion, and one imagines one's experience of the sounds to be one's experience of it.

Music sometimes induces actual feelings and sensations in listeners, not just imaginings of such, and it sometimes affects our actual moods, if not our emotions. There are tricky questions about how best to describe the various effects music has on listeners. A lot will depend on what intentional content one takes the various psychological states to involve. It is more plausible to say that music makes listeners tense or relaxed or exuberant or agitated, in ordinary instances, than that it arouses in them genuine, as opposed to imagined, anguish or determination or confidence

[27] Elliott, "Aesthetic Theory and the Experience of Art," p. 152.
[28] Budd, *Music and the Emotions*, pp. 127–31.
[29] Ibid., pp. 131, 135.
[30] Elliott makes it clear that *expression* of an emotion is, for him, not limited to behavior ("Aesthetic Theory and the Experience of Art," p. 146).

or pride or grief (although the experience of vividly imagining feeling anguish or determination or grief is likely itself be an emotional one). A person who is deeply depressed might only imagine being exuberant, when she listens to an exuberant fugue, whereas an originally cheerful listener might be made genuinely exuberant. I don't doubt that even someone who is depressed may become genuinely less depressed as a result of imagining being exuberant, in response to the music. Instead of trying to sort out merely imagined feelings from genuine ones, I will understand the notion of imagined feelings to include genuine ones as well. Music that induces me actually to feel exuberant thereby induces me to imagine feeling thus, and music might induce me merely to imagine feeling anguish when I don't really.[31]

That listeners' experiences of music include such imagined feelings (whether they are actual or not) fits nicely with the tendency of music to elicit behavioral responses like foot tapping, dancing, or swaying with the music. Some people sing along with music; some are inclined to sing along but know better. When music swells, one may swell with it. These are the beginnings of behavioral expressions of feelings—feelings of exuberance, agitation, gaiety, anguish, pride. They may manifest, if not actual feelings of these kinds, the vivid imagining of experiencing them. Compare the filmgoer who suddenly tenses, and perhaps screams involuntarily, as he imagines being attacked by a slime and being terrified. In this case also, vividly imagining experiencing certain feelings is intimately tied up with behavior expressive of the feelings; the imagining elicits the expressive behavior, and the person imagines this behavior to express actual feelings of the kind in question.

I tried earlier to explain how music might portray feelings directly rather than via their behavioral expressions. Now we see that behavior— the listener's expression of the feelings she imagines experiencing—has come back into the picture. But this does not mean that the music portrays an instance of the feeling by portraying someone's behavioral expressions of it. It may be that some music which can be taken to portray a person behaving in certain ways and thereby expressing certain feelings might alternatively be understood to involve the *listener's* behavior. (It might be understood in both ways, as we shall see.) But it doesn't *portray* the listener's behavior—certainly not in anything like the way a film about me portrays my behavior if it shows me expressing my feelings. Behav-

---

[31] "The affections of the will itself, and hence actual pain and actual pleasure, must not be excited, but only their substitutes, that which is in conformity with the *intellect* as a *picture or image* of the will's satisfaction, and that which more or less opposes it as a *picture or image* of greater or lesser pain" (Schopenhauer, *The World as Will and Representation*, 2:451; italics in original).

ior is likely to come into the picture because in listening I, or any of us, may be induced to imagine not only experiencing certain feelings but also expressing these feelings behaviorally.

Wallace Stevens describes the intimate connection between hearing music and imagining feeling (or actually feeling) as follows. Notice that he doesn't indicate anything about observing, even to empathize with, a consciousness distinct from the listener, presented or represented or portrayed or suggested by the music:

> Just as my fingers on these keys
> Make music, so the selfsame sounds
> On my spirit make a music, too.
>
> Music is feeling, then, not sound;
> And thus it is that what I feel,
> Here in this room, desiring you,
>
> Thinking of your blue-shadowed silk,
> Is music. It is like the strain
> Waked in the elders by Susanna.
>
> Of a green evening, clear and warm,
> She bathed in her still garden, while
> The red-eyed elders watching, felt
>
> The basses of their beings throb
> In witching chords, and their thin blood
> Pulse pizzicati of Hosanna.[32]

Sounds are curiously unusual in their tendency to elicit responses like foot tapping and singing along. Visual designs in motion have no comparable tendency. I have no inclination to tap my feet or dance or even sway back and forth to abstract motion pictures, even ones with a "beat," a regular persistent rhythm. It is hard to imagine jiving with a blinking traffic light, or even a battery of traffic lights operated by a jazz percussionist. People who dance at sound and light shows dance to the sound, not the light.

There may be reasons why sounds are better suited than sights to play the role I have claimed sounds often do play—reasons to expect that if there is an "introspective" art of the kind I have described, as opposed to

---

[32] Wallace Stevens, "Peter Quince at the Clavier," in *Collected Poems* (New York: Knopf, 1951), stanza 1.

a perceptual one, it is more likely to be a sound art than a visual one. Aural experiences may be better suited than visual ones to count as, fictionally, experiences of feelings or emotions; experiences of sounds, as we construe them, may be more naturally imagined to be experiences of feelings or emotions than experiences of sights are. How might this be?

Here is an easy first point: hearing is something we cannot easily turn off; we can't close our ears as we can close our eyes. The same is true of our introspective "sense." We can't simply turn off at will feelings of agitation or serenity or anguish, or a sense of foreboding or of well-being—or our access to such feelings. In this and other ways also, seeing is a more active sense than hearing is. When our eyes are open we choose what to look at. Short of moving to a different location, we can't choose what sounds we hear, although we can to some extent ignore certain sounds and pay attention to others. Likewise, we don't have much direct control over what we feel, short of changing our situation or circumstances. We can concentrate on some feelings and ignore others, to an extent. But there is nothing in feeling, any more than in hearing, much like looking at one thing rather than another.

Other analogies between hearing and feeling are related to what I call the Cavell-Calvino observation about sounds. Stanley Cavell remarked that we think of sounds as independent entities separate from their sources, in a way we do not think of sights; we reify or objectify sounds.[33] We speak of clatters, bangings, whinnys, murmurs, echoes, creaks, clangs, rustles, grumbles, gurgles. Sounds—like smells—fill rooms and cross streets; sights don't do that. Italo Calvino puts the point well, in "A King Listens":

> The music comes and goes, in gusts, it oscillates, down in the rumbling groove of the streets, or it rises high with the wind that spins the vanes of the chimneys.
>
> And when in the darkness a woman's voice is released in singing, invisible at the sill of an unlighted window . . . what is it? Not that song, which you must have heard all too many times, not that woman, whom you have never seen: you are attracted by that voice as a voice, as it offers itself in song.
>
> That voice comes certainly from a person; a voice, however, is not a person, it is something suspended in the air, detached from the solidity of things.[34]

[33] Stanley Cavell, *The World Viewed*, enlarged ed. (Cambridge, Mass.: Harvard University Press, 1979), chap. 2.

[34] Italo Calvino, "The King Listens," in *Under the Jaguar Sun*, trans. William Weaver (San Diego: Harcourt Brace Jovanovich, 1988), pp. 50, 53–54.

We reify or objectify feelings and sensations, as we do sounds, and we conceptualize them and our relations to them in similar ways. We think of feelings of exuberance or anguish as entities distinct from their sources, and sometimes as leaving their sources and surrounding or entering us. A feeling, like a sound, may come over me. It may permeate my consciousness. Both feelings and sounds wax and wane, independently of changes in their sources. They get more intense, or diminish and then disappear; they can be overwhelming or hard to detect. The same loss may cause grief of more or less intensity in different people, just as the same train causes louder or softer sounds at different distances. Sounds and feelings both are individuated sometimes by their sources, sometimes by their perceivers. And we are of two minds about whether either can exist unperceived. We reify feelings and sounds complete with their intentional properties (while thinking of them as distinct from their intentional objects). The sound of a bell may waft through the house. Anguish about a particular event may eat at me for months afterward; determination to succeed as a pianist may permeate one's life; pangs of jealousy seep into one's consciousness. (There is, I expect, a lot more to say on this score.)[35]

We do sometimes objectify sights distinct from their sources—glimmers, reflections, flashes of light, sheens, and so on. But it is only in fairly special instances that we think of things like these as the objects of our vision; usually we think of ourselves as seeing physical objects—trees, houses, people, mountains. And a glimmer or a sparkle, if not identical to the thing that glimmers or sparkles, is thought of as attached to it. Glimmers and sparkles don't come to us from things that glimmer and sparkle, as sounds do from the sounding object.

Maybe it shouldn't be surprising that auditory rather than visual experiences are imagined to be experiences of feelings of exuberance or anguish or foreboding or well-being.[36]

There is no incompatibility between a work's inducing an appreciator to imagine someone else feeling exuberance or anguish, and its inducing the

---

[35] Susanne Langer claims that particular feelings and particular sounds have similar "logical structures" (*Philosophy in a New Key*, pp. 226, 228, 244; and Langer, *Feeling and Form* [New York: Scribners, 1953], p. 27). But my point is that feelings in general and sounds in general are conceived in analogous ways. It is possible that conventions of some sort have a place in the explanation of how particular sounds get associated with particular feelings. And it is possible that the natural affinity Langer finds between certain sounds and certain feelings is a result of, rather than the source of, the tendency of the sounds to get us to imagine experiencing those feelings.

[36] "As tone is itself inwardness and subjectivity, it speaks to the inner soul" (G. W. F. Hegel, *Hegel's Philosophy of Nature*, vol. 2, trans. Michael John Perry [London: Allen and Unwin, 1970], p. 71).

appreciator to imagine feeling this herself. It may do both at once. Visual depictions often do both when they elicit empathy for a character.

Empathizing with someone, I assume, involves imagining feeling the way one takes the person to feel. I see someone slice her hand with a kitchen knife. I wince and jerk my hand back.[37] I am not in pain. But I imagine (spontaneously, unreflectively, perhaps subliminally) the knife slicing through my flesh as I watch it cut her, and I imagine feeling pain. My imagining this explains my wincing and my jerking my hand back.

What stimulates my empathetic reaction in this case is what I see happening to my friend, not, or not directly, how she feels or how she responds. But other instances are different. If I am watching my friend's face as she is cut, I might respond empathetically to the pain I see on her face. I may not even see or know about the accident. One may simply observe a person's facial or behavioral expressions and find oneself behaving sympathetically, spontaneously mimicking his expressions, contorting one's face as he contorts his. This reaction is empathetic, and I take it to consist in imagining feeling what one observes him feeling. (Maybe one actually does feel as he does, in some respects; some aspects of the feeling, as well as the expression, may be contagious.) One may empathize with a dancer or an athlete, feeling one's muscles tense and relax in sympathy. (When a visual object is or represents a person, it can evoke responses akin to foot tapping.)

We respond similarly to fictional characters, imagining feeling as we perceive them (fictionally) to feel. When I look at a portrait I may contort my face in sympathy with the portrayed character's facial expressions, just as I contort my face in sympathy with a real person. So a picture may induce me to imagine someone else feeling anguish or elation and also, at the same time, to imagine (myself) feeling this way. I imagine her feeling anguish or elation and I imagine feeling the same in response to her.

When music (vocal music, for instance) portrays a more or less definite character, we are likely to have this kind of empathetic response. But what needs to be emphasized is that even when there is no definite character in the music, it can get us to imagine feeling in certain ways. The music swells, and I swell with it. I imagine feeling anguish or ecstasy as these qualities are expressed in the music; I imagine experiencing a sense of foreboding, as the music changes suddenly from a major key to the parallel minor. In such cases I probably do not think of the music as portraying a person (distinct from me) who swells or feels anguish or

[37] The example is borrowed from Richard Moran.

foreboding. My experience, phenomenologically, does have some affinity with that of one who watches another person's facial expressions and responds empathetically. But I may not have much of a sense of empathizing with someone at all. No doubt this is partly because I do not imagine perceiving anyone, when I listen, and because music is so fuzzy about the individuation of particulars. The difference between imaginatively recognizing and feeling with another person and merely imaginatively experiencing certain feelings oneself, as one listens to the music, can be very subtle, especially given that the imaginings are often implicit or subliminal. I am sure that sometimes there is no fact of the matter as to which is the case. But it would be a serious distortion of listeners' experiences to suppose that whenever music gets listeners imaginatively to feel, it must be doing so by eliciting imaginative empathy with a person portrayed in the music.[38]

There are other instances in which something gets us to imagine feeling a certain way without getting us to empathize with anyone. I see my friend's knife slip and strike the cutting board. I see a guillotine operate without a victim. In both cases I wince and draw back. But I don't observe someone else being hurt. I do imagine being cut or guillotined. A film of a hurtling roller coaster empty of passengers may nevertheless get us to imagine riding in it. Just looking at a comfortable rocking chair may induce one to imagine sitting in it.

Music differs from these last cases in that it often gets us to imagine having certain experiences not by showing us circumstances that would produce them but by doing something more like showing or indicating either behavioral expressions of the experiences in question or (somehow) the experiences themselves—but still (often) without in any very definite way portraying someone (distinct from the listener) exhibiting the expressive behavior or having the experiences. It is as though the music provides the smile without the cat—a smile for the listener to wear. How music manages this trick is a good question. But the trick itself, the result, is not mysterious. Music gets us to imagine experiencing a certain feeling, and possibly expressing it or being inclined to express it in a certain manner. It often does this without getting us to imagine knowing about (let alone perceiving) someone else having that experience or expressing it in that manner.

---

[38] Elliott sometimes characterizes experiencing music, or a poem, "from within" as putting oneself in the shoes of another person, e.g., the poet.

Is Expression Representation?
Game Worlds Without Work Worlds

I have a lot of imagining going on in the appreciation of music, a lot of imagining *de se*. There is a game world full of life. But what has happened to the work world, the fictional world of the music itself? If there were a cat, it would be in the work world. But if there is only a smile, and the smile is mine—the listener's—maybe there isn't even a place for a cat; maybe there is only a game world. The work world is supposed to contain fictional truths generated by the music alone. But the only fictional truths there are may be ones generated by the listener's experience with the music, ones that belong only to the game world.

In the case of a picture of a dragon, there is a fictional world, the world of the work, even when no one is looking at the picture. This is a large part of what it means to say that the picture is representational. The picture, standing alone, establishes a fictional world. But in music, insofar as appreciation involves imagining experiencing feelings in the way I described, there are game worlds but no work worlds. This gives us an important sense in which music is not representational.

Dragons exist independently of anyone's perceiving or knowing about them, if they exist at all. If there is a dragon in my garden, it is there regardless of whether or not I see it. When it is fictional that a dragon exists, it is fictional that it exists independently of its being perceived. So it isn't surprising that we should understand something that actually does exist independently of perceivers to make it fictional that a dragon exists. A picture fills the bill. It is there whether or not anyone sees it, and it, by itself, makes it fictional that a dragon is there, whether or not it is fictional that anyone sees the dragon. Work worlds comprise fictional truths generated by the work alone. But feelings (of agitation, foreboding, ecstasy) do not exist independently of people who feel them. (Even if they can exist "unperceived" or unnoticed, they don't exist *unowned*.) So there is no pressure to regard the music itself as establishing a fictional world in which there are feelings (unless it is fictional that there is a person distinct from the listener whose feelings they are). It is the listener's auditory experiences that, like feelings, cannot exist apart from being experienced, which make it fictional that there are feelings. When the listener imagines experiencing agitation herself, there is no reason to think of the *music* as making anything fictional. It is the listener's hearing of the music that makes it fictional that she feels agitated. The only fictional world is the world of her game, of her experience.

The absence of a work world goes a considerable way toward recovering the "abstractness" or "nonrepresentationality" of music, toward explaining the impression that music is not representational in the way that painting and literature are. Insofar as music is expressive in the manner I have described, it does not have fictional worlds of the kind that (figurative) paintings and novels do.[39] The music itself is not a prop, as a painting or a novel is. What the music does is supply us with experiences when we listen to it, and we use these experiences as props. It is the auditory experiences, not the music itself, that generate fictional truths. I can step outside of my game with a painting. When I do, I see the picture and notice that it represents a dragon, that it calls for the imagining of a dragon (even if I don't actually imagine this). But when I step outside my game with music and consider the music itself, all I see is music, not a fictional world to go with it. There is just the notes, and they themselves don't call for imagining anything.[40]

The absence of a work world does not, however, prevent the listener's imagination from running wild, as she participates in her game of make-believe.

---

[39] There is a work world insofar as music portrays characters behaving expressively. And as I mentioned, most or all music has a fictional world and is representational in the way nonfigurative painting usually is, though the fictional worlds in these cases differ importantly from the worlds of figurative painting and literature.

[40] It is misleading or worse to say, as Susanne Langer does, that the sounds are *symbols* for feelings, even "nondiscursive" symbols (whatever that is supposed to mean). "If music has any significance, it is semantic. . . . Music is *about* feelings, it is their logical expression" (*Philosophy in a New Key*, p. 218). I disagree. Langer's obscure notion of *presenting* emotions for our contemplation, however, might be understood as getting us to imagine experiencing them.

4

Musical Idiosyncrasy and
Perspectival Listening

KATHLEEN MARIE HIGGINS

Friedrich Nietzsche lampoons Western philosophy's quest for objectivity, which demands

> that we should think of an eye that is completely unthinkable, an eye turned in no particular direction, in which the active and interpreting forces, through which alone seeing becomes seeing *something*, are supposed to be lacking; these always demand of the eye an absurdity and a nonsense. There is *only* a perspective seeing, *only* a perspective "knowing"; and the *more* affects we allow to speak about one thing, the *more* eyes, different eyes, we can use to observe one thing, the more complete will our "concept" of this thing, our "objectivity," be.[1]

I shall argue that Western philosophy has tended to posit not only an aperspectival eye but an aperspectival ear as well. The "scientific" aspirations of post-Enlightenment musical aesthetics have distorted musical experience in multiple ways, among them by failing to acknowledge the differences among individual listeners.

I will be using the term "idiosyncrasy" polemically to refer to the whole range of responses that depend on the individual listener's particular character and background. Although the Enlightenment idealized uni-

[1] Friedrich Nietzsche, *On the Genealogy of Morals*, trans. Walter Kaufmann and R. J. Hollingdale (together with *Ecce Homo*, trans. Walter Kaufmann) (New York: Random House, 1967), p. 119.

versality and thus directed attention to those features of experience that would be standard for all individuals, the experience of music is diminished when its many resonances with the particularities of its listeners' lives are belittled or ignored. Among these particularities are both the contingent facts of the listener's biography and the diverse cultural contexts for interpretation that are generally assumed within a society, but far from standard outside it. I will term both types of responses "idiosyncratic" because both appear eccentric—even quirky—from the analytic standpoint that seeks to explain musical experience in terms of what is common to all listeners.

One might ask whether theoretical analysis has much direct concern with musical *experience*. After all, musicologists tend to analyze musical structures, not experiences; and philosophers similarly tend toward structural accounts and concern with experiences only to the extent that they are dictated by structures. One might also doubt that scholars have much influence on listeners, who typically enjoy music unperturbed by intellectual analyses.

I concede both points, but I insist that such disconnection between listeners and scholars is symptomatic of a problem. Scholarly analysis of music should, I think, be grounded in concern with enhancing musical experience (even if those who benefit directly from such analysis constitute a small subset of the listening public). Moreover, in our society, where scholars are a significant force within the relatively small elite that are culturally acknowledged as "experts" on music, their view carries weight outside their ranks. If they, by their practice, encourage the view that the less standardized responses to music are intellectually inferior to standardized responses, their orientation is likely to be understood by many as a touchstone of which responses are respectably found in music and which are, at best, déclassé.

I will be suggesting that some responses that might enhance the value of music within our own society have been largely ignored within our scholarly analyses of music. Even if this orientation influenced only scholars, this would be an unfortunate consequence. I suspect, moreover, that because our society discourages the average listener from having confidence in his or her own musicality,[2] the attitudes of scholars toward

[2] See John Blacking, *How Musical Is Man?* (Seattle: University of Washington Press, 1973), for a discussion of the musical elitism of Western society. Blacking finds this elitism paradoxical: "'My' society claims that only a limited number of people are musical, and yet it behaves as if all people possessed the basic capacity without which no musical tradition can exist—the capacity to listen to and distinguish patterns of sound" (p. 8). See also Henry Kingsbury, *Music, Talent, and Performance: A Conservatory Cultural System* (Philadelphia: Temple University Press, 1988). Kingsbury describes in detail the inculcation of music students within a conservatory, and he contends that the notion of "talent" (and the related

idiosyncratic responses to music have impact beyond academia, although I will not attempt to demonstrate this here.

I will concern myself, instead, with the reigning philosophical approach to analyzing music. This approach aspires to "objectivity" in the spirit of the Enlightenment. After indicating the ways in which this ideal features in certain influential accounts within musical aesthetics, I will consider some characteristics of musical experience in non-Western cultures that are not easily embraced by the Western "objective" paradigm. These, I contend, are features that depend upon the cultural history of particular societies, those bases for interpretation which particular societies do not necessarily share with their neighbors. I will then consider the parallel case of those responses to music within our own culture that depend on the biographical background and individual characteristics of the listener. Both categories of "idiosyncratic" experiences, I will contend, are experiences of value that should be encouraged, not foreclosed, by philosophical analysis. Along the way I will argue that musical aesthetics has placed inappropriate emphasis on formalistic musical scores. I will nevertheless conclude that a reassessment of aesthetic "objectivity" would result in a different appreciation of the score and its significance.

The Objectification of Western Classical Music

Many historical developments in Western music have contributed to music's "objectification."[3] Nevertheless, Hanslick's influence has led to a culmination of the tendency for aesthetics to see music as a class of objects.[4] Hanslick, insisting that proper aesthetic appreciation attended exclusively to "tonally moving forms," sought to ground musical aesthetics on a scientific basis, formulated in terms of musical laws. He pursued this goal by means of a dubious but influential assumption: "Philosophically speaking, the composed piece, regardless of whether it

---

notion that most individuals lack musical talent) is central to the social production of Western classical music.

[3] This point is made in Lewis Rowell, *Thinking about Music: An Introduction to the Philosophy of Music* (Amherst: University of Massachusetts Press, 1983), pp. 34–36. See also Lydia Goehr, *The Imaginary Museum of Musical Works* (Oxford: Clarendon Press, 1992), p. 267: "Formalism has increasingly inclined toward positivism to the extent that reference to 'subjective' principles having to do with personal, 'pathological' feelings has effectively been banned from the account."

[4] I discuss Hanslick at some length in Kathleen Marie Higgins, *The Music of Our Lives* (Philadelphia: Temple University Press, 1991), pp. 67–72.

is performed or not, is the completed artwork."[5] Accepting Hanslick's terms and aspirations, the field of musical aesthetics has subsequently tended to understand "music" in terms of "musical structure," something accessible to all intelligent listeners and usually notated in a score.[6]

The tendency to seek an objective philosophical account remains evident in more recent musical aesthetics. Leonard B. Meyer has reinforced Hanslick's hierarchy of intellectual above physical/emotional appreciation in his discussion of "sensuous/associative" and "syntactic" levels of understanding music. Although acknowledging the role of the former in everyone's experience of music, he considers the syntactic level the most useful for assessing the value of music, again because it is not subject to idiosyncratic variation.[7] This was precisely the argument that Hanslick used to dismiss emotional associations in aesthetic accounts: "I share completely the view that the ultimate worth of the beautiful is always based on the immediate manifestness of feeling. However, I hold just as firmly the conviction that, from all the customary appeals to feeling, we can derive not a single musical law."[8]

Meyer's commitment to the pursuit of an objective account of musical meaning is evident in his theory of musical emotion developed in *Emotion and Meaning in Music*.[9] There, Meyer correlates experienced affect with defiance of expectation. Given appropriate awareness of the conventions of a given style, one can determine what listeners have been led to expect, and thereby ascertain where expectations have not been fulfilled and where affect, consequently, is produced.[10]

Significantly, Meyer contends that so long as one has proper awareness of stylistic conventions, the score is an adequate guide to musically produced affect. In other words, the "objective" transcript (or, more aptly, stated instructions) of a musical work is all one needs to determine when

[5] Eduard Hanslick, *On the Musically Beautiful*, trans. Geoffrey Payzant (Indianapolis: Hackett, 1986), p. 48.

[6] My discussion appears in Higgins, *The Music of Our Lives* (Philadelphia: Temple University Press, 1991), pp. 99–128.

[7] See Leonard B. Meyer, "Some Remarks on Value and Greatness in Music," in *Music, the Arts, and Ideas: Patterns and Predictions in Twentieth-Century Culture* (Chicago: University of Chicago Press, 1967), p. 36. Even while defending the primacy of the syntactic level of musical understanding, however, Meyer feels the need to reassert the importance of association in the context of discussing profound music (p. 38).

[8] Hanslick, *On the Musically Beautiful*, p. xxii.

[9] Leonard B. Meyer, *Emotion and Meaning in Music* (Chicago: University of Chicago Press, 1956).

[10] Meyer is not committed to saying that affect is always produced by defying expectation. Someone who takes an analytic point of view may instead appreciate deviation from expectation intellectually instead of emotionally. The fact that Meyer considers intellectual and emotional response to be alternatives, however, indicates the extent to which he is unconcerned with the actual experience of emotion by any particular listener.

during its performance emotion will be aroused in receptive and knowl-edgeable listeners. A corollary claim is that we can expect such listeners to feel comparable emotion at the same points in a performance of a work. Meyer's account similarly predicts agreement among all who assume an analytic point of view. Thus individual idiosyncrasy in response to music can be accommodated by his account only as irrelevant or as a symptom of ignorance with respect to the work's style.[11]

The predominance of the score as a basis for philosophical analysis of music is evident even in Diana Raffman's "cognitive" approach to musical understanding, an approach that explicitly sets out to account for musical nuances, those features of musical experience that are too subtle to be cap-tured within our analytical grids. Drawing on Fodor's cognitive theory of perception and on Lerdahl and Jackendoff's generative grammar for tonal music, Raffman describes musical understanding in terms of various levels of abstraction to which the listener's mind refers what it hears: "As you hear the incoming musical signal, you mentally represent it (you recover the score more or less) and analyze it according to the grammati-cal rules; that is, you compute a *structural description* of the piece."[12] Raffman analyzes the alleged ineffability of music partly in terms of our ability to refer features of our musical experience to abstract categories: "Very roughly, it turns out that certain features of the musical signal are likely to be recovered at such shallow processing levels (i.e., so 'near' to the peripheral sense organs) that they fail to be mentally categorized in the manner thought necessary for the learning of verbal labels. Therein lies their ineffability, which I call 'perceptual ineffability.'"[13]

Raffman's analysis certainly does not minimize the importance of non-notated features of music for musical enjoyment. Admirably, she takes pains to qualify her position in this connection; and she links the "inef-fability" of musical experience, often cited in rhapsodic terms by listen-ers, to features not designated by the score. The fact that even Raffman

[11] I have argued elsewhere that Susanne K. Langer and Peter Kivy both adopt a structural approach to music in their respective accounts of emotion in music. See Higgins, *The Music of Our Lives*, pp. 100–108, 119–28.

[12] Diana Raffman, "Toward a Cognitive Theory of Musical Ineffability," *Review of Meta-physics* 41 (June 1988): 690. For Raffman's more complete account of musical ineffability, see Diana Raffman, *Language, Music, and Mind* (Cambridge, Mass.: MIT Press, 1993).

[13] Raffman, "Toward a Cognitive Theory of Musical Ineffability," p. 688. In her longer study, *Language, Music, and Mind*, Raffman analyzes three species of musical ineffability. These include "structural ineffability" (the ineffability that arises from the instability of the most high-level structures of a piece of music and their resultant susceptibility to multi-ple analyses); "feeling ineffability" (the incommunicability of the "feel" of a musical instance to someone who does not have appropriately similar background experience); and "nuance ineffability" (the type of ineffability that is termed "perceptual ineffability" in Raffman's "Toward a Cognitive Theory of Musical Ineffability").

(following Lerdahl and Jackendoff) takes the score as the basis for the "series of increasingly abstract mental representations of the environment" to which we refer music, however, is evidence of the extent to which scores are privileged in the philosophical accounts of music in our tradition.[14] The long-standing philosophical tendency in the West is to consider the score an adequate—and indeed, the only sufficiently objective—basis for a philosophical account of music; and even accounts that look beyond the score still tend to see it as an appropriate model for philosophical analysis.

Recently, however, musical aesthetics has been subjected to internal critique for its reliance on a "scientific" model and its predominant concern with scores. Lydia Goehr, for instance, observes that the scientific model has led aesthetics to neglect the role of history in making sense of music. "The dominant model of analysis for all areas of philosophy—ethics, aesthetics, and science—has come to be characterized as one governed by 'positivistic' standards of objectivity and logic."[15] Besides treating the terms in which music is analyzed as "historically and ideologically neutral,"[16] Goehr argues, this approach has involved the equation of "music" with "musical works."

> Even the apparently harmless belief that all or many kinds of music can be spoken of in terms of works can serve as evidence for the inappropriate stance of analysis. Generally, it seems not to have occurred to theorists (at least until recently) that the work-concept might not function in all musical practices of whatever sort. Thus where attention has been given to the concept of music (or the concept of art, more generally), it has automatically been given to the concept of a work of music (or art). . . . Why the focus on classical music? Why the focus on the concept of a musical work? And why not a focus on the concept of music in as broad a sense as it can be understood?[17]

[14] Certainly, Raffman seeks to pinpoint where scores and the analytical grids related to them are incapable of articulately transcribing what we experience in music. I think, however, that the quest for a detailed grid remains pronounced throughout her analysis. Indeed, her description of musical nuances as "fine-grained" suggests the aspiration for a grid that is as detailed as possible, even if her analysis concludes that, human perceptual memory being what it is, we will never have a sufficiently fine grid to make all nuances "effable." See Raffman, *Language, Music, and Mind*, p. 65, for example. Raffman also accepts Jackendoff's assumption that the listener, as a music processor, seeks a "unique best structural description" of what he or she hears (see ibid., p. 28). I see this as further indication that Raffman considers such a description of an instance of music to be desirable, even if not fully attainable.

[15] Goehr, *The Imaginary Museum of Musical Works*, p. 71.

[16] Ibid., p. 78.

[17] Ibid., pp. 79–80.

I will attempt to follow Goehr's suggestion that "music" be understood in as broad a sense as possible while I proceed to consider certain cases in which disparate cultural assumptions affect the musical experience within certain non-Western societies. By surveying some of the findings of ethnomusicologists who have worked in a variety of non-Western societies, I will indicate features of music that have been underemphasized in Western analyses of classical music. While I recognize that Western classical music is designed to emphasize structural features of pitch and metrical rhythm over some of the features that are prominent in the musics of other societies, I suspect that more attention to such features (many of which fall into the category that Raffman describes as "nuances") would enhance our experience of our own music, as well as enable us to make greater sense of music from cultures not our own.

My primary purpose in the following section is to suggest the range of responses that other societies expect from their musics, responses that from the standpoint of a universalistic or positivistic approach appear idiosyncratic. I intend also to suggest (although I do not defend this suggestion here) that our musical lives might be fuller if we expected and sought more interconnections between our music and the rest of our experience.[18]

Ethnomusicology versus Musical "Objectivity"

Study of musics outside the Western world has prompted a number of ethnomusicologists (along with a growing number of musicologists) to criticize the "objective" aspirations of Western musical aesthetics; and accordingly, they attempt in their own work to maintain awareness of their inherently subjective position with respect to various musics and musical discourse. At the very least, these ethnomusicologists claim, the bases on which Western musical aesthetics is formulated serve as an inadequate basis for dealing with "music in as broad a sense as it can be understood." Responding to Alan Merriam's account of the assumptions of Western musical aesthetics, Charles Keil, for example, remarks,

> I judge that few, if any, of the six factors which Merriam's excellent analysis . . . finds underlying the Western notion of an esthetic can, if taken as criteria, be met by many preliterate societies: (1) "psychic distance" or "objectivity" or "sense of non-utility"; (2) "manipulation of form for its own sake"; (3) "attribution of emotion-producing qualities to music conceived

---

[18] I argue for this claim at length in *The Music of Our Lives*.

strictly as sound"; (4) "attribution of beauty to the art product or process"; (5) "purposeful intent to create something esthetic"; (6) "presence of a philosophy of an esthetic."[19]

Keil's expression "preliterate" might be taken to imply that an aesthetic of the Western sort is an acquisition that some non-Western societies have so far failed to achieve. This is far from Keil's intention, however. Indeed, he believes that music in Tiv society plays a role that Western society has lost.[20] Many ethnographic studies similarly suggest that where music is concerned, the relative failure is on the side of the West. The detachment of music from the everyday life of most Westerners is, in their view, a sign that Western musical experience is relatively impoverished.

The Aboriginals of Australia, by contrast, consider music to be central to socialization. For them, music is far from being a formal structure disconnected from everyday concerns. Instead, Aboriginal music is encoded with multilayered information regarding the proper conduct of life. This music is intelligible at some level to every member of Aboriginal society but fully penetrated only by those who have reached the apex of maturity and the practical insight that comes with it. Catherine J. Ellis reports,

> For the tribal person, music is an essential part of life, a force without which his known world crumbles. Learning music is a means of entering the highest reaches of his culture's intellectual and spiritual development. Whether or not an individual is capable of progressing through the entire process of learning, his awareness of the fact that some of his own people can do this is a security to him in a world which is otherwise frequently bewildering and sometimes hostile to him. Without this security his sense of identity collapses. With it, he has before him a means of education which will develop his individual abilities to the full (provided he makes the necessary effort) and will at the same time develop his whole personality.[21]

Some societies consider music to be an essential aspect of medicine. The Navajos consider specific songs to be so valuable for curing certain ailments that those who know them guard them as commodities that can command a considerable market price.[22] The Temiar tribe of Malaysia,

---

[19] Charles Keil, *Tiv Song* (Chicago: University of Chicago Press, 1979), p. 187.
[20] See ibid., pp. 257–58.
[21] Catherine J. Ellis, *Aboriginal Music: Education for Living* (St. Lucia: University of Queensland Press, 1985), p. 129.
[22] See David McAllester, *Enemy Way Music: A Study of Social and Esthetic Values as Seen in Navaho Music*, Papers of the Peabody Museum of American Archaeology and Ethnology, Harvard University, 41:3 (Cambridge, Mass.: Peabody Museum, 1954), p. 66.

similarly, considers the most important function of music to be its role in mediumistic healing rituals.[23] Although music therapy is becoming increasingly employed in Western contexts, the West is arguably behind other societies in learning how to utilize music for healing.

Even if one resists the temptation to insist on the superiority of one or another approach to musical value, the Westerner is bound to be struck by the unfamiliar but intriguing uses to which music is put in various societies of non-European origin. Music is used by many societies as an explicit means of establishing and mapping one's place in time and space.[24] Keil sees the organization of music of the Tiv tribe in Africa as reflecting and reinstating cultural notions about the complex circles of kinship within that society.[25] Steven Feld reports that the songs of the Kaluli tribe of Papua, New Guinea, map locations within the rainforest and reinforce connections to ancestors, whom the songs typically lament.[26] Marina Roseman points out that the healing songs of the Temiar also serve as maps, indicating important features of the local landscape such as mountains, plants, and so on. These features are believed to have souls like human souls, which teach songs to human mediums through dreams. "Landforms traversed or cultivated become landmarks that are further anthropomorphized when their souls are dreamt and sung."[27] The songs themselves present knowledge, which is metaphorically understood in terms of "paths."

The details of the Temiar perspective on music are likely to sound foreign to most Westerners. But Roseman notes that this perspective serves to focus cultural attention on a matter of growing concern within our own society: the importance of adapting to the environment. Besides inculcating an ecological consciousness toward nature,[28] the Temiar perspective on music facilitates social adaptation and adjustment to the rapid transformations of the modern world.

In addition to providing a format for expressing mutuality with the rainforest environment, the theory of dream revelation provides a space for

[23] See Marina Roseman, *Healing Sounds from the Malaysian Rainforest: Temiar Music and Medicine* (Berkeley and Los Angeles: University of California Press, 1991).
[24] Simon Frith contends that we in the West employ popular music for this purpose and stresses the importance of developing an aesthetic of popular music. See Simon Frith, "Towards an Aesthetic of Popular Music," in *Music and Society: The Politics of Composition, Performance and Reception*, ed. Richard Leppert and Susan McClary (Cambridge: Cambridge University Press, 1987), pp. 133–49.
[25] Keil, *Tiv Song*, pp. 200–202.
[26] See Steven Feld, *Sound and Sentiment: Birds, Weeping, Poetics and Song in Kaluli Expression* (Philadelphia: University of Pennsylvania Press, 1990).
[27] Roseman, *Healing Sounds from the Malaysian Rainforest*, p. 62.
[28] See ibid., p. 177.

Temiars to incorporate new experiences with technological devices of the developing Malaysian world. The ever-changing environment of the Temiar has increasingly included airplanes, parachute drops, perfume oils, wristwatches, Malays, Chinese, the British, Japanese (during World War II), and anthropologists, all of which have emerged in dreams and given songs to Temiar mediums. The theory of dream revelation also offered strategies for adjusting to changes in social organization as the Temiars interacted historically with traditional Malay headmen and courts, and as they interact with the contemporary Malaysian government bureaucracy. . . . The Temiar theory of dreaming thus becomes a dynamic resource for interpreting and formulating new responses to the natural and social world.[29]

Even if one restricts one's attention to "purely musical" concerns, the "objectivity" of Western notation ignores much that is musically important in other traditions. Steven Feld points out that one of the central aesthetic goals in Kaluli music is "lift-up-over-sounding" (*dulugu ganalan*, in the Kaluli language), a layered, nonsynchronous overlap among multiple voices, including the "voices" of the rainforest soundscape. "Lift-up-over-sounding" is a textural ideal, achieved by the particular interaction of variously timbred voices in a specific performance. Feld considers this Kaluli concept a challenge to the approach to music practiced by traditional Western aesthetics, an approach that emphasizes quasi-scientific analysis of structures and deemphasizes the temporal and participatory features of music experienced in the context of actual performance.

> *Dulugu ganalan* is, at the least, a forest of trees falling, crashing down and shaking the grounds of any general aesthetics that privileges vision, visual objects, and visualism, privileges product over process, melody and rhythm over timbre and texture, syntax over semantics, structure over emotion, form over participation, linearity over simultaneity, force over flow, transcendental over temporal, top-heavy over egalitarian, vertical harmony over the moving groove.[30]

The testimony of many ethnomusicologists suggests that the universalistic emphases of recent Western musical aesthetics would miss much that is musically important outside the domain of Western classical music. Extending the focus to "music in as broad a sense as it can be understood" will require that musical aesthetics make more concessions to diversity than its current tools encourage. In the following section, I will indicate a

---

[29] Ibid., pp. 68–70.
[30] Steven Feld, "Aesthetics as Iconicity of Style, or 'Lift-Up-Over-Sounding': Getting into the Kaluli Groove," *Yearbook for Traditional Music* 20 (1988): 105.

further limitation of the aesthetic rage for objectivity. Although rooted in the individualistic West, this pursuit has ignored and demeaned one of the joys of individuality—the possibility of genuine idiosyncrasy among listeners.

Idiosyncrasy in Musical Experience

A corollary to Hanslick's "objective" musical aesthetics was that idiosyncratic responses to music were aesthetically insignificant. Indeed, Hanslick treated idiosyncratic enjoyments with condescension. The more idiosyncratic, in Hanslick's opinion, the less relevant was a response to aesthetics. Hanslick was particularly scornful of those who listened "pathologically," enjoying their own sensations in response to music without focusing their intellect on tonal forms. ("Incidentally, for people who want the kind of effortless suppression of awareness they get from music, there is a wonderful recent discovery which far surpasses that art. We refer to ether and chloroform."[31]) Yet Hanslick also denied the aesthetic relevance of idiosyncratic responses based on associations (and hence on the diverse experiences of listeners) even when these involved attention to musical development. The only associations that Hanslick deemed remotely respectable from an aesthetic standpoint were associations of emotional dynamics with musical dynamics—associations that would be essentially the same for everyone. Yet even in this case, Hanslick considered the "objective" vocabulary of musicology most appropriate for discussing musical dynamics. Different listeners used emotion terms too variably to rely on their terminology.

Hanslick's snobbish characterization of those who listen idiosyncratically suggests that the intelligent and informed will be more similar in their listening experience of the same music than will the thoughtless and uninformed. This remains the implication of "objective" musical aesthetics—insofar as a response is aesthetically important, it is common to all knowledgeable listeners. This characterization does not, however, explain the idiosyncrasies wrought by being intimately involved in performing music. When I make this suggestion, I have in mind three anecdotes that reveal a dimension of musical experience that is typically ignored:

First, a student in one of my graduate seminars,[32] an oboist, described his experience of playing the same symphony in two different orchestras. In one orchestra he played the first oboe part; in the other he played the

---

[31] Hanslick, *On the Musically Beautiful*, p. 59.
[32] Tom Porcello, who has received his Ph.D. from the University of Texas at Austin.

second oboe part. When I asked whether this affected his experience of listening to the symphony, he replied, "I know now that there are at least two ways of listening to this symphony: the first oboe way of listening, and the second oboe way of listening."

On another occasion, a pianist complained to me that she could not relax while recordings of piano music were playing in her presence. Having devoted years to mastering the piano, and frequently having listened to recordings of skillful performers for the details of their articulation, she could no longer listen without focusing on technique. Hearing piano music, she felt as though she should be "working" on it.

Finally, being a pianist myself, I feared the eventual moment when I would no longer be able to relax when I heard piano recordings. Self-scrutiny revealed that I did attend to technique and articulation. Nevertheless, I never reached the point of finding piano music intrinsically unrelaxing. (Perhaps this testifies to the fact that I do not and never did intend to make a career of performing, whereas the pianist who could not relax while hearing piano recordings did.) I discovered, instead, a different peculiarity of my listening experience. When I hear a recording of a piano work that I have at one time performed, my attention becomes riveted. I have difficulty attending to conversation. This is so even if the volume is low, and the music is functioning as background music (not an uncommon situation in certain restaurants).

In such situations I feel at every moment something akin to bated expectation for the next musical event. Although I know exactly what the next chord or melodic element will be, I feel an almost magnetic desire to hear it. My only comparable experience occurred in childhood, when I wanted to hear a well-known story exactly as I had heard it every time before. At every point during a story, I was eager to hear the very next detail. I awaited even the appearance of the Wicked Witch in "Sleeping Beauty" with something akin to desire, even though I hated and feared her, so long as she appeared at the precisely correct moment.

In his book *Musical Elaborations*, Edward W. Said similarly observes that prior familiarity with a work of music conditions and heightens his response upon hearing it. During a concert in Carnegie Hall, Said reports, Alfred Brendel performed a transcription of a Brahms sextet. Said found this part of the recital of particular interest, for he was well acquainted with the original sextet: "Strangely, I think the effort of correspondence held me much more rigorously to the music than is usually the case: I assimilated, I actively bound my hearing to, an earlier but still lively experience of the score with Brendel's performance."[33]

[33] Edward W. Said, *Musical Elaborations*, Welleck Library Lectures at the University of California, Irvine (New York: Columbia University Press, 1991), p. 80.

Nietzsche seems to have had a similar sense of at least some familiar works, judging from the following passage:

> This is what happens to us in music: First one has to *learn to hear* a figure and melody at all, to detect and distinguish it, to isolate it and delimit it as a separate life. Then it requires some exertion and good will to *tolerate* it in spite of its strangeness, to be patient with its appearance and expression, and kindhearted about its oddity. Finally there comes a moment when we are used to it, when we wait for it, when we sense that we should miss it if it were missing; and now it continues to compel and enchant us relentlessly until we have become its humble and enraptured lovers who desire nothing better from the world than it and only it.
>
> But that is what happens to us not only in music. That is how we have learned to love all things that we now love.[34]

Nietzsche intimates here that familiarity can result in such an intensely personal engagement with a work of music to warrant the description "love."

These anecdotes have some interesting implications for musical idiosyncrasy:

First, some of those best educated to appreciate scores "objectively" have the most idiosyncratic perspectives. Practicing musicians would seem to be among the very individuals one would expect to be the most expert at "intellectually processing the score." In fact, however, these musicians are perhaps least likely to be simply attending to "tonally moving forms" when they hear a familiar work.

Second, the idiosyncrasies involved in these cases are musically motivated and musically conditioned. They are not reveries that take music as a mere stimulus or point of departure. Nor are they the consequence of willfully perverse listening (e.g., listening for the fourth beat of every measure, or listening so attentively for the appearance of Neapolitan second chords that one effectively ignores the rest of the music). These idiosyncrasies emerge from intimate familiarity with and attention to music by individuals who are well-acquainted with the stylistic context of the music they are hearing.

Third, what is salient to listeners varies with their individual musical (and generally artistic) backgrounds. Said emphasizes the "ideal purity of the individual experience," although he conscientiously acknowledges "its public setting, even when music is most inward, most private."[35] One wonders if this focus is not related to the fact that Said's instrument is the

---

[34] Friedrich Nietzsche, *The Gay Science, with a Prelude in Rhymes and an Appendix of Songs*, trans. Walter Kaufmann (New York: Random House, 1974), no. 334, p. 262.
[35] Said, *Musical Elaborations*, p. xiv.

piano, an instrument well suited to solo performance. Said's background as a literary critic may also be relevant. Said applauds Proust's reference to "the melody which in each author is different from the ones to be found in all other authors,"[36] for Proust aptly indicates "the ultimately solitary intimacy by which the special music of an author impresses itself upon a receptive critical intelligence."[37] Perhaps, as one whose career is founded on intimate acts of reading, Said is especially inclined to approach music as affording private encounters with composers.

Performers of orchestral instruments and members of bands, I suspect, would be much less likely than Said to extol the private experience of music. Their experiences encourage them to see music as a social enterprise, of a sort suggested by Alfred Schutz's title "Making Music Together." I have frequently been struck, discussing music with members of orchestras and bands, at our different perspectives on the "sociability" of music. My brother, who has played the drums in a number of rock bands, is attuned to the idiomatic predilections of particular musicians (one likes inserting drones and pedal points against the music played by other performers, for example) in a way that is largely unfamiliar to me as a pianist who has almost exclusively played solos.

Finally, musicians and other knowledgeable listeners form something like personal relationships with particular works of music. An explanation is offered by Feld's suggestion that all musical listening involves the listener's active efforts to relate the music to his or her broader experience. In listening, Feld maintains, we dynamically relegate some aspects of the music to the background, drawing others to the foreground, making judgments that relate them to a whole schema of relations to other, often extramusical concerns. These judgments, or "interpretive moves," involve "the action of pattern discovery as experience is organized by the juxtapositions, interactions, or choices in time when we encounter and engage obviously symbolic objects of performances."[38] Music is interpreted in terms of its relationship to locations, categories, associations, reflections, and evaluations relevant to the listener.

Relevance to the listener is crucial in this account. Feld emphasizes the extent to which many interpretive judgments are specific to social groups. This makes sense, given that one's sense of group membership often depends on shared location, classification schemes, backgrounds, experiences, metaphors, and values. Feld's account would also seem to imply,

---

[36] Marcel Proust, *Contre Saint-Beuve* (Paris: Gallimard, 1971); as translated and cited in Said, *Musical Elaborations*, p. 92.

[37] Said, *Musical Elaborations*, p. 92.

[38] Steven Feld, "Communication, Music, and Speech about Music," *Yearbook for Traditional Music* 16 (1984): 8.

however, that differences in individual backgrounds, whether or not they conform to specific group patterns, will have significant impact on the way particular individuals will interpret the music they hear. The unique set of an individual's personal experiences may influence which locations, categories, associations, reflections, and evaluations that individual will draw upon in interpreting music as personally relevant.

The personal relevance of music is a facet of its value that the objective emphasis of musical aesthetics does not accommodate. Yet music is important to human beings largely because they do find it personally relevant. Even if one is skeptical of Schopenhauer's broad metaphysical interpretation of will (and of his basic aesthetic theory), he is surely right in claiming that we relate to music as animate and identify with its movement.[39] Hanslick himself admits that the dynamics of musical tones naturally remind us of the dynamics of our own emotions. Peter Kivy argues further that we tend to associate music with the dynamics of our own activity because we tend to endow everything in our environment with animate qualities.[40] Donald Callen describes our listening experience as an inner singing, which expresses our identification with musically suggested emotions.[41] Roger Scruton similarly refers to our experience as listeners as "inner dancing."[42]

All these images underscore the importance of personal engagement with music. When we are really appreciating music, we engage our entire sense of ourselves. In order to do this, we have to be receptive as the entire individuals that we are. This implies our openness not only to recognitions of the sort indicated in the preceding examples but also to what Said describes as "fleeting, often banal nonmusical associations."[43]

Oddly, the very features of music used to justify the traditional philosophical focus on objectivity with respect to music are the ones that make possible personal engagement with music. Music's relative nonspecificity invites listeners to incorporate it into their own lives. Simon Frith links music's direct emotional intensity to its abstract character: "Because of its qualities of abstractness (which 'serious' aestheticians have always stressed) music is an individualizing form. We absorb songs into our own lives and rhythms into our own bodies; they have a looseness of reference

[39] Arthur Schopenhauer, *The World as Will and Representation*, 2 vols., trans. E. F. J. Payne (New York: Dover, 1969), 1:259.
[40] Peter Kivy, *The Corded Shell: Reflections on Musical Expression* (Princeton: Princeton University Press, 1980), pp. 57–59.
[41] Donald Callen, "Transfiguring Emotions in Music," *Grazer Philosophische Studien* 19 (1983): 88.
[42] Roger Scruton, "Musical Understanding and Musical Culture," in *What Is Music? An Introduction to the Philosophy of Music*, ed. Philip Alperson (New York: Haven, 1988), p. 357.
[43] Said, *Musical Elaborations*, p. 86.

that makes them immediately accessible."[44] Schopenhauer, too, considered the abstract character of music to be the basis for its powerful emotional impact:

> It does not . . . express this or that particular or definite joy, this or that sorrow, or pain, or horror, or delight, or merriment, or peace of mind; but joy, sorrow, pain, horror, delight, merriment, peace of mind themselves, to a certain extent in the abstract, their essential nature, without accessories and therefore without their motives. Yet we completely understand them in this extracted quintessence. Hence it arises that our imagination is so easily excited by music, and now seeks to give form to that invisible yet actively moved spirit-world which speaks to us directly, and clothe it with flesh and blood, i.e., to embody it in an analogous example.[45]

A Reassessment of Musical Scores

I have been arguing that the quest for "objectivity" in musical aesthetics has distorted the value of idiosyncratic (i.e. nonuniversal) musical responses and the importance of personal engagement with music. Suppose musical aesthetics did abandon objectivity as a goal. What would this mean for the field's approach to musical scores?

In the first place, scores would continue to function in many of their current roles within the field.[46] They would still allow us to "point" to features of given works. This function is bound to be vital so long as musical aesthetics endeavors (as I think it should) to support theory with particular examples. I am convinced that recordings and computer-generated transcriptions of performances offer us new resources for pointing. I am just as convinced, however, that aestheticians will want to talk about works independent of specific performances for as long as musical "works" retain their prominence in Western practice to any significant degree.[47]

A more experientially based approach to musical aesthetics would, however, suggest reasons for appreciating the score's detailed notation apart from apparent objectivity. An important, underacknowledged

---

[44] Frith, "Towards an Aesthetic of Popular Music," p. 139.

[45] Arthur Schopenhauer, *The World as Will and Idea*, trans. R. B. Haldane and J. Kemp, vol. 1 (London: Trübner, 1883), p. 338.

[46] Outside of musical aesthetics, scores would, of course, retain their pedagogical and communicative roles in musical practice. I presume that musicologists would continue to analyze scores for the intrinsic interest of their structures.

[47] Lydia Goehr analyzes the development of the "work concept" in Western music in *The Imaginary Museum of Musical Works*.

reason for appreciating detailed Western notation is that it has made possible an art form based upon the sharing of very detailed, unfolding temporal structures. In absolute music, these structures are appreciated in their own right, not as a mere scaffolding for some more focal content. The unfolding of temporality as such is underemphasized in Western experience, as I have argued elsewhere;[48] thus an art based upon it is particularly significant. Moreover, as Schutz reminds us, this focal sharing of temporality involves simultaneously the personal engagement of each listener, a conjunction basic to music's vividness and affective power.[49] Said similarly links music's value to its temporal linearity, which integrates the unique presence of individual sonorities and the unfolding attention that we share with other listeners.[50]

A more experiential, less objectivist approach to musical aesthetics would reveal yet another basis for valuing scores. Scores make possible fairly exact repetition of extremely complex musical details. Repetition, although basic to music,[51] is underestimated by the "objective" orientation of Western musical aesthetics. Meyer goes so far as to claim that "in the West, for instance, exact repetition is felt to be wasteful and pointless."[52] This is an overstatement; consider, for instance, the formulaic da capo of classical sonata form.[53] Nevertheless, Meyer rightly recognizes that the value of repetition is less than obvious if we assume that all musical significance lies with the details of musical structure. He contrasts the Western view of repetition with

the example of primitive music. Here apparently repetition is not only enjoyed, it is prescribed. The difference lies in the cultural situation. In primitive culture music is not separated from other aspects of living—it is not placed in a special, "aesthetic" category. It is one with ritual and religion; and perhaps their inherent conservatism—particularly when their

48 Higgins, *The Music of Our Lives*, pp. 185–86.
49 Alfred Schutz, "Making Music Together," in *Symbolic Anthropology: A Reader in the Study of Symbols and Meanings*, ed. Janet L. Dolgin, David S. Kemnitzer, and David M. Schneider (New York: Columbia University Press, 1977), p. 118.
50 Said, *Musical Elaborations*, pp. 75–76.
51 Herndon and McLeod emphasize the importance of repetition in music: "Music is always redundant in comparison with other forms of human activity. This is frequently expressed by stating that music is highly patterned." Marcia Herndon and Norma McLeod, *Music as Culture* (Darby, Pa.: Norwood Editions, 1980), p. 112.
52 Leonard B. Meyer, "On Rehearing Music," originally in *Journal of the American Musicological Society* 14, no. 2 (1961): 257–67. In Morris Weitz, *Problems in Aesthetics: An Introductory Book of Readings*, 2d ed. (New York: Macmillan, 1970), p. 530.
53 The typical explanation of the latter, of course, is that the ignorant bourgeois, for the first time enjoying serious music, needs to get the basic themes firmly in mind in order to appreciate their later appearance in altered form during the development and recapitulation. Meyer might say that this is a functional repetition—what would otherwise be pointless has its point in allowing appreciation in variety.

existence is threatened by alien cultures—accounts for the tendency toward exact repetition.[54]

Meyer hints that "primitives" can enjoy exact repetition because they intimately connect between music and the rest of life. Although I am skeptical of his dichotomy between Western and primitive music, I think that Meyer is onto something in this insight. Repetition, when music is understood to address one's other concerns in living, is not monotonous. For the restatement of the "objectively" identical takes on new significance in the divergent contexts that life itself provides.[55]

In this connection, once again, the idiosyncrasies of listening become important. Said claims that "the private possibilities" of the listening experience can render a familiar work quite new. Proust's emphasis on these possibilities strikes him as

> very moving, obviously because in its poignancy and psychological richness it has helped me to comprehend a great deal about my own experience of music, experiences that seem to me like an unceasing shuttle between playing and listening privately for myself and playing and listening in a social setting, a setting whose constraints and often harsh limitations (for example, the dreary sameness of most concerts, the failing capacities of hand, eye, memory, and mind that come with age, the comic, entirely parodistic familiarity with what Adorno calls "alienated masterpieces" enabled by record players and electronic gadgets) only suddenly and very rarely produce so novel, so intense, so individualized, and so irreducible an experience of music as to make it possible for one to see in it a lot of its richness and complexity almost for the first time.[56]

Marcia Herndon and Norma McLeod emphasize the importance of repetition and familiarity in another important, albeit rare, kind of musical experience, which they designate "flow." The flow experience is an experience of performers who achieve a condition of "merging" with the music. Loss of ego awareness and a simultaneous sense of complete control of one's actions are among the characteristics associated with this experience. Herndon and McLeod stress the value of knowing one's material "quite well" as a precondition to "communicating directly with . . . [one's] instrument."

> The mind is freed of the necessity to be totally involved in simply producing the effect. The overarching sense of control over performance is such

[54] Meyer, "On Rehearing Music," pp. 529–30.
[55] Indeed, I would contend that this is precisely the basis for pleasure in the appearance of a cantus firmus in Western music. See Higgins, *The Music of Our Lives*, pp. 179–80.
[56] Said, *Musical Elaborations*, p. 76.

that some of the attention can then be diverted from mere mechanics. In such moments, the performer can move into a new awareness of the piece being performed which is transcendent of himself and his formal view. Where group performance is involved and all are competent, the concept of oneness in the entire performing group, or "communitas" takes over. In these circumstances, an orchestra may suddenly become a living orchestra.[57]

Herndon and McLeod consider the "shifting [of] personal awareness" to be a basic capacity of music.[58] Flow is one type of musical experience that accomplishes such shifting. Flow is yet another basis for valuing musical scores as vehicles for detailed repetition. Because they provide one possibility for achieving a high degree of familiarity with one's material, scores facilitate the achievement of flow.

Herndon and McLeod describe another rare but valuable type of musical experience, one that returns us to the topic of idiosyncratic response among listeners. They designate this type of experience "flash."

In "flash," there is an intensification of awareness of the entire environment, a consciousness of the importance of the moment and a need to mark it in some way. . . . One type of "flash" . . . is the state of mind in which the attention is so firmly focused on what is happening that the rest of the environment blanks out, and the listener is totally unconscious of everything else. In circumstances of this kind, he may be immobilized; his arms and legs cease to function. Another common concomitant of this state is the raising of the hair on the back of the neck, the tingling of the scalp and other indications of psychic shock. This state of mind may last for some time after the performance is finished. . . .

There is a "flash" experience in which time is shifted or becomes meaningless into a psychological "now," as Wachsmann puts it. Unlike those occasions on which the environment is burned into the awareness, in this variety, the environment is excluded and concentration is only on the object or performance. After such an experience, one tends to babble.[59]

Herndon and McLeod suggest that some of the most striking aesthetic responses to music are those in which a listener's normal sense of individuality is transcended. Ironically, perhaps, this is one of the most important reasons for musical aesthetics to attend to idiosyncratic listening response.

[57] Herndon and McLeod, *Music as Culture*, pp. 93–94.
[58] Ibid., p. 124.
[59] Ibid., pp. 94–95.

Even when listening occasions less striking responses than flash, aesthetics should attend to the remarkable in musical experience. Aesthetics should ask listeners, Did this music give you goose bumps?[60] Such a question depends on more than the "objective" details of musical structure. Nuances of performance as well as the listener's background and condition are all factors in musical magic.

Conclusion

In our historical moment and place, "difference" has, at least in academic circles, become trendy ad nauseum. The differences considered most salient have to do with the unique natures of particular ethnic and religious cultures. This climate offers us the temptation to accept prematurely the idea of radical difference between the musical practices of various societies. Ironically, it also tempts us to consider any given musical culture (including our own) as more monolithic than it actually is.

In defending appreciation of idiosyncrasy, I aim to counter both temptations. Differences certainly abound, among listeners with similar backgrounds as well as between listeners from different musical cultures. Nevertheless, even the fashionable notion of "difference" depends on some prior notion of a large measure of potential intersubjectivity among listeners. The operative notion of "music" employed by DJs of radio shows with an "eclectic" bent presupposes, I think, a common humanity (or more general common vitality, as, for example, when whale song is included among the "musical" offerings). Such programming assumes that an open-ended sharing of musical productions is possible, even if it is not sharing in every respect.

What, then, is the value of openness to idiosyncrasy? Such openness, minimally, is a necessary by-product of being receptive to certain unusual (but potentially intersubjective) experiences in connection with music. Openness to idiosyncratic responses is also an aspect of what, I submit, is an optimum way of relating to music—specifically, that of developing full personal relationships with music in a manner that resembles the development of personal relationships with other people. In both kinds of relationships, the details that determine who one is become increasingly important, including the details that differentiate one from other individuals.

Aesthetics is surely concerned with when and why music has an impact, and with how music can have its fullest impact. If so, it cannot afford to ignore the idiosyncratic nature of musical response.

---

[60] My thanks to John L. Swanay for this way of focusing the question.

II

MUSIC AS STORY-TELLING:
THE LITERARY ANALOGY

5

Music as Drama

FRED EVERETT MAUS

Recent professional music theory and analysis has tended to avoid certain large questions. Theorists have written little, explicitly at any rate, about the value of music or the nature of musical experience. Stanley Cavell has noted that

> whatever the cause, the absence of humane music criticism . . . seems particularly striking against the fact that music has, among the arts, the most, perhaps the only, systematic and precise vocabulary for the description and analysis of its objects. Somehow that possession must itself be a liability; as though one undertook to criticize a poem or novel armed with complete control of medieval rhetoric but ignorant of the modes of criticism developed in the past two centuries.[1]

Joseph Kerman has also expressed regret at the limitations of professional theory and analysis. Kerman suggests that "the appeal of systematic analysis was that it provided for a positivistic approach to art, for a criti-

I am grateful to Milton Babbitt, Edward T. Cone, Joseph Dubial, Patrick Gardiner, Eric Graebner, Marjorie Hess, Katharine Eisaman Maus, Alan Montefiore, James K. Randall, Eric Wefald, Peter Westergaard, and Richard Wollheim for valuable advice and encouragement in response to earlier versions of this essay.
[1]. Stanley Cavell, *Must We Mean What We Say?* (Cambridge: Cambridge University Press, 1976), p. 186.

cism that could draw on precisely defined, seemingly objective operations and shun subjective criteria."[2]

Cavell and Kerman agree that the precision, definiteness, and clarity of theory and analysis have worked to discourage the study of more obscure and demanding aspects of music. It would be hard to relinquish the precision and detail that musical analysis can offer; the problem is to integrate theory and analysis somehow into a more comprehensive understanding of music.

At times theorists seem simply oblivious to such issues. Allen Forte, in a paper on Schenker that is probably the best introduction to Schenker's late work, concludes with a list of unsolved problems in music theory, suggesting that Schenker's work might contribute to solutions. He mentions, for instance, the lack of a theory of rhythm in tonal music, and the lack of helpful analytical techniques for music outside the standard eighteenth and nineteenth century repertoire. Forte does not ask whether Schenker's work can lead to a better understanding of the importance of music, or to a convincing account of musical experience. In this Forte is more reticent than Schenker himself, whose writings are full of evaluations and speculations that go far beyond Forte's range of concerns. But Forte is silent about Schenker's broader claims, except for a footnote in which he tersely dismisses "Schenker's frequent indulgence in lengthy ontological justification of his concepts."[3] Forte's paper assumes that one aspect of music, its "structure," can be distinguished from other aspects and studied separately. Other fields might concern themselves with other aspects of music, but music theory and musical analysis, as the study of "structure," can progress independently of those other fields.

Some theorists are more explicit than Forte in acknowledging areas of aesthetic inquiry that they have set aside. Fred Lerdahl and Ray Jackendoff, in *A Generative Theory of Tonal Music*, write that

> an artistic concern that we do not address here is the problem of musical affect—the interplay between music and emotional responses.... Like most contemporary theorists, we have shied away from affect, for it is hard to say anything systematic beyond crude statements such as observing that loud and fast music tends to be exciting. To approach any of the subtleties

---

[2] Joseph Kerman, *Contemplating Music*, p. 73.
[3] Allen Forte, "Schenker's Conception of Musical Structure," in *Readings in Schenker Analysis and Other Approaches*, ed. Maury Yeston (New Haven: Yale University Press, 1977). Kerman has commented on Forte's article to show the self-imposed restrictions of professional theory and analysis.

of musical affect, we assume, requires a better understanding of musical structure.[4]

David Epstein writes that "the matter of expression in music is beyond the confines of these studies. . . . The question of what music 'says' is vast and complex and deserves separate study." Like Lerdahl and Jackendoff, Epstein suggests that an understanding of "expression" presupposes an understanding of "structure": "In attacking this problem it is first of all essential clearly to perceive, to recognize, and to comprehend what it is we hear, free of external or misconstrued meanings."[5] These two sources imply the existence of a *dichotomy* between, on one hand, issues of musical "structure" and, on the other hand, those of "affect" or "expression." In referring to "affect," Lerdahl and Jackendoff link that part of the dichotomy to *emotion*. Epstein, more cautiously, relies on two different for-mulations, referring to "expression" and to "what a piece 'says,'" using scare-quotes and commenting that the terms are imprecise. But evidently Epstein sees a dichotomy between structure and an aspect of music anal-ogous to the meaning of human language or gesture.

Whether or not they acknowledge the existence of larger aesthetic issues, theorists generally defend the autonomy of their own studies. Even Kerman, while castigating analysts for their narrowness, seems to leave room for such an independent area of inquiry:

> Their dogged concentration on internal relations within the single work of art is ultimately subversive as far as any reasonably complete view of music is concerned. Music's autonomous structure is only one of many elements that contribute to its import. Along with preoccupation with structure goes the neglect of other vital matters—not only the whole historical complex . . . but also everything else that makes music affective, moving, emotional, expressive.[6]

According to Kerman, analysis has usurped the place in musical institu-tions and education that should be occupied by a more ambitious music *criticism*. But Kerman writes of the "autonomous structure" of music as though such a component can be isolated unproblematically: it is one,

---

[4] Fred Lerdahl and Ray Jackendoff, *A Generative Theory of Tonal Music* (Cambridge, Mass.: MIT Press, 1983), p. 8. In a footnote they add a further comment: "The affective content of music, we believe, lies in its exploitation of the tonal system to build dramatic structure." This suggestion is in accord with my argument here, though Lerdahl and Jackendoff would probably find my presentation unacceptably informal.
[5] David Epstein, *Beyond Orpheus* (Cambridge, Mass.: MIT Press, 1979), p. 11.
[6] Kerman, *Contemplating Music*, p. 73.

though only one, of music's "elements." Criticism, then, would supplement descriptions of structure with considerations of historical context and with—again—an area of concerns linked somehow to human emotion.

In trying to understand what music theory can contribute to a more general understanding of music, it would be natural to begin with this well-entrenched dichotomy between "structure" and "affect" or "expression." Many musicians and writers on music believe that some such dichotomy exists. If they are right, then an understanding of the distinction between these different aspects of music, and—once they are clearly distinguished—an understanding of the relation between them, would be a crucial step in integrating the insights of music theory into a larger picture.

In reflecting on this dichotomy, theorists can now turn to work by the philosopher Peter Kivy, who has recently distinguished between "technical" and "emotive" descriptions of music, arguing for the musical importance of emotive qualities. Kivy's essay *The Corded Shell* begins by noting a "paradox of musical description": "Either description of music can be respectable, 'scientific' analysis, at the familiar cost of losing all humanistic connotations; or it lapses into its familiar emotive stance at the cost of becoming, according to the musically learned, meaningless subjective maundering."[7] Kivy distinguishes two kinds of musical description, and he associates each kind with a different readership: trained musicians prefer technical description, whereas "musically untrained" music-lovers are likely to find emotive description attractive. So in evaluating emotive description, Kivy addresses not only a general aesthetic issue but also a practical problem about criticism. Professional musicians may enjoy "the healthy atmosphere of amphibrachs and enhanced dominant relationships," but such technical description

> leaves a large and worthy musical community out in the cold. Music, after all, is not just for musicians and musical scholars, any more than painting is just for art historians, or poetry for poets. It seems both surprising and intolerable that while one can read with profit the great critics of the visual and literary arts without being a professor of English or the history of art, the musically untrained but humanistically educated seem to face a choice between descriptions of music too technical for them to understand, or else

[7] Peter Kivy, *The Corded Shell: Reflections on Musical Expression* (Princeton: Princeton University Press, 1980), p. 9. Kivy expects that his dichotomy between ways of describing music will not be novel for his readers. As he puts it, musicians write technically at a "familiar" cost; the alternative is the "familiar" emotive stance.

decried as nonsense by the authorities their education has taught them to respect. (pp. 8–9)

How should one address this issue? According to Kivy, "What needs doing, rather than to take cheap shots at technical language, is to make emotive description once again respectable in the eyes of the learned, so that it can stand alongside of technical description as a valid analytic tool" (p. 9). So Kivy intends his defense of emotive description as a defense of the criticism that amateurs can read—at any rate, those amateurs who are "humanistically educated." But Kivy is not only, perhaps not primarily, concerned with the needs of musical amateurs. Kivy argues that ascriptions of emotional properties can be intelligible, objective, and relevant to aesthetic evaluation. If Kivy is right that emotional properties often contribute to the value of a composition, then anyone who cares about music should want to know about them.

The emotive description that interests Kivy has two defining traits. It ascribes emotional expressiveness to the piece, rather than ascribing emotions to the composer or listener (pp. 6–7), and it should be taken literally, not as "nonsense" that somehow guides the listener's perception (pp. 9–10). Kivy associates emotive criticism especially with the writings of Donald F. Tovey, whose famous *Essays in Musical Analysis* originated as program notes for concerts in which Tovey appeared as conductor or pianist.[8] Kivy is astute in choosing Tovey to exemplify popular criticism: not only are Tovey's essays accessible to readers with diverse musical backgrounds, but many professional musicians and musical scholars consider Tovey one of the most insightful analysts, in his program notes no less than in his more professionally oriented works.[9] Many musicians would grant that an interpretation and defense of Tovey's criticism is a valuable undertaking.

Though one is grateful for Kivy's clarity, his project is much too simply conceived. If Kivy succeeds in defending emotive description so that it can "stand alongside of technical description," he is left with an obvious puzzle about musical experience. When he concludes his defense of emotive description, it seems that music can be described in two very different ways. These two ways use quite different vocabularies, and many

---

[8] Kivy introduces the discussion of emotive criticism by quoting some of Tovey's analytical writing (p. 6), and at the end of his essay he indicates that his arguments have vindicated Tovey's critical practice (p. 149). Kivy mentions only one other contemporary writer, H. C. Robbins Landon, as a practitioner of emotive description (p. 120).

[9] According to Joseph Kerman, "For richness, consistency, and completeness, Tovey's Beethoven stands out as the most impressive achievement, perhaps, yet produced by the art of music criticism" (Kerman, "Tovey's Beethoven," in *Beethoven Studies* 2, ed. Alan Tyson [London: Oxford University Press, 1977], p. 191).

people can understand only one kind of description, although both ways of describing music constitute "valid criticism." Assuming that the two kinds of description bring out different aspects of music, what is the relation of these aspects? What is it like to hear a composition that has such diverse qualities? How might the experiences of listeners with different vocabularies differ? Do the two vocabularies record two completely different ways of experiencing music? Or do perceptions of musical structure and perceptions of emotional expression simply "stand alongside of" each other in musical experience? Or is there some way of unifying these different aspects within a single coherent experience?

At several points Kivy's essay touches on the relation between emotional aspects of music and other aspects. Kivy wonders whether it is possible to listen to music without perceiving its expressiveness:

> Some people claim to, and I suppose we should take their word for it. I suspect, though, that the most plausible way of looking at it is as a matter of selective attention. A listener can, I think, decide to focus on the expressive qualities of music, or to focus on some other aspect instead. Whether one can totally extirpate one's perception of musical expressiveness I tend to doubt, but am prepared to believe if brought to it. (p. 59)

This is an intriguing suggestion, but Kivy's claim that one can focus selectively on different aspects of music does not commit him to any view about the way a listener might integrate those aspects.

When Kivy presents his theory of musical expression, he argues that various features of pieces, identifiable under technical descriptions, are naturally or conventionally expressive. For example, he connects musical contour with expressive inflection in speech, the diminished triad with restlessness, and the minor triad with "the darker side of the emotive spectrum" (pp. 46–56, 71–83). But such correlations leave the relation between different aspects of music obscure, for it seems that emotive and technical descriptions interpret the same features of a piece in quite different ways. A conventional musical analyst might try, for instance, to understand the motivic relations among the details of the piece, and he or she might try to place the details in a larger musical progression described in technical vocabulary. Kivy's approach takes the details one by one and associates them with emotional states, presumably interpreting their succession in terms of a coherently developing *series* of emotional states. This leaves a variant of the original puzzle about Kivy's position: can the two kinds of description come together in a single unified description of a piece, or do they reflect two fundamentally disparate ways of regarding the same details?

No account of music as a loose conjunction between ingeniously patterned sounds and expressions or evocations of various emotional states will be plausible. A better account must consider, much more centrally than does Kivy's essay, the extent to which a composition can *unify* its different aspects.

Given the confusing, fragmented image of music in Kivy's treatment, it is easy to see why theorists like Lerdahl and Jackendoff, or Epstein, have suggested the priority of theory and analysis over more humanizing forms of interpretation. Edward T. Cone has argued similarly: "If verbalization of true content—the specific expression uniquely embodied in a work—is possible at all, it must depend on close structural analysis."[10] Instead of dismantling music into loosely related components, these writers argue, one should begin with what is solidly established—the insights of theory and analysis—building from this knowledge toward an understanding of "affect," "expression," "content," "meaning," . . .

The discussion so far points toward an attractive but inadequate position on the relation between music theory and the broader issues of music criticism and aesthetics. The position can be summarized in four claims: (1) Music theory and musical analysis constitute an autonomous discipline, capable of establishing its methods and achieving results without drawing on other ways of interpreting music. (2) Theory and analysis study one aspect of music, namely its "structure." (3) The "structure" of a composition is only one of its aspects. Among the others, one is particularly crucial for criticism and aesthetics. It is hard to name, because the common designations—"expression," "affect," "content," and so on—all imply controversial commitments. But this other aspect is closely linked in some way to human feeling or emotion, and it may also have affinities with linguistic meaning. (4) An attempt to articulate this unnamed humanistic aspect of music must draw on the solid achievements of theory and analysis. Ignoring the findings of theory and analysis will lead to a fragmentary, unconvincing account of other aspects of music.

I am in partial agreement with this position. Certainly it improves upon Kivy's views. Theory and analysis have achieved many insights into tonal music, and a more ambitious aesthetic theory must draw on those insights and place them in a convincing relation to its own claims. But I find the received notion of musical "structure," as an aspect of music that can be distinguished from "meaning," to be vague and obscure. Further, the position that I have summarized places far too much weight on the role of emotion in musical experience.

It will take considerable exposition to clarify and motivate these points of disagreement.

[10] Edward T. Cone, "Schubert's Promissory Note," *19th-Century Music* 5, no. 3 (1982): 233.

Example 5.1. Beethoven String Quartet Op. 95, beginning of first movement

Example 5.1. (Continued)

Reflections on a Passage by Beethoven

To move toward a more general understanding of music, it will be helpful to reflect at length on a particular musical example. The beginning of Beethoven's Quartet Op. 95 (example 5.1) is richly complex, inviting close scrutiny. In this section I begin with detailed description of the first seventeen measures, interrupting the description twice for some preliminary commentary. I have not restricted the description to the language provided by conventional music theory; rather, I have tried to articulate my understanding of the passage as clearly and flexibly as possible, using music-theoretical language along with other kinds of description. After the Beethoven analysis, I move to a more general consideration of the kind of musical thought instantiated in the description.[11]

Analysis. Loud, aggressive, astonishingly brief, surrounded by silence—the initial abrupt outburst leaves much unresolved complexity, even confusion. It is strangely timed as a whole, arriving forcefully and apparently decisively—no uncertainty among the instruments about the proper course—but ending so quickly, as though that gesture could feel complete and self-sufficient. It is palpably incomplete. The clumsiness of the passage, its awkward incompleteness, comes largely from its internal

---

[11] By working from a detailed analysis to more general claims, obviously I run the risk that some readers will disagree with some or much of the analysis. Such readers may still find interest in the generalizations that follow, provided they believe that there are satisfactory analyses that conform to my generalizations. (In any case, I offer the analysis as *one* way of regarding the passage, one option among many for me or for any other listener.)

timing. The change from sixteenths to eighths articulates the opening strangely; the placing of D♭ and C creates rhythmic conflict and confusion. The sixteenth notes, along with the repetition of the opening F, suggest a quarter-note pulse, and to some extent that pulse gives greater weight to the D♭ than to the C. But this creates a bizarre neighboring motion, the elaborated note altering between its two appearances! The pitches are easier to understand as a line descending from F to C and returning to F, passing through the pitches that most conventionally appear in ascents and descents in minor. But this latter pitch structure gives special weight to the C, contrary to the implied quarter-note pulse.

Rhythmic ambivalence comes along with harmonic uncertainty. Heard as rhythmically stressed, the D♭ creates some sense that D♭ rather than C goes together with the emphasized Fs and the top A♭ to make a background triad for these two bars; this sense is muddled or contradicted by the D♮ in the ascent to F—muddled rather than wiped out. C, taken as part of a background triad, would give a second inversion, that is, a dissonant, unstable form, of the F–A♭–C triad. Perhaps the C can be heard as resolving D♭, but as standing for a V chord (extending through a consonant E at the end of the bar). This last might be the most satisfactory structure for the passage, but still the rhythmic location of the implied V is vague, and the passage does not in itself suggest such importance for the E; so this interpretation feels more like the listener's desperate imposition of a familiar stereotype than a report on the harmonies projected by this very passage.

Commentary. The analysis uses traditional music-theoretical vocabulary and relies on traditional assumptions about tonal music—that pitch and rhythm go together most simply when their hierarchies align, that neighboring structures normally begin and end with the same pitch, not with an altered version of the same scale step, and so on. Correct labeling using theoretical vocabulary, and comparison of the Beethoven passage to the common procedures of musical succession summarized in theoretical generalities, are essential parts of the analysis. But the analysis begins by calling the opening a loud, aggressive, abrupt outburst, calling it clumsy, incomplete. These are not technical terms of music theory. Nor do they name emotional qualities, though they do anthropomorphize the passage somewhat, describing it as one might describe a person or a human action. In the analysis they function as general descriptions of the music, the theoretical description serving to amplify and substantiate. The clumsiness or incompleteness of the music is not hard to hear, but it is heard more precisely when one is sharply aware of the disproportion created by the sixteenth notes, dividing the music into a short span—but not an upbeat!—set against a much longer, slower span, or when one is sharply aware of the particular lack of focus created by skewing of pitch structure and meter. Both sorts of description—"technical" or music-theoretical, and "dramatic" or anthropomorphically evocative—belong, interacting, to the analysis.

If the "specifically musical" descriptions do not *supplant* the others, then the more animistic or anthropomorphic descriptions, attributing to the piece qualities of human action—"an aggressive, abrupt outburst, forceful and apparently decisive"—need further attention and reflection.

Analysis, continued. The next outburst (mm. 3–5) invites comparison to the first: again, loud, aggressive, and surrounded by silence, but this second attack is not quite so brief; indeed, it is long enough to seem very repetitious by the end, even while it sustains the sense of frustratingly halting succession. The increased duration feels like a response to the excessive brevity of the first passage, while the repetitiousness marks the response as less than successful.

In other respects as well the new passage registers an awareness of peculiarities of the opening and an effort to clarify, but again there is abruptness throughout, and new peculiarities appear. Response to the earlier problems comes in various ways. The rhythmic complexities of the opening yield to an almost obsessional clarification and simplification. In m. 3 the first violin refers to the stressed second beat of m. 1, but now the emphasis belongs to what is obviously an offbeat pattern, clearly subordinated to the stronger beats stressed by the lower instruments. The lower instruments also emphasize a division of the bar into halves, responding to the uncertain articulation of the third beat in m. 1. In the next measure all four instruments join to divide the bar neatly in half. And when, in the next bar, the earlier stress on the second beat appears, it no longer subverts the strength of the first or third beat, rather appearing as an aftereffect to the strong downbeat, almost an echo. Not only does the pulling-in of the register and move from a full triad to a bare octave subordinate the second beat to the first, but the silence on the third beat is a natural continuation of this fading away. This last effect, then, refers to the opening bar, divided into 1 + 3 beats, reproducing the disproportion but rendering it appropriate and undisturbing.

The passage also refers to the pitch-related obscurities of the opening, offering clean, simple reworkings of the pitch material. The whole three-bar passage harps on the dominant triad, vaguely suggested at the opening; and in particular, the outer parts pound on the pitch C on strong beats (even the first violin's offbeat pattern places C in stronger positions than in m. 1). Earlier there was an obscure suggestion of a second-inversion F triad; now such a triad appears unequivocally, emerging from and resolving into V chords. The definiteness of the dominant harmonies, with subordinated tonic harmonies distinctly interposed, makes the possible glimpse of V in m. 1 seem, in retrospect, too dim to be believable. To some extent this second outburst reshapes the first as essentially a long tonic chord to be succeeded by a long dominant. However, the sound of that tonic remains cluttered with intimations of other harmonies.

Throughout there is, strangely, no hint of the pitch D♭, or of the D♮ that was at odds with it. And even more disturbing is the registral discontinuity between the two outbursts, the second disregarding until quite late the lower register of the first, while opening without transition an area extending a tenth above the original upper boundary. This upper region contains only first violin Cs, which perhaps associates the pitch and registral peculiarities of this response especially with something like hysteria on the part of the first violin. More generally, the completely unmediated contrast of textures—octave-doubled theme followed by tuneless chords—gives the two passages a mutual repulsion that keeps them from settling into any persuasive continuity.

So far, then, the events of this piece are a rough, abrupt initial outburst, and a second outburst that responds to many peculiar features of the opening but also ignores some of its salient aspects, matching the roughness and abruptness of the opening and combining urgent response to the first passage with a strained disjunction.

Commentary. The analysis continues to include specific description in music-theoretical terms, again in interaction with general descriptions that do not use specifically musical vocabulary. A crucial element becomes prominent: events are *explained,* the analysis gives *reasons* for their occurrence. The analysis treats the second passage as in many ways a reasoned *response* to the first. The first passage was rhythmically confused; that gives a reason for the second passage to respond with corresponding rhythmic clarifications; rhythmic features of the second passage are explained by citing such reasons. The first passage was harmonically obscure; that gives a reason for the second passage to respond with corresponding harmonic clarity, retrospectively simplifying the harmonic feel of the first passage somewhat and integrating the two passages into a single clear harmonic succession, or trying to.

Analysis of the next few measures will show a continuation of this drama of abrupt action and response, confirming the appropriateness of the analysis so far but introducing no new modes of interpretation.

Analysis, concluded. The next passage, from m. 6 to the first beat of m. 18, retraces the preceding events: there is a return to the motive of the opening, then something that is like the second outburst in amounting to a long, decorated V chord. As mm. 3–5 responded to mm. 1–2, so mm. 6–18 respond, more adequately, to all the preceding events. The passage is long and continuous, continually purposeful, neither abrupt nor repetitious.

Addition of an explicit chord to the cello's repetition of the opening motive makes the harmony unambiguous. Because the harmony is clear, and because a meter has already been established, the placement of a passing tone on the third beat raises no special problems. In the present setting the motive seems much more straightforward.

That second-beat chord hardens the break between the sixteenth notes and eighths in the cello motive, reviving and intensifying the earlier disproportion. But relatively unemphatic syncopations (mm. 8, 10, 12) refer quietly to the chordal attack, placing softer attacks in a metrically straightforward context, absorbing the blow until by m. 14 rhythms align simply with the meter—a gradual, tactful procedure.

The previously slighted D♭ now exerts its influence: the opening returns in G♭ major, which bears the same relation to the tonic key that the pitch D♭ bears to C, and a key in which D♭ is part of the tonic triad, as the first violin demonstrates. From this starting point there is a slow move to the dominant. Not only does the move to V (mm. 8–9) spell out the semitone relation between the keys of G♭ and F (their dominants are connected by an utterly literal semitone descent), but the D♭ to C connection is singled out as special by delays of both pitches. The strategy: because previously there was an outburst with a problematic D♭, and a response that seemed to ignore the D♭, compensate by imitating the first outburst but doing something *wilder* than the D♭ was (but *like* the D♭), and resolve it *explicitly* to something like the initial response. The beginning of the response is a little startling; it creates another sharp break between contiguous gestures, having little to do with the tonic and dominant chords that immediately precede it; but because its motive and harmony link it primarily to the first gesture of the piece, this local disjunction is not as disturbing as the contrast between the first and second outbursts.

Explicit resolution of the D♭ to C continues in the first violin tune (mm. 12–15), twice by putting D♭ in a much weaker rhythmic position than C, once by putting the D♭ on the third beat of the measure and resolving it unambiguously to C. The first violin in this passage sticks to the new register it opened in m. 3; the high register was abruptly and irrelevantly opened, but now the first violin assimilates it to the other registers that have been used by repeating in this register the features of lower registers (an F triad with C as the lowest note, Cs neighbored by D♭s).

Mm. 13–15 refer back to the earlier alternating tonic and dominant chords, but slowly, smoothly. And instead of eliminating the problematic D♭, these measures include it, along with D♮, in clear relation to the primary chords. And then, recalling the possible mingling of D♭ and F triads at the opening, m. 16 places a D♭ triad in the position that might have been occupied by F minor, leading the D♭ up to D♮ while placing a chromatic lower neighbor to C, as if to diminish the import of the D♭ by providing a symmetrical semitone neighbor, the two closing in on the structurally focal C. In place of the earlier disregard of the problematic D♭, here is elaborate, lucid acknowledgement of the pitch, placing it in vivid, definite relation to F minor. The D♭ triad also does much to assimilate the G♭ sound, absorbing it and placing it in the governing tonality.

The present passage occupies the combined registral spread of the opening outbursts, forming one seamless space from registers that had contrasted sharply. The piece now seems to have opened a wide registral span by successively opening two subspans. Within this space the cello has a special role. Having begun the passage by retrieving the opening motive, the cello maintains a special concern with the beginning of the piece: its remarkable ascent and descent (mm. 10–17) occupy the registral spread that was occupied at the opening by the entire ensemble, referring to those boundaries but showing them to have been narrow.

The earlier textural discontinuity is absorbed into a single developing process. What felt like a jarring succession of extremes—line versus chords—now appears within a process of increasingly independent instrumental parts. Stages of the process: octave doubling; chords, with some rhythmic diversity; line *and* chords; polyphonically independent, rhythmically diverse parts.

The return to the opening motive and texture in m. 18 groups the first seventeen measures together as a separate stage of the action, and the analysis of those measures has already provided sufficient basis for the following discussion. However, it is worth noting briefly that the issues arising in the opening measures remain fundamental concerns in the continuation of the piece. The abrupt return to the opening raises new questions about the status of D♭ and now G♭ as well, and the subsequent tonicization of D♭ attempts to draw the disheveled pitch materials into a new equilibrium. The major mode return of this material in the recapitulation reenacts the suppression of D♭ in mm. 3–5, giving urgency to the final return of F minor. Concern about the metrical placement and resolution of D♭ persists to the last measures of the movement. Of course, to explore these later developments fully would require a lengthy analysis.

It would be natural to call the quartet a conspicuously *dramatic* composition, and the analysis makes the sense of drama concrete by narrating a succession of dramatic *actions*: an abrupt, inconclusive outburst; a second outburst in response, abrupt and coarse in its attempt to compensate for the first; a response to the first two actions, calmer and more careful, in many ways more satisfactory.

I suggest that the notion of action is crucial in understanding the Beethoven passage. A listener follows the music by drawing on the skills that allow understanding of commonplace human action in everyday life. In transferring those skills from the context of ordinary human behavior to the more specialized context of musical events, a listener can retain some forms of interpretation relatively unchanged, while other habits of thought must be changed to fit the new context.[12] In order to understand the use of these skills in understanding music, it will be helpful to begin with some generalizations about nonmusical contexts.

The related notions of action, behavior, intention, agent, and so on figure in a scheme of explanation or interpretation that applies to human beings (also, more controversially or problematically, to some animals and to sophisticated machines, such as chess-playing computers). The scheme works by identifying certain *events* as *actions* and offering a distinctive kind of *explanation* for those events. The explanations ascribe sets of psychological states to an agent, states that make the action appear reasonable to the agent and that cause the action. The explanatory psychological states can be divided roughly into epistemic states (beliefs and the like) and motivational states (desires and the like). Ascriptions of psychological states are constrained by the need for the agent to shape up as an intelligible person: fairly coherent, consistent, rational, and so on. Besides beliefs and desires, one important class of explanatory states includes character traits, moods, and emotions. These function in a variety of ways: they can affect epistemic and motivational states, and they sometimes help to explain failures of consistency or rationality.[13]

---

[12] In focusing on musical action, and most obviously in my discussion of fictional "musical agents," I have been influenced by Edward T. Cone's excellent study *The Composer's Voice* (Berkeley and Los Angeles: University of California Press, 1974). The importance of that book has not yet been sufficiently recognized by music theorists. See my "Agency in Instrumental Music and Song," *College Music Symposium* 29 (1989): 31–43, along with other essays on Cone in that issue of *College Music Symposium*; also Carolyn Abbate, *Unsung Voices* (Princeton: Princeton University Press, 1991). My work on anthropomorphism has been influenced by unpublished work of the late Flint Schier and the art criticism of Adrian Stokes and Michael Fried. I encountered Roger Scruton's fine essay "Understanding Music" (in his *The Aesthetic Understanding* [London: Methuen, 1983]) after formulating the claims and arguments of this essay, but I am pleased by the similarity of our positions.

[13] For careful and influential explorations of the point, see Donald Davidson, *Essays on Actions and Events* (New York: Oxford University Press, 1980). My account draws largely on Davidson's views. Along with Davidson's work, G. E. M. Anscombe, *Intention* (Ithaca: Cornell University Press, 1957), was crucial in establishing the study of action as a central preoccupation of current analytic philosophy. Sophisticated, engaging recent work includes Daniel Dennett, *Brainstorms* (Montgomery, Vt.: Bradford Books, 1978); Christopher Peacocke, *Holistic Explanation* (New York: Oxford University Press, 1979); Adam Morton, *Frames of Mind* (New York: Oxford University Press, 1980); and Jennifer Hornsby, *Actions* (Boston: Routledge and Kegan Paul, 1980).

What shows that an event is being regarded as an action? Some words are consistently associated with actions; to say that some event is a theft is always to classify that event as an action. Other words sometimes designate actions, sometimes not; knocking down a snowman might be an action, but if I slip on the ice, bumping the snowman by accident, and it falls, my knocking it down is not an action. More generally, it is a necessary condition for an action that it can be explained by citing the agent's reasons, by ascribing an appropriate configuration of psychological states.[14]

The Beethoven analysis includes some terms that always indicate actions. An abrupt outburst, for instance, is always an action, and so is a reasoned response. But also, the explanations the analysis gives for events in the piece, beginning especially in the description of mm. 3–5, cite reasons consisting of psychological states, explaining the events of the piece just as actions are explained. Consider again the analysis of mm. 3–5: many features of the second outburst are explained by ascribing an intention to respond to the first outburst and beliefs about the precise points of unclarity in the opening gesture. For instance, the description points out that the passage presents certain pitch material, which was more obscurely presented before, and in depicting this as a response, it ascribes *thoughts* that refer to the opening, that is, thoughts that the opening had certain features that make a compensating action appropriate. Something like this: "That outburst left a vague, equivocal sense of a dominant triad. That is unsatisfactory, and one way to deal with the situation is to present a dominant triad more straightforwardly, leaving no doubt about what I mean." The thought is ascribed to explain an action, the action that the thought shows as rational. More formally, one can identify beliefs—"There was something vague about the harmony at the opening; a straightforward alternation of tonic and dominant would be much clearer"—and a desire—"I want to replace the sound of the opening with something clearer"—combining to give a reason for acting.

Saying that the passage *harps on* the dominant suggests that the response is repetitious and perhaps a little out of control. Although the contents of mm. 3–5 warrant this description, there is a further suggestion that the same *mood* or *character trait* that led to the initial outburst continues to operate, infecting the response with a certain clumsiness, both internally and in its relation to the first outburst. As with the ascription of thoughts, the ascription of mood or character to explain events resembles explanation of actual behavior.

---

[14] These generalizations simplify, but not in ways that affect the musical application. For discussion of necessary and sufficient conditions for an event to be an action, see Davidson, *Essays on Actions and Events*, and Peacocke, *Holistic Explanation*.

In general, the description of the Beethoven passage *explains* events by regarding them as *actions* and suggesting *motivation, reasons* why those actions are performed, and the reasons consist of combinations of psychological states.

But to whom are these ascriptions of action and thought made? It might be thought that these descriptions are straightforward accounts of what the composer did in composing the piece, or what performers do in performing it. Two considerations show that these suggestions are too simple.

First, if the analysis contains description of an action or motivation that cannot be ascribed to the composer or performers, and if this fact does not show that the analysis is wrong, then it seems the analysis involves the ascription of at least one action to an imaginary agent. Consider again the account of mm. 3–5: the second outburst is an abrupt, clumsy response to the first outburst. But that does not mean that Beethoven penned the opening, noticed its unresolved complexities, and hastily penned a rough response. (Maybe he did, but that is independent of what the analysis claims.) Neither is it the case that Beethoven *pretended* to respond roughly and hastily; there is no sense of play or pretense about that response, which sounds earnest. Nor does the analysis describe the actual response of the members of the string quartet. An essential part of the passage is the feeling that the first outburst has taken someone somewhat by surprise, and that the roughness of the second outburst comes from unpreparedness. But the members of the quartet know what is coming next.

A second consideration is more general. In listening to a piece, it is as though one follows a series of actions that are performed now, before one's ears, not as though one merely learns of what someone (Beethoven) did years ago. And in following the musical actions, it is as though the future of the agent is open—as though what he will do next is not already determined. But then the actions are not straightforwardly those of the composer, whose (relevant) actions are all in the past, or those of the performers, whose future actions are already prescribed.

But these considerations are not conclusive. They indicate that some kind of imaginative activity or construction of fiction figures in understanding music. That might involve the ascription of actions and psychological states to fictional characters; but it might equally, for all these arguments have shown, involve the creation of fictionalized versions of the composer or performers. For instance, if I follow musical actions as though they are currently taking place, I could be following the actions of imaginary agents, but I could rather be *imagining* that the *composer* is currently performing those actions. Or if I follow actions of which the future is open, I could be following the actions of imaginary agents, or I could be imagining that the *performers* are *improvising*.

The analysis does not answer these questions about agency; indeed, at many points the Beethoven analysis is evasive about specifying an agent. For example, "The next outburst . . . registers an awareness of peculiarities of the opening and an effort to clarify. . . . The whole three-bar passage harps on the dominant triad." The first sentence mentions an outburst, an awareness of something and an effort, without identifying anyone to whom these thoughts and actions belong. The second sentence seems to say that a passage does something: but perhaps this is a way of saying that the passage *is* a harping on the dominant, again without specifying a musical agent.

Such evasions might seem to be *omissions*, gaps that a fuller analysis would fill. I suggest, however, that the gaps belong in the analysis, that they record an aspect of musical experience. The evasions reflect a pervasive *indeterminacy* in the identification of musical agents. Sometimes it seems appropriate to think of the whole texture of a piece as the action of a single agent. In other contexts a differentiation of agents within the texture may be more natural, conspicuously in concerto style, where a solo part interacts with an orchestra, but also in many less extreme contexts. For instance: "The first violin refers to the stressed second beat of m. 1. . . . The lower instruments also emphasize a division of the bar into halves." What questions about individuation does such a passage answer? Does it, for instance, show that the first violin part in this passage corresponds to the activity of a single agent, determinately set apart from the rest of the ensemble? But why not think of the first violin part as somewhat like one limb of an agent who has several limbs and can do several things at once? And what about the other three instruments—are they three agents cooperating, or a single agent producing chords? Further, the distinction between first violin and lower instruments is sharp in m. 3 of the Beethoven (as described by the excerpt just quoted) but decreases in the following measures; the first violin retains individuality in that it contributes only Cs, while the other instruments play more different pitches, but the rhythmic unison suggests a single chord-producing agent. And— whatever is shown by the dissociation of the first violin from the other instruments—this is only a small part of a piece in which the four instruments continue to play; what does the temporary distinctness of the first violin mean for the dramatis personae of the rest of the piece?

Indeed, what is the relation, in terms of the identity of the agent, between the opening outburst and mm. 3–5? The indeterminacy here is reflected by another evasion in the language of the analysis: nowhere is it clear whether the response to the first outburst is made by the same agent or agents. If the continuity in the performing forces suggests continuity of the musical agency, the registral discontinuity and utterly different treatment of the ensemble may suggest that a distinct agent or agents have entered to respond. (Consider, also, the prominence of the first violin in m. 3 especially; at the opening, the first violin merely doubles the second, so at m. 3 the first violin enters somewhat as a new character.)

Questions like these arise naturally, and they do not invite determinate answers. The actions that a listener follows in listening to the Beethoven passage do not belong to determinately distinct agents. More precisely, as the listener discerns actions and explains them by psychological states, various discriminations of agents will seem appropriate, but never with a determinacy that rules out other interpretations. The claim is not that *different listeners* may interpret the music differently (though they undoubtedly will) but rather that a *single* listener's experience will include a play of various schemes of individuation, none of them felt as obligatory.

If this is correct, then the thoughts connected with music are not just a matter of imagining the composer's actions as occurring in the present. Were that the case, indeterminacy about the musical agent would not be possible: there would be one agent, whose actions give rise to the entire musical texture, determinately continuous from the beginning to the end of a piece. Nor does a listener simply imagine that the performers before him are improvising, or otherwise cast them in dramatic roles like actors in a play; once again, a determinate set of agents would result. However, it remains possible that the play of interpretations within this indeterminacy would include interactions involving fictionalized representations of the composer and performers.

As indicated in the commentaries, the analysis mingles standard music-theoretical vocabulary with other sorts of description. The anthropomorphic language, I suggested, belongs to the analysis because the analysis reports an experience of the music as a succession of actions. A crucial question remains: what is the relation between the actions I have discussed—outbursts, attempts to resolve—and the music-theoretical language of the analysis? The musical terminology includes some phrases (e.g., "mm. 7–10") that serve mainly to locate parts of the score, but also phrases (e.g., "the change from sixteenths to eighths," "a rhythmic strong point," "the pulling in of the register and move from a full triad to a bare octave") that describe the way the music sounds in performance. It is the latter language, and its relation to the more dramatic language, that is interesting.

The first point to observe is that the technical language and the dramatic language offer descriptions of *the same events*. That event at the opening of the quartet, according to the analysis, is an outburst, and it is also a unison passage with an obscure relation between metrical hierarchy and pitch hierarchy. The technical vocabulary of the analysis describes the actions that make up the piece.

To develop this point into something more interesting, further reflection on ordinary nonmusical action will be helpful. Suppose I write an address on an envelope. That action has many different descriptions; for example, I have addressed a letter, used some ink, misspelled part of the address, embossed the address on one page of the enclosed letter, moved my hand in an elaborate pattern, and so forth. Some of these descriptions, but not all of them, are pertinent in understanding why I want to perform the action; or to put the point differently, the action is intentional under some descriptions but not under others. I intentionally address a letter; I do not intentionally misspell some words. Again, my action can be evaluated in various ways, according to various criteria; and given certain criteria, some descriptions will be pertinent to evaluating the action, while others will not. Descriptions that bear on evaluation will not necessarily be the same as those under which the action is intentional. For an evaluation of my social skills, it may be important that there are misspellings and that the pen has made indentations on the letter in the envelope.

Much of the theoretical language of the analysis not only describes the actions of the piece but describes them in ways that show the intention with which the action is performed. To explain the second outburst, the analysis implies an intention to respond to harmonic obscurity with a clear alternation of dominant and tonic chords. Other language, not providing a description of an act as intentional, nonetheless provides descriptions that pertain to evaluations that motivate subsequent actions. The metrical and harmonic obscurities of the first outburst, as it is depicted in the analysis, seem consequences of its haste and abruptness, not features intended by the musical agent or agents.[15] Those obscurities, though, are recognized and motivate later attempts to compensate. The theoretical language provides a description that bears on an evaluation of the passage; that description then figures in the thoughts of the

---

[15] This point depends on a crucial distinction between Beethoven's historical intentions and those of the agents in the piece. Suppose a dramatist writes that a character should trip and fall at a certain point in his play. The dramatist intends the clumsiness, but in an important sense it is not *the dramatist's* clumsiness, and within the world of the play the clumsiness is not intentional. A similar distinction holds for the quartet. Perhaps Beethoven intended the passage to be clumsy. Still it makes sense to say that this is not Beethoven's clumsiness, and that it is not intentional in the world of the quartet.

agents of the piece when they evaluate the first outburst and formulate a response.[16]

In short, the music-theoretical language in the Beethoven analysis gives descriptions of the actions in the piece, bringing out aspects that are pertinent in describing and evaluating the events *as* actions. This point is not trivial: it should not be taken for granted that descriptions of actions happen to be pertinent to their explanation and evaluation. Consider, for instance, the descriptions that a physiologist might give of my bodily movements in addressing a letter, sealing it, and walking to the mailbox. The physiologist might produce accurate anatomical descriptions of my actions, but those descriptions would not show how I thought of the actions in deciding to perform them, nor would they be relevant to most criteria of evaluating my actions. Because of the relevance of the theoretical descriptions in explanation and evaluation, that language also figures in *attribution of thought* to the musical agents.

While the theoretical language of the analysis most obviously designates actions, a further indeterminacy concerning agency enlarges the possible functions of theoretical language. In everyday contexts, there is a sharp distinction between agent and action. Agents and actions are different sorts of thing: an agent is, for instance, me—an animal of a certain size, shape, and history—whereas my actions are transient events. But in musical thought, agents and actions sometimes collapse into one another. An F-minor triad or the opening motive of the Beethoven might be regarded as actions, perhaps typical actions of some recurring character; but they might instead be regarded as agents, as characters within the composition. This issue does not arise in the language of the Beethoven analysis, except perhaps in its evasiveness, but Schoenberg, for instance, writes that "a piece of music resembles in some respects a photograph album, displaying under changing circumstances the life of its basic idea—its basic motive,"[17] and similar descriptions are common. In Schoenberg's description a motive is treated as a *dramatic character*. This indeterminacy between sounds as agents and as actions is possible because a musical texture does not provide any recognizable objects, apart from the sounds, that can be agents. If the sound is regarded as action, the listener

---

[16] The last three paragraphs are indebted to Davidson. See especially "Agency," "The Logical Form of Action Sentences," and "The Individuation of Events," in *Essays on Actions and Events*. Davidson's views are controversial. Other positions on the individuation of actions and events would allow me to make the same points, but in a more cumbersome way.

[17] Arnold Schoenberg, *Fundamentals of Musical Composition* (London: Faber and Faber, 1967), p. 58.

may also, seeking a perceptible protagonist, attribute those actions to the sounds as agents. In music, Yeats's enigma—how to tell the dancer from the dance—arises continuously and vividly.

I shall summarize these points about the Beethoven analysis by comparing the Beethoven passage to a stage play. Comparisons between drama and music, especially music of the classical period, are commonplace, but the Beethoven analysis makes it possible to specify the comparison in considerable detail.[18] It will be useful, for purposes of comparison, to sketch a somewhat simplified, idealized notion of a "normal stage play." Four properties will be relevant: (1) a play presents a series of actions; (2) the actions are performed by fictional characters (or fictionalized representations of mythical or historical figures); (3) for the audience, it is as though the actions are performed at the same time as the audience's perception of the actions; and (4) the series of actions forms a *plot* that holds the actions together in a unified structure. I have suggested that the quartet, like a stage play, presents a series of actions, performed by imaginary agents and perhaps fictionalized versions of the composer and performers, and that these actions are heard as taking place in the present. Regarding the fourth property of a "normal stage play," the structuring of events into a plot, it may seem obvious that the issue arises only for an entire movement or multimovement composition rather than for the opening fragment of a piece, but in fact a definite plot structure is discernible within the opening bars of the quartet. For a pertinent account of plot one can turn to the work of the contemporary literary theorist Tzvetan Todorov. According to Todorov, "An ideal narrative begins with a stable situation that some force will perturb. From which results a state of disequilibrium; by the action of a force directed in a converse direction, the equilibrium is re-established; the second equilibrium is quite similar to the first, but the two are not identical."[19] Todorov's remarks are very suggestive for the general issue of musical plot; musicians will find it easy

---

[18] Tovey and Rosen have written influentially about the dramatic character of the classical style. For characteristic passages, see Donald F. Tovey, "Sonata Forms," in his *Musical Articles from the Encyclopaedia Britannica* (London: Oxford University Press, 1944), pp. 208–32; and Charles Rosen, *The Classical Style* (New York: Norton, 1972), pp. 70–78. Stanley Cavell, "The Avoidance of Love: A Reading of *King Lear*," in his *Must We Mean What We Say?*, pp. 267–353, includes insightful suggestions about music and drama. Cavell writes about music on pp. 320–22 and 352–53, but the point of his remarks depends on much of the rest of the essay. Elliott Carter describes his own music as dramatic in conception. See, for instance, his remarks on the Second String Quartet, in *The Writings of Elliott Carter*, ed. Else Stone and Kurt Stone (Bloomington: Indiana University Press, 1977), pp. 278–79.

[19] Tzvetan Todorov, *Introduction to Poetics*, trans. Richard Howard (Minneapolis: University of Minnesota Press, 1981). Todorov has contributed some of the best work toward the construction of a "grammar" of narrative, analogous to the grammar of a language. Some other important works in this area are Vladimir Propp, *Morphology of the Folktale*, trans.

to think of many ways in which compositions can conform to Todorov's schema. (A particularly obvious example of an "ideal narrative" would be sonata form.) In applying the schema to the opening of Beethoven's quartet one should remember that Todorov is describing an *ideal* narrative in which the plot structure is simple and complete. The Beethoven passage can be understood as involving a *modification* of Todorov's schema, in two respects. First, the opening gesture *combines* the functions of establishing an initial state of stability and introducing an imbalance or "disequilibrium": to put it in a very general way, the first two bars establish a certain tonality and meter, but they do so in an obscure or confusing way, thereby introducing a problem that needs to be resolved. A second modification of Todorov's schema appears in the occurrence of *two* attempts to establish stability—one (in mm. 3–5) that is only partly successful, and a second (in the rest of the passage) that responds more successfully to the opening five measures. The existence of such condensation and overlapping suggests that the Beethoven passage not only organizes its events into a plot but does so in a particularly sophisticated way.

The analogy between the opening of the quartet and the "normal stage play" holds up fairly well. Two points that emerged earlier qualify the analogy in important ways. First, the actions in the music are not as close to everyday actions as are the actions of nonmusical drama. In a stage play, characters perform actions that occur in everyday life; they make promises, argue, marry, murder, and so on. In the Beethoven passage, the actions have general descriptions that can be satisfied by everyday actions: for instance, there are two *outbursts* at the beginning of the piece, and the second one is an attempt to *respond* to the first and *compensate* for it. But these actions also have more detailed descriptions that are "specifically musical": for instance, the second outburst responds to the first by establishing a straightforward metrical pattern, by clarifying the pitch structure, and so on. Second, a stage play normally involves a

---

Laurence Scott (Austin: University of Texas Press, 1968); Claude Lévi-Strauss, "The Structural Study of Myth," in his *Structural Anthropology*, trans. Claire Jacobsen and Brooke Grundfest Schoepf (Garden City, N.Y.: Anchor Books, 1967); and Roland Barthes, "Introduction to the Structural Analysis of Narrative," in his *Image—Music—Text*, trans. Stephen Heath (London: Fontana, 1977), and *S/Z*, trans. Richard Miller (New York: Hill and Wang, 1974). These studies are by now somewhat dated: theoretical work on narrative has recently concentrated more on political, psychoanalytic, or rhetorical issues rather than the narrowly formal issues of structuralist analyses. However, the structuralist accounts remain promising for work on musical narrative. Typically such accounts *abstract* from specific actions and individual characters while generalizing about the patterns of events within "well-formed" narratives: accordingly, in light of my remarks above, this approach seems peculiarly well suited to bring out similarities between musical and nonmusical narratives.

definite number of fictional characters that can be reidentified as the *same* characters at different points in the play. Hamlet is a different character from Gertrude, and Hamlet in act 5 is the same character as Hamlet in act 1 (otherwise one could not contemplate the extent to which Hamlet may have *changed* in the course of the play). But the agents in the Beethoven passage are indeterminate.

It may seem strange at first to think of music as a kind of drama that lacks determinate characters. The position may seem less strange if one recalls that Aristotle, in the *Poetics*, considers the traits of individual characters to be less important for a tragedy than the intelligibility and unity of the series of actions in the plot: "The most important of all is the structure of the incidents. For Tragedy is an imitation, not of men, but of an action and of life. . . . Dramatic action, therefore, is not with a view to the representation of character: character comes in as subsidiary to the action, and of the agents mainly with a view to the action."[20] For Aristotle, the imitation of agents in tragedy serves the more essential purpose of imitating an action. Perhaps Aristotle's remarks can help one grasp the suggestion that music can be dramatic without imitating or representing determinate characters *at all*.

Musical Structure as Dramatic Structure

In light of the preceding discussion, what is the *structure* of the Beethoven passage?

The analogy to drama suggests that the structure of the music is its *plot*. The structure could be summed up as three large actions, the second responding to the first, and the third responding to both earlier actions. Or, following Todorov, one could describe the structure in terms of equilibrium and imbalance, in the slightly complicated way that I indicated.

But these structures do not imply any distinction between structure and other aspects of the music, for all the detail of the analysis simply provides fuller specification of its plot. Nor does this account of structure permit a distinction between structure and a more "humanistic" or "emotive" aspect of the music: humanistic aspects—more precisely, the drama and anthropomorphism that I have discussed—are also present as aspects of the plot.

But this notion of dramatic structure is different from the notion of "structure" that appeared in the first section of this essay. There, I cited

[20] Aristotle, *Poetics*, trans. S. H. Butcher (New York: Hill and Wang, 1961), pp. 62–63.

writers who agreed in distinguishing a particular aspect of music, "structure," that is studied in isolation from other aspects by theorists and analysts. How would one isolate the structure, in that sense, of the Beethoven passage? In particular, does the dramatic or anthropomorphic language contribute to a description of "structure"? Or is it closer to the pole of "meaning" and "expression"?

This question is hard to answer with any conviction. The notion of structure seems stable when it is vaguely specified as some sort of "patterning of sounds" and placed in opposition to "affect," "emotion," and so on. When the picture is complicated—and given greater verisimilitude—by introducing the dramatic aspects I have presented, the contrast breaks down.

The contrast breaks down at both ends. In light of a detailed narration of musical drama, it becomes implausible that *emotion* occupies a privileged role in musical experience. A writer who believes that emotion is the only link between music and ordinary human life will stress emotion heavily in explaining the importance of music. But the Beethoven passage is connected to everyday life by action, belief, desire, mood, and so on.[21]

In short, the quartet analysis, along with my subsequent commentary, does little to support the notion of musical structure as a patterning of sounds, the appropriate subject matter of a technical discourse that remains aloof from aesthetic issues. For at least some music, a satisfactory account of structure must already be an aesthetically oriented narration of dramatic action.

---

[21] Peter Kivy's *The Corded Shell*, as I indicated earlier, relies uncritically on a sharp distinction between technical and emotive description of music. Curiously, however, there is a brief passage in which one can glimpse a promising unification of Kivy's account of musical experience, along the same lines that I have been exploring. Kivy observes that to regard a piece as expressive is to regard it animistically. In order to defend the ascription of emotional expression to music, Kivy argues that ascription of emotion to music figures in a much more general pattern of animistic construal: "Only a moment's reflection on the way we talk about music will reveal, I think, how deeply 'animistic' our perception of it really is. A musical theme is frequently described as a 'gesture.' A fugue subject is a 'statement'; it is 'answered' at the fifth by the next 'statement' of the theme. A 'voice' is still what musicians call a part in a polyphonic composition, even if the part is meant to be played on an instrument rather than sung by a voice. . . . We must hear an aural pattern as a vehicle of expression—an utterance or a gesture—before we can hear *its* expressiveness" (pp. 58–59). According to Kivy, the vocabulary of technical description reveals that musical events are sometimes construed as utterances or gestures, and it is such utterances or gestures that provide the basis for the ascription of emotion.

The dichotomy between technical and emotive aspects of music governs Kivy's thinking so powerfully that he can even sketch a position that *eliminates* the dichotomy, without being led to question the fundamental importance of the dichotomy.

Evaluation and elaboration of the claims I have made can come from two obvious sources: further detailed analyses, and close interpretation of major texts in music theory and aesthetics to see whether dramatic models operate in these texts. The latter task is both important and promising: in fact, it turns out that some of the finest and most influential theorists understand music as a drama of interacting agents. I mentioned Schoenberg's dramatic construal of motivic patterning; more generally, Schoenberg's *Harmonielehre* construes pitches and harmonies as agents, struggling for supremacy, and it is notable that his language becomes *more* animistically dramatic when he addresses the most crucial foundational concepts. Schenker's early work depends on a similar dramatization of pitch relations, and his later work remains pervasively animistic in the context of a very different theory. Tovey is perhaps the most obvious example of a major analyst who explains music by providing a dramatic narrative. (Ironically, Kivy's central example of an *emotive* analyst turns out to be predominantly concerned *not* with emotion but rather with *narratives* in which dramatic and technical language mix freely, as in my Beethoven quartet description.) The prerequisite for such further explorations is a clear, if provisional, exposition of the concepts of musical agency, drama, and so on, which I have attempted to provide in this essay.[22]

---

[22] I have developed ideas from this paper in several subsequent publications: "Hanslick's Animism," *Journal of Musicology* 10, no. 3 (summer 1992): 273–92; "Music as Narrative," *Indiana Theory Review* 12 (Spring–Fall 1991): 1–34; "Ashbery and the Condition of Music," in *World, Self, Poem*, ed. Leonard Trawick (Kent, Ohio: Kent State University Press, 1990), pp. 178–86. An extended account will appear in *Humanism and Musical Experience*, forthcoming from Cambridge University Press.

6

Action and Agency in Mahler's
Ninth Symphony, Second Movement

ANTHONY NEWCOMB

I understand the essence of at least the particular kind of music on which I focus here to lie in transformational successions of events in sound, transformational successions of sounding events designed by a human being. In this view, music as heard—whether in the concert hall or in the head of the practiced score-reader or frequent record-listener—is a representation and reenactment of a complex pattern of intentional human action.[1] A question that arises soon, if not immediately, when one understands music this way is this: if music is (or represents) actions and events, who is acting? One can put together quotations from everyone from Hanslick to philosophers and hard-nosed music analysts of the post–World War II era, each of which implicitly recognizes this question without trying to explore its ramifications.

I want to zoom in as quickly as possible on the specifics of my subject in an individual piece, but I will first take a moment to locate the subject at least sketchily in the larger landscape of which it forms a part. I shall start with Richard Wollheim's (and perhaps many others') three fundamental powers of (in this case) painting: the powers to represent, to express, and to delight (or, as he puts it, to "induce a special form of

---

[1] I mean intentional, at least for now, in Donald Davidson's sense that anything understood as an action must be understood as intentional, not in Richard Wollheim's more direct connection with the fulfilled intentions of the specific artist. See Donald Davidson, *Actions and Events* (Oxford: Oxford University Press, 1980), esp. the essay "Agency"; and Richard Wollheim, *Painting as an Art* (Princeton: Princeton University Press, 1987).

pleasure").[2] A large component of most music lies in its power to do the last, to delight with its patterns in sound. (Hanslick likened music to the arabesque and the kaleidoscope.)[3] But in some music these patterns seem to force upon some of us recognition of meaning connected to other aspects of our life—of a representational and expressive power. As Wagner put it, something in the successions of such music elicits from us the question, Why? What does it *mean* that it happened just that way, there?[4] It is discussion of Beethoven's symphonies that brings Wagner face to face with his question, and Beethoven's was the music that most unavoidably forced the question of musical meaning on musicians of 1800 and after.[5] It was a question that was to preoccupy their writings about music—writings of which Hanslick's pamphlet is but a fraction of a percent.

If music was in fact meaningful, what, or how, did it mean? That, of course, was the question that Hanslick proposed to answer and that his supporters and opponents have debated from well before he was born (1825) up to the present day. Hanslick's answer was to locate those higher powers in the power to induce a special, nonrepresentative form of pleasure, in what Wollheim calls "the much maligned property of the decorative," Hanslick's arabesque.

But for the many opponents that Hanslick's influential pamphlet called forth, his was an answer that robbed some music of much of its power over our imagination.[6] For these writers music was heard as in some sense re-presenting patterns of external and internal human behavior—actions and emotions. And many nineteenth-century musicians invented stories—patterns of external and internal human actions—to go with many of the pieces they valued most, including their own. These nineteenth-century musicians were, as we would think now, fairly naive in

[2] Wollheim, *Painting as an Art*, p. 45.

[3] Eduard Hanslick, *Vom Musikalisch-Schönen* (Leipzig: Weigel, 1854), chap. 3, "Das Musikalisch-Schöne," pp. 33–37.

[4] Richard Wagner, "Zukunftsmusik" (September 1860), *Gesammelte Schriften*, 6th ed. (Leipzig: Breitkopf und Härtel, n.d.) 7:112, 129.

[5] Beethoven implied the question in his laconic note at the top of the first page of the sketches for the "Pastoral" Symphony: "Mann überlässt es den Zuhörer sich selbst die Situationen aufzufinden." See *Beethoven: Ein Skizzenbuch zur Pastoralsymphonie op. 68 und zu den Trios op 70. 1 und 2*, ed. Dagmar Weise (Bonn: Beethovenhaus, 1961), p. 2, fol. 2r. Cited in Owen Jander, "The Prophetic Conversation in Beethoven's 'Scene by the Brook,' " *Musical Quarterly* 77 (1993): 510.

[6] To name just some chronologically close and influential examples: Richard Wagner, "Über Liszt's Symphonische Dichtungen" of early 1857 (*Gesammelte Schriften*, 5:182–99); Adolph Kullak, *Das Musikalisch-Schöne* (Leipzig: Matthes, 1858); and A. B. Marx, *Ludwig van Beethoven, Leben und Schaffen* (Berlin: Otto Janke, 1859).

their handling of agency in the stories they invented. Sometimes (for example, in Wagner's Beethoven programs) they referred it back to the composer in an unmediated fashion, in the characteristic belief that in biography lay the key to musical hermeneutics. Sometimes they referred it to other individuals (e.g., Napoleon or Faust) or, as in Schumann's case, the Doppelgänger protagonist pair from Jean Paul's *Flegeljahre*. Sometimes the agency was a more generalized public one (*marcia funebre*, "Festklänge"). But to conceive of some music as actions and emotions, as many did, raised—for some at least—the question, Who is acting or feeling?[7]

We have now more sophisticated metaphors for musical agency. One is voice. Instrumental music does not have this, in the literal sense of the sound produced by air forced through the vocal chords of a living being. It does have voice (or voices) in the metaphorical sense, in which we speak of the author's, or perhaps the narrator's, voice in literature. Another such metaphor is persona, as in dramatis persona, which is much closer as a metaphor to the view I shall go on to develop here.[8] The overlap of our use of the word "character" for a character (dramatis persona) in a play and "character" as in *Charakterstück* and "he has 'character'" is something I shall return to in connection with the displaying of expressive properties in music.

Whatever metaphor we use, it is important to realize that in music as in the other arts (verbal, filmic, literary, painterly) *aspects of agency are not continuously displayed, nor are aspects of narration*. Both are only intermittently operative. Even the most "expressive" music (to use a favorite nineteenth-century term for what I take to be music having clear elements of narration and agency) at times simply swirls or dreams or chugs along in its decorative function. But in this it is essentially no different from painting and literature. It may differ from them only in the balance of these functions. (For example, large swaths of the marked surface of many a painting are there for reasons of proportion or ornament.)

One might go on to ask here, What aspects of an agency and what kind of agencies can be represented or expressed in instrumental music? I

---

[7] See Otakar Hostinsky, *Das Musikalisch-Schöne und das Gesamtkunstwerk vom Standpunkt der formalen Aesthetik* (Leipzig: Breitkopf und Härtel, 1877), esp. pp. 51–56. Hostinsky explicitly raises the question, If music expresses feeling, *wer fühlt*? His answer is quite close to that developed by Richard Wollheim in *Art and Its Objects*, 2d ed. (Cambridge: Cambridge University Press, 1980), essay 5, "Seeing-as, Seeing-in, and Pictorial Representation," and further developed in *Painting as an Art*, chap. 2, "What the Spectator Sees."

[8] See Edward T. Cone's seminal book *The Composer's Voice* (Berkeley and Los Angeles: University of California Press, 1974); and, more recently, Jerrold Levinson, *Music, Art, and Metaphysics* (Ithaca: Cornell University Press, 1990), esp. chap. 13.

would begin to offer some examples as follows: instrumental music can represent institutional agencies, such as city, country, court; it can represent natural agencies, such as storm, wind, thunder; it can represent some aspects at least of sentient agencies, such as animals (Haydn's *The Creation* and *The Seasons*; Saint-Saëns's *Carnival of the Animals*), and, of course, humans. If we focus on this last, what aspects of a human agent can be represented or expressed? At least some external ways of behavior can be well represented by music (as I shall try to show presently). But much, perhaps most, musical representation is of internal characteristics ascertainable only by introspection—what most call expression of emotions and feelings.

Here as well, we must answer the question, To whom are these emotions and feelings attributed? In a painting or sculpture, the issue of the expressive agencies is, I think, less problematic, partly because, in figurative painting or sculpture at least, there are often human simulacra—an anguished "expression" is on the face or in the gesture of some human figure. But also because a painting or statue is a frozen moment.[9] In a reenacted human action, which is what I take the imagination or performance of music to be, the question becomes more complicated and finally, I believe, less avoidable. I claim that in music we do understand (we say we "hear," by which we mean understand from aural input) behavior patterns, which we associate with separable agencies (that is, separable from us). In stage drama we also see and hear patterns of behavior, but there the separate (fictional) agencies are physically presented to us. In music they are not. In music we must go about isolating and identifying the characteristic or expressive elements in the behavior patterns (as we must also in drama). Then we must in addition decide how to group them into agencies, as we need not in drama. This is a distinctive aspect of the representation of agency in music, and one that, I will propose, lies at the root of music's being able to represent and express in a way that other media cannot.

Is this indeterminacy of grouping of a different order from the initial indeterminacy involved in isolating the expressive or representative attributes in any art? It is additional, but it may not be of a different order. In both cases the same issues arise: *where* (which attributes of a work are expressive); *what* (what do they express), and *how specific* (at what level of particularity—for representation: any woman, a particular class or kind of woman, the Empress Josephine).

[9] But cf. the fascinating narratives and agencies viewers felt moved to invent when confronted with a newly discovered classical sculpture in the Renaissance: Leonard Barkan, "The Beholder's Tale: Ancient Sculpture, Renaissance Narratives," *Representations* 44 (Fall 1993): 133–66.

I want now to move to a specific piece of music, to try to flesh out in practice how I propose to answer some of these questions. Let me begin by proposing that the imagination of agency in music works, in schematic form, as follows:[10]

1. The selection of musical attributes that "stand out," that we might call "characteristic" (in the sense of "full of character"). This involves contrasting the way the particular musical gesture behaves with the way such gestures should behave in the normative world of a particular musical style. The "character" (i.e., the representative or expressive element) of these musical attributes may be located in any of various musical elements—for example, in instrumentation, tempo, texture, interval vocabulary, metric design, rhythmic motive or style, harmonic support, and so on.

2. The interpretation of these musical attributes as attributes of human character or behavior, in those instances where the attribute or context suggests human agency (as opposed to, for example, a storm or a magic helmet). This step in the operation seems to me to be parallel to Richard Wollheim's finding of "correspondences."[11]

3. The combination of these human attributes in various configurations, as possible or plausible human agencies. (Both the composer and the listener do this, as part of different aspects of the listening activity.)[12]

4. The understanding of this fictional agency or these fictional agencies as relevant in the unfolding of a plausible chain of human actions and events—including, of course, the development of new attributes and agencies—which is one's understanding of the section, movement, or piece. (This last element may take me beyond the topic of agency in the strictest sense into what I call the narrative element of the piece, but it has a great deal to do with the understanding of the meaning of the piece as a transformational succession of events.)

In this interpretation, human agency is represented in a distinctive fashion in these unattached, in that sense abstract, attributes—unattached, that is, to any specific human simulacrum (including any specific instrument or player, save perhaps in some movements of concertos and accompanied sonatas). The composer's activity of combining musical attributes, and the listener's activity of isolating and interpreting them to construct

---

[10] See also Levinson, *Music, Art, and Metaphysics*, p. 330, for a somewhat similar formulation.

[11] Cf. n. 7 in this essay.

[12] Composers or pieces do this by combining, juxtaposing, or otherwise interrelating various musical attributes; listeners do it by responding to these suggested interrelations.

plausible agencies, is a distinctive part of the musical representation of agency. Just as music can present thematic generality (for example, what I call an archetypal plot)[13] without having to attach it to any specific situation, so it can present shifting constellations of attributes that do not *have* to be attached to specific (fictional human) figures.

The result is that *musical* attributes—attributes of instrumentation, tempo, interval vocabulary, metric design, rhythmic motive or style, and harmonic support—can recombine or shift so as to produce unexpected transformations in the cluster of metaphorically or anthropomorphically interpreted attributes making up a character or agency. One presumed agent, a unified combination of musical attributes in a given section of music, can even unobtrusively take on musical attributes from another presumed agent, attributes that one thought to be distant, thus producing surprisingly rapid, oblique psychological shifts in the configurations or constellations of human attributes—bringing together by a small change in harmonic vocabulary or metrical placement psychological worlds that one had thought widely separated. Wagner, of course, was the master of this.

What is important to emphasize here is that agency in music is not locatable in any *one* musical attribute. The agency is not identifiable with, or located in, the trumpet or the harmonic progression or the intervallic pattern of the melody. It lies in the momentary combination (by the composer) of these elements, which can shift and recombine with unparalleled fluidity, because the attributes are not attached to any fixed physical embodiment (any human simulacrum, as I have put it). This indeterminacy of location of "characteristic" musical attributes (which is where I locate expressive properties) is distinctive to musical agency.[14]

Let me now exemplify the operations proposed in the preceding on a single piece—or at least the beginning of a single piece. I pick a piece of considerable extension because, as I have said earlier, the complexity of agency and expressive meaning that I find in the most interesting music comes not from any single brief slice of music, any of which may be relatively simple or general in expressive meaning, but from the succession, interrelation, and transformation of these slices in the course of an entire piece.

The piece I have chosen is the second movement, corresponding to the scherzo-trio-scherzo of the four-movement sonata cycle, from Mahler's

---

[13] Anthony Newcomb, "Narrative Archetypes and Mahler's Ninth Symphony," in *Music and Text: Critical Inquiries*, ed. S. P. Scher (Cambridge: Cambridge University Press, 1992), pp. 118–36.

[14] The musician can literally transfer musically embodied psychological characteristics from one agent to another, something a playwright or prose author cannot easily do.

Ninth Symphony. Let me start by referring to the first slice, the very opening of the movement (mm. 1–27).

According to the series of steps I have outlined, what stands out here? I will suggest a provisional conclusion and propose that the opening musical idea projects a characteristic way of behavior that one might call "clumsy" or perhaps "rustic." This is embodied (notice the word) in several stylistically unusual (or conspicuous) musical attributes:

— the downbeat double-drones in the lower strings, bringing up resonances of bagpipe music, perhaps via Haydn symphonic trios;
— the repeated down-bows (instead of properly grouped up- and down-bows) in the violin parts (which Mahler marks "like fiddles")—violin playing as a series of rough downstrokes);
— the assembly of a tune and, as the section goes on, of countermelodies out of commonplace fragments of the diatonic scale in various concatenations, and their combination in a counterpoint that is rough at best (one of these, the horn phrase in m. 13, is marked "cheeky" [*keck*]);
— the simple harmonic support; and
— the generic reference of the tempo and rhythmic style of the moderate-tempo Ländler.[15]

I claim that the immanent musical attributes of this section will lead the attentive and culturally attuned listener to begin imagining an agency that is "clumsy." I might now mention that Mahler prefaces the movement with the direction *etwas täppisch und sehr derb* (somewhat clumsy and very sturdy, earthy, coarse); the entrance of the tune in the violins he marks not only like "fiddles" but also *schwerfällig* (ponderous, bear-like), as if to make sure that the expressive intent not be missed. But I maintain that, even were the words to fall away, the meaning would be there for the culturally prepared and attentive performer or listener.[16]

As the brief section continues, other attributes stand out, now attributes depending on succession and order: the incapacity to conclude a thought properly, the tendency to treat succession as a series of somewhat crude, loud interruptions. These are complemented by one of the most subtle of

[15] I note that "clumsy" is not an emotion; it is principally a way of behavior. I also note that these attributes do not depend for their meaning on the order in which they are presented. So far, transformation and order in a succession of events are not important elements of meaning but simply the combination and juxtaposition of various musical attributes.

[16] Many modern performers do in fact smooth out this clumsy rusticity, preferring a refined and lovely sound to an expressive one. The best recording I know is of a live performance by the Vienna Philharmonic conducted by Bruno Walter on 16 January 1938. My copy is Vox/Turnabout 65008/9; the master is an EMI property.

the musical attributes suggesting the human attribute "clumsy": the ungainly, inelegant, asymmetrical, additive (rather than balanced and complementary) phrase structure of this first section, whose phrases continually either fall short of or run beyond the "proper" four- and eight-measure units of the style. This is an important factor also in projecting the interruptive or petering-out impression in the phrases—they end either before or after they properly should. This is not well-formed discourse.[17]

The contrast between, on the one hand, initial assertiveness and brusque interruptions and, on the other, inability to conclude—this contrast evokes something of insecurity, bombast, even bluster to add to this rustic clumsiness. The world evoked by the characteristic style of the Ländler and the rough, simple counterpoint also add an element of physical setting to the section: the rural atmosphere of, say, the third movement of Beethoven's Pastoral symphony (to which Mahler's movement may well be understood to allude).

I note finally that it is the protagonist of the piece, the imagined agency of the piece, that acts this way. It is not the piece, which—unlike much other late nineteenth-century expressive or representative music—is itself neither clumsy nor bombastic. And it is not the performers or the composer who are clumsy or bombastic (as has been elegantly demonstrated by Fred Everett Maus in "Music and Drama," in this volume); it is an imagined agency within the music that acts this way.

In the way this first section ends (if this is the word) or is replaced by another, one hears most clearly the inability properly to conclude the musical unit, the tendency to begin emphatically and peter out, that marks the behavior of this first agency. It lays itself open, so to speak, to the violent act of possession by the second agency (see example 6.1).

What are the characteristic musical attributes in this new agency?

An important one is a sudden leap in the level of harmonic complexity—no longer the diatonic simplicity of what I call Dance A on table 6.1 (see p. 143). A more specific and complicated harmonic attribute derives from a harmonic progression that originated in the previous movement (the first movement): the descending movement by major thirds and the associations that this progression had come to have there

---

[17] The initial four-measure phrase is answered by a three-measure one. The second half, or consequent phrase (mm. 14ff.), of the opening "tune" (mm. 10ff.) is cut off almost immediately by the interruption of the opening woodwind cadence (mm. 15–16) to give another three-measure consequent. The next try at the "tune" (mm. 19ff.) runs well past its expected cadence in m. 26. Its seeming inability to recognize or accept the cadence is put to rest only by the brusque nonmodulation to IV in mm. 32–33.

with loss of center, with violation of innocence, and with alienation.[18] This attribute I cannot present directly in the local illustration, nor will it come into clear form in the first occurrence of the new musical idea/agency. It is part of the transformational succession I referred to previously—part of the evolution of this agency. I will point it out in later occurrences.

Example 6.1. Mahler, Ninth Symphony, second movement, end of Dance A, beginning of Dance B (mm. 82–97)

[18] An association that one might understand as immanent in the progression itself, whose symmetrical division of the octave gives one no orientation within it. The point is developed more fully in my "Narrative Archetypes and Mahler's Ninth Symphony."

Example 6.1. (Continued)

Even in its first appearance, one cannot mistake the raw vigor with which the new agency rushes, so to speak, onto the stage—the energy of its interruption. And anyone sensitive to the stylistic world out of which Mahler's movement comes would also recognize immediately the new characteristic style—the waltz—in the new section. I have proposed that this moment represents the introduction of another agency, another action-force. Whether this action-force comes from within a single pro-tagonist or from a separate agency coming from outside is, I believe, finally indeterminate. This is a distinctive aspect—and a potential strength—of musical agency. The action-force can be simultaneously understood (1) as an *external* agency—for example, urbanness, or a par-ticular social group of which urbanness is a large generalization; (2) as *another person* (as in Charpentier's *Louise*, a wildly successful new opera that Mahler conducted repeatedly in Vienna in the years leading up to the Ninth and that uses the waltz as the sounding symbol of the corrupting forces of the city that bring down the simple lass of the title role); or (3) as *an element within the protagonist's own personality*—this last a particularly powerful possibility in a culture fascinated with multiple personality manifestations and disorders.

Were space to permit it, I would want to develop fully the argument that, for the movement as a whole, the most fruitful view is in fact this last—to see a complex of distinct and contradictory agent-like forces focused in a single protagonist. I would develop this line principally on the basis of shared and transformed musical attributes among the various agencies presented and developed in this movement. I shall point out examples presently.

But first let me point out that in music it is distinctive—and a power-ful source of complex meaning—that the question *need not* be resolved as to whether or to what degree the action-forces come from within or from without the protagonist. No view is exclusively prescribed by the music. This does not mean that in interpreting this music anything goes. It means that at least several appropriate versions can coexist in the mind of the listener.

This question of "within or without" aside, my claim is that the partic-ular way in which the section is introduced—the way in which the music behaves at this transitional point—produces a particular meaning. To summarize grossly: in the first section we have emphatic, rustic, some-what self-assertive behavior, but with a tendency to peter out; that is then replaced in a violent interruption or incursion from somewhere by another set of attributes, another musical idea or musical agency. Like the first idea, this one is characterized, at least in its entrance, by some-what obstreperous, unmediated, inelegant, almost irrational behavior (in musical terms, we might ask, Where the hell did that come from?).

But it is something quite different—another action-force or another characteristic style. In brief, the differences in musical attributes are of tempo (particularly important in this movement), of harmonic language, and of rhythmic and metrical style (the waltz). But there are shared attrib-utes as well: melodic motive (the stepwise descending third), the repeated violin down-bows, and the rough, additive phraseology. If, following this hint, one conceives of the action of the movement as involving shifting forces within the personality of a single protagonist, the accumulated units are already painting an emotional picture of some considerable complexity.

I should qualify here the adjective "emotional." Often when used in music-aesthetical discussion, it means "emotional states" (e.g., "sad," even the more complex "melancholy"). But I am using it here in another, uncontroversial meaning: the tendency to certain kinds of behavior over time (as in irritability, excitability, fearfulness, volatility, aggressivity, passiveness, confidence, and so on)—even an evolving pattern of emotional or psychological states over time (for example, growing confidence). Such things can be represented only by longer patterns of the succession, transformation, and substitution of characteristic events, not by the single brief slice of musical action.

As I appeal to these longer patterns of succession, I must leap across considerable stretches of music, although to do so almost contradicts my entire enterprise, since music's meaning, as I propose it, is located in the particularity of its moment-to-moment successions and their accumulating interrelations. I would ask the reader, in order to test my interpretations, to go back finally and read through or listen through the entire movement. Meanwhile, I will simply have to assert that the nature of the agency in this next, sizable section of the movement (Dance B in table 6.1) can be located in the following important musical patterns of succession:

1. its gradual achieving (in not so subtle steps) of what would be recognized in an actor on stage as a clear mode of expressive behavior: namely, "a very confident stride" (something easily represented in music and incorporated into the metaphorical language of our supposedly technical descriptions—cf. "stride bass");

2. the gradual coarsening of the musical idea of Dance B itself into something simpler, more banal, as stride, confidence, momentum, and tempo accumulate; and

3. the incorporation (eating up) of the first musical agency (Dance A) by the second (Dance B—as its own midsection).

All these musical elements are ones of process, ones depending on order of presentation, no longer ones that can be located in the brief musical slice.

1. Examples 6.1 (mm. 90–97) and 6.2a–b (mm. 132–42, 260–68) give the three successive embodiments of the main material of Dance B. The initial occurrence of the material (example 6.1) shares with Dance A its irregular, awkward metrical structure. The downbeat figures of its opening measure stumble over each other in melodically active top and bottom

Table 6.1.

	Dance A (a moderate-tempo Ländler)
	Opener: (mm. 1–4: an opening gesture and a cadence)

Dance A (a moderate-tempo Ländler)
  Opener: (mm. 1–4: an opening gesture and a cadence)
    Theme A: (seven measures, not eight—closing with the above cadence)
  Opener and Theme A repeated in varying combinations, including a small
  central section in IV, and a following series of repetitions, eventually
  disintegrating without a cadence (cf. example 6.1 and end of movement).

m. 90　Brusque interruption of **Dance B** (a faster waltz)
    Theme B: at first a somewhat awkward tune (**Theme B¹**), it gradually
    straightens out metrically to a "well-built" eight-bar waltz tune
m. 148　 (**Theme B²**).
m. 168　 **Dance A. Opener** interrupts, but without breaking the hold of
    Tempo B. After four attempts to find a proper cadence,
m. 180　 **Theme B²** interrupts and proceeds to accumulate speed and a new
    merry-go-round trumpet tune. (In here Mahler writes *Flott*.)

m. 208　Brusque interruption of a low **D**; brief transition and motivic transformation.

m. 217　**Dance C** (a slow Ländler)
    a　**Theme C:** a nostalgic recall of the 3̂–2̂ falling whole step of the first
      movement, with a counterpoint made up of bits of **Theme A**.
    b　A midsection made up of **Opener** and bits of **Theme A** from **Dance A**.
    a'　The start of a return of **Theme C**, which loses its way to the cadence.

m. 260　Brusque interruption by **Dance B**
    Theme B¹: a new version, now a "well-built" eight-bar tune plunging
    down the circle of thirds, which runs through a series of increasingly fast
    and orgiastic repetition-variations (cf. mm. 180ff.)

m. 323　Brusque interruption by low **C**: brief transition (cf. mm. 208ff.)
m. 332　**Dance C:** as before, fails to find a cadence and drifts to a complete stop
    (fermata).

m. 368　**Dance A: Opener** intervenes. Several failed attempts to stabilize a proper
    cadence are followed by fragments of **Theme A**. These are *gradually*
    infected by motives of **Theme B¹**, accompanied by a *gradual* acceleration
    toward the
m. 403　tempo of **Dance B**. The previously interruptive low notes of mm. 208 and
    323 appear, with the accompanying gesture of the rising sixth, but these
    fail to stabilize on a pitch or to slow the tempo. Instead of the expected
    move to **Dance C** (as at mm. 208 and 323) we get
m. 422　**Dance B: Theme B²** takes over completely. Again (cf. mm. 180ff.) gets
    faster and faster. After a cadence parallel to that at m. 304, the material of
    Dance C attempts to intervene but cannot slow the tempo or break
    through the noisy textures. It lasts for only six measures.

m. 522　Brusque interruption by **Dance A** and Tempo I. Fragments of motives from the
    Opener and of **Theme A**, now heavily colored by the minor mode and by
    motivic inflection from **Theme B**, drift through the disintegrating textures
    of the movement, which expires as if exhausted by the repeated
    interruptions and confrontations.

voices (mm. 93–95) toward a rebeginning in m. 96. After a brief contrast
(to which I shall return), the main material of Dance B recurs in a metrically smoothed out form (example 6.2a), in which an initial pair of three-
measure, melody-plus-accompaniment phrases is answered by a pair of

Example 6.2a. Mahler, Ninth Symphony, second movement, mm. 132ff.

Example 6.2b. Mahler, Ninth Symphony, second movement, mm. 260ff.

two-measure precadential phrases. After a larger contrast, the main material returns once more, now as a fully regularized, confident pair of four-measure phrases. It is in the last version that the harmonic progression by descending major thirds to which I referred is first realized as a full cycle covering an octave (example 6.2b, mm. 260–63).

2. The brief contrast between first and second occurrences of the main material of Dance B (mm. 123–31) contains the kernel from which the increasingly banal secondary material of Dance B (Theme B^2 on table 6.1) will sprout. The descending triadic figure of the trombones in mm. 123–24

grows with weed-like vigor and rapidity into the athletic eight-measure phrase of mm. 148–55 (example 6.3a). This tune in turn, taking the cue from an accompanimental mutation in the trumpets (mm. 187–90), is transformed into the merry-go-round music of mm. 444–52 (example 6.3b). This version is shrilled out by the woodwinds plus piccolo and E♭ clarinet near the climax of the intoxicated triumph of Dance B, whose material gains confidence, stride, banality, and tempo as the movement progresses.

3. Tempo itself is a primary carrier of musical structure and meaning in this movement. Three contrasting tempos are explicitly defined and played off against one another in the movement, like tonalities in Haydn. Thus the fact that the material of Dance A, introduced in the central section of Dance B shortly after example 6.3a here, is unable to impose its own tempo is an important carrier of meaning (mm. 168–79: *Immer*

Example 6.3a. Mahler, Ninth Symphony, second movement, mm. 147ff., arrangement for piano–four hands by J. V. Wöss (Vienna: Universal, 1912)

Example 6.3b. Mahler, Ninth Symphony, second movement, mm. 444ff., arrangement for piano–four hands by J.V. Wöss (Vienna: Universal, 1912).

dasselbe Tempo [II] writes Mahler). In fact it is swept away after only twelve or thirteen measures by the material in example 6.3a.

I shall now skip ahead to the last of the distinctive characters/agencies/ways of behaving in this movement—the one I have designated Dance C on table 6.1. It is in yet another tempo and characteristic style (slow Ländler). As in other sectional joints both small and large in this piece, much information about the agencies is contained in the way in which one thing succeeds, becomes, or replaces another. Example 6.4 gives the transition from an increasingly giddy Dance B (in a headlong version marked *flott* [racy, chic] by Mahler) to Dance C. The impression of willful intervention to stop the headlong rush of Dance B is given by the arresting (literally) gestures of the low Fs and Ds, and the subsequent effortful striving toward the new behavior represented musically by the turning around of the falling sixths of Dance B and their gradual, slow

Example 6.4. Mahler, Ninth Symphony, second movement, mm. 197–222, short score by the author

Example 6.4. (Continued)

rise to the tune of dance C—as well as, of course, by the effortful pulling
down of the tempo, the breaking of the momentum of B.

Who, or what, did this? In music, the answer to this question *must*—or,
I would say from the positive side, *can*—remain indeterminate. In prose,
drama, or film, the author could—would probably need to—answer this
question, with something such as the visit of a childhood sweetheart or

friend, or the chance turning up of a photograph, or the unexpected whiffing of a smell touching off this reaction in our protagonist. The *nature* of the new behavioral and emotional world is much less ambiguous. The characteristic style, tempo, and rhythms of the slow Ländler tell us already something of the relaxed country setting, as does the pastoral sound of the oboe in the second phrase. Most important as a carrier of meaning, however, is the appearance of the transformed head of the first theme of the first movement as the head of this theme. In the first movement, this theme had been a symbol of a primary Arcadian innocence, toward whose recovery the movement continually strove in effortful transitions, following repeated crises and collapses. Here the melodic fragment reappears after a similar transition and with the same meaning.

Another element of meaning derives from the relation between the musical material of Dance C and that of Dance A. (Recall that the material of Dance B had swallowed, or, one might almost say, run over, that of Dance A.) Here Dance A is incorporated, first, as a harmonious if somewhat chunky counterpoint to Dance C (see example 6.4—end, bottom voices). It then becomes the midsection of Dance C, *but in its own proper tempo* (mm. 229–50). The two coexist in combination and juxtaposition, the identity of neither one suppressing that of the other.

The final attribute of this agency (or section, or way of behaving musically) comes from the way it ends, or fails to end, and is replaced by Dance B. Here again, as with Dance A, we have failure to achieve closure. In Dance C this failure is reinforced not so much by the disintegration of the texture as in Dance A as by the gradual chromaticization (sophistication) and loss of center of the harmony, by the explicit and undirected droop of the melodic lines, and by the near total loss of rhythmic energy, momentum, and direction (mm. 255–59).

Dance B interrupts as before, sweeping away the agency or set of attributes in a burst of vigor. (The version of Dance B here is the first occurrence of the fully confident stride—the version of example 6.2b shown here, with the full instance of the descending progress by major third.)

Before leaving this section and agency, I should like to propose that one could defensibly apply to it, among others, the subtle emotional predicate "nostalgic."[19] The most complicated definition in my dictionaries for "nostalgia" reads "wistful or excessively sentimental, sometimes morbid, yearning for return to or of some past period or irrecoverable condition"

---

[19] My purpose here is to contest the assertion made by Peter Kivy that music can possess "gross expressive properties" (such as "sad" or "happy") but not "subtle expressive properties." See Peter Kivy, *Sound Sentiment* (Philadelphia: Temple University Press, 1989), chap. 14, "Newcomb's Problems." This chapter is itself a response to my article "Sound and Feeling," *Critical Inquiry* 10 (1984): 614–43.

(Webster, *New Collegiate Dictionary*, 1969 ed.). We have in the Mahler the past period—the object of the emotion—through the varied recall of the first movement's theme. If one accepts my analysis of the meaning of that movement, we have an irrecoverable condition in another sense than just the past—the sense of Arcadian innocence, the naive of Schiller's naive and sentimental dichotomy.

Do we have yearning ("a kind of urgent desiring," my dictionary tells me)? I would say yes. As a superficial gesture, we have it in the transposition of the first-movement motive from an upbeat motive to a downbeat-afterbeat one. Combined with the stepwise fall, this is a classic musical embodiment of the sigh. More intrinsic to the process and more complex in its meaning is the effort represented in the transition—the willful stopping of the runaway process of Dance B and the slow, effortful climb to Dance C indicate a strong and sudden motivation that could be little else than a desire for the condition striven for and attained—if fleetingly.

Even the "wistful" element (Webster: "yearning with little expectation of gratification") is captured in the drooping lines of the entire musical section (Dance C), in the relative lack of energy in the rhythmic activity, and, most strikingly, in its inability to reach closure. Thus I would claim that this relatively brief section, when put in the entire context of which it forms part, prescribes for our protagonist an emotional predicate of a relatively complex sort. I have tried to show that the conceptual contents of this emotional predicate are in fact represented by musical attributes, which direct our imaginations in a relatively precise way.

In defense of understanding the agency of Dance C as coming from the same personality as that of Dance A (the connection between Dances A and B has already been pointed out) I would point out not only the appearance of A as counterpoint then midsection to C in its own tempo but also the pastoral color of the instrumentation of both and the characteristic Ländler style common to both. If, as I would want to suggest in a more developed analysis, we are directed to put the various characteristics of this agency together with other contradictory emotional and behavioral attitudes or susceptibilities in the agency's makeup, as represented in Dances A and B and their transitions, the agency thus formed is a psychologically highly complex and conflicted one—even before we proceed to the rest of the movement (we have reached m. 260 of 620).

Table 6.1 summarizes in schematic form the rest of the movement. I shall not go through it in detail here (although it repays as well as the first part of the movement detailed attention with the kind of approach taken in the preceding). After a transition similar to the previous one, Dance C tries once more to establish itself but fails even more drastically than before, drifting to an inconclusive, noncadential complete stop (m. 367, *morendo*). Dance A then intervenes, but it too fails to find a proper cadence, or even a consequent phrase in the same key. It is gradually infected by elements of Dance B, which finally takes over completely, this time by a process of gradual subversion or infiltration. A final feint at the material of Dance C (m. 515—cf. m. 332) does not succeed in even slightly retarding the headlong rush of Dance B's tempo and survives for only six measures. Dance A returns in a thoroughly etiolated version, fragmented and full of motivic material from Dance B. As always unable to find a proper end, it disintegrates and evaporates, its coarse bluster worn away to nothing.

Let me now summarize the complex series of actions and agencies (action-forces) toward which we have been quite firmly directed by purely musical attributes and successions. The simple predicate "clumsy in a rustic way" was indicated by the opening musical "slice." (Or if one prefers, the proposition "X is clumsy in a rustic way" was indicated.) Attributes of rough-hewnness, coarseness, ponderousness began to accrue to it as the section proceeded. The implications of "sturdy" in these was qualified by an implication of insecurity and lack of substance indicated by the combination of, on the one hand, swagger—"cheeky" horn calls, and the loud beginnings and interruptions—with, on the other, the inability to finish a thought or action properly and to design well-formed, as opposed to crude and interruptive, successions. Something of emotional impulsiveness and lack of self-control and of self-discipline are suggested by these behavioral styles as well.

What I call a new action-force sweeps away this blustery but inconsistent first one. The foreground change is, in my reading, the intrusion of the urban (the waltz) and the sophisticated (the harmonic language and the wide range of the melodies). But attributes of the previous agency remain in the background (its melodic motive, $\hat{3}$–$\hat{3}$–$\hat{2}$–$\hat{1}$, and its somewhat ungainly phrase structures), suggesting that we have here an internal interaction of forces within the protagonist's psyche—the first set of attributes (the first agency) swept away, or at least suppressed, by the forces represented by the new agency. Tempos and their characteristic styles are especially important carriers of meaning in this movement, thus the incorporation of the original material of Dance A into Dance B without tempo reversion to Dance A and the almost immediate subsequent invasion of the material of Dance A by that of Dance B points strongly to the lack of resistance that the first agency can or does put up to the second.

The effortful transition by which the runaway triumph of Dance B (the waltz) is stopped (just as it has become *flott*), plus the style and the melodic material of the new Dance C introduces another element into this portrait: a strength and a will to resist that we might not have suspected, plus a kind of sweet melancholy that can be called nostalgia comes into the makeup of our protagonist. Again, that these are part of the same agency is suggested by the musical motivic connections that I pointed out earlier.

But this agency or set of attributes, too, is eroded by the same inability to sustain effort, to maintain attention and complete a thought. That our protagonist allows this set of attributes, this style of behavior for which he had striven with some real effort of will, to be easily swept away, as if in a moment of dreaminess and lapsed attention, by the glittering urban world of Dance B, indicates his susceptibility to this force, this world, which, for the first time at this point, incorporates the full harmonic cycle of disorientation/alienation from the first movement.

One could follow further the story and the evolution of this protagonist (which one might think of as a class rather than as an individual). It is in my view one of the more powerful embodiments of one of the classic archetypal plots of the time, the corruption of the individual by modern urban society—again I cite Charpentier's *Louise*. There is a struggle in Mahler's movement, but it is not at all a heroic struggle. Foregrounded are issues of weakness of will, of lapses of attention, of addiction to external glitter, entertainment, and the racy life, of banalization and brutalization of the initial clumsy, rustic image, and of the realization only intermittently and too late of the need to resist. This archetypal plot could perhaps be done as a heroic struggle, but this particular instance ends, as some readers may remember, like that of another modernist antihero, not with a bang but with a whimper—with evaporation rather than cadence, with as close to nonclosure as this style will permit.

7

Shostakovich's Tenth Symphony and the Musical Expression of Cognitively Complex Emotions

GREGORY KARL and JENEFER ROBINSON

In his influential book *Vom Musikalisch-Schönen,* Eduard Hanslick argued that it is impossible to represent the emotions in music because music cannot represent the "conceptions" or cognitive content that help to define the emotions. "The feeling of hope cannot be separated from the representation of a future happy state which we compare with the present; . . . Love cannot be thought without the representation of a beloved person, without desire and striving after felicity, glorification and possession of a particular object."[1] Yet music cannot represent these ideas or objects; all it can do is represent the "dynamic" aspects of emotional life.

Hanslick's words have echoed down the years, influencing both philosophers of music and music theorists and critics. Among philosophers, Susanne Langer repeats almost verbatim Hanslick's strictures on emotional expression in music, claiming that music can represent only the dynamic aspects of emotional life, its patterns of motion and rest, tension and relaxation. On her view, music "reveals the rationale of feelings, the rhythm and pattern of their rise and decline and intertwining, to our minds."[2] Unlike Langer, Peter Kivy believes that music *can* express par-

[1] Eduard Hanslick, *On the Musically Beautiful,* trans. Geoffrey Payzant (Indianapolis: Hackett, 1986), p. 9.
[2] Susanne Langer, *Philosophy in a New Key,* 3d ed. (Cambridge, Mass.: Harvard University Press, 1957), p. 238.

ticular emotions. In *The Corded Shell* he argues that some musical phrases mimic human gestures that are expressive of a particular state of human feeling, and other musical features are expressive of particular feelings by virtue of some conventional association. Music can sound like a person loudly lamenting or joyfully jumping; or it can sound sad just because music in a low register and a minor key conventionally signifies sadness.[3] Significantly, however, virtually all the musical examples of expressive music that Kivy cites are confined to a very limited set of feelings, mostly joy, sadness, and restlessness. The vast majority are also accompanied by words, which of course help to establish expressiveness. In his *Music Alone*, which deals with "pure" or "absolute" music, Kivy continues to maintain that music can express particular emotions, but he echoes Hanslick in arguing that the emotions music can express are only those that need not be directed toward any kind of object. Music can be sad or joyful or restless without being sad, joyful, or restless *about* anything in particular.[4] This requirement would seem to rule out the possibility that music can express cognitively complex emotions. Like Hanslick, Kivy seems to think that it simply can't be done.

Tendencies in twentieth-century music and music theory have helped to establish the notion that music cannot express complex human emotions. In the second quarter of the century, for example, Igor Stravinsky was at the forefront of a reaction against romantic music and musical aesthetics, claiming that "music is, by its very nature, essentially powerless to express anything at all,"[5] while cultivating a more reticent neoclassical style. Somewhat later the serialists and advocates of aleatoric music began to experiment with mathematical procedures that increased the temptation to think of music in the medieval way, as belonging with arithmetic, geometry, and astronomy in the quadrivium. More recently, the dominant theoretical systems, including Schenkerian theory and set theory, have tended to concentrate on what they take to be music's internal relationships, emphasizing rigidly recursive structural hierarchies and quasi-mathematical manipulations and terminology, respectively.

[3] Peter Kivy, *The Corded Shell* (Princeton: Princeton University Press, 1980). The view is summarized on p. 83.

[4] Peter Kivy, *Music Alone* (Ithaca: Cornell University Press, 1990), esp. pp. 174–77. Kivy cites Daniel Putman, "Why Instrumental Music Has No Shame," *British Journal of Aesthetics* 27 (1987). However, the basic idea derives from Hanslick. According to Kivy, the only exception to the doctrine that emotions expressible by music are those that require no objects are feeling states such as prideful pomposity, which have a characteristic expressive behavioral pattern or "contour." See *Music Alone*, pp. 178–79.

[5] Igor Stravinsky, *Igor Stravinsky: An Autobiography* (London: Calder and Boyars, 1975), p. 51. Although Stravinsky's position ultimately proved more flexible than this statement suggests, his pronouncement both reflected and helped to shape contemporary opinion on musical expression.

In the last decade, however, a number of highly respected musical scholars, including Joseph Kerman, Edward T. Cone, Leo Treitler, and Anthony Newcomb,[6] have called attention to the limited scope of recent musical analysis and have advocated a broader focus that includes attention to issues of musical expression and criticism. At the same time, recent philosophical work on musical expression has begun to question Hanslick's assumptions and to explore the possibility that music can perhaps express more than just varieties of sadness and joy.

I

Among music theorists Edward T. Cone has proposed a model of musical expression that construes music "as emanating from personas or characters who subsist only by virtue of the musical composition."[7] He suggests that we think of pure instrumental music as a kind of expressive utterance. Whereas language has both a semantic and a gestural function—it both communicates a content and conveys an attitude—music, by contrast, has only a gestural function: it cannot communicate a specific content, but it can function as a system of expressive gestures. According to Cone, "these gestures are symbolized by musical motifs and progressions, and they are given structure by musical rhythm and meter, under the control of musical tempo. The vocal utterance of song emphasizes, even exaggerates, the gestural potentialities of its words. Instrumental utterance, lacking intrinsic verbal content, goes so far as to constitute what might be called a medium of pure symbolic gesture."[8] The musical gestures are to be heard as the gestures of the composer's musical persona, the "implied author" of the musical piece.[9] What emotion is actually being expressed by the musical gestures is a function of the "context" in which they are heard—for example, the context provided by an accompanying

---

[6] See Joseph Kerman, *Contemplating Music* (Cambridge, Mass.: Harvard University Press, 1985); Edward T. Cone, *The Composer's Voice* (Berkeley and Los Angeles: University of California Press, 1974), *Music: A View from Delft*, ed. Robert P. Morgan (Chicago: University of Chicago Press, 1984), and "Schubert's Promissory Note: An Exercise in Musical Hermeneutics," *19th-Century Music* 5 (1982): 233–41; Leo Treitler, *Music and the Historical Imagination* (Cambridge, Mass.: Harvard University Press, 1988); and Anthony Newcomb, "Sound and Feeling," *Critical Inquiry* 10 (1984): 623–41, and "Once More 'Between Absolute and Program Music': Schumann's Second Symphony," *19th-Century Music* 7 (1984): 233–50.

[7] Cone, *The Composer's Voice*, p. 160.

[8] Ibid., p. 164.

[9] Cf. Wayne Booth, *The Rhetoric of Fiction* (Chicago: University of Chicago Press, 1961), for the idea of an "implied author." For the idea that style should be viewed as the expression of character or personality in an implied author, see Jenefer Robinson, "Style and Personality in the Literary Work," *Philosophical Review* 94 (1985): 227–47.

verbal text. Where there is no accompanying verbal text, as in pure instrumental music, then "each listener supplies his own context, out of the store of his own experience."[10] The different contexts brought to the music by different listeners are "linked by their common isomorphism with the musical structure."[11]

This is a promising beginning to a theory of musical expression, but it does not explain how music can be heard as the expression of a musical persona. Nor does it explain how pure instrumental music can express particular cognitively complex human emotions. The requirement of "structural isomorphism" between the musical gestures and some emotional state or kind of human situation may be necessary for the expression of particular emotions, but it hardly seems to be sufficient. When Cone employs his own theory in an interpretation of the Moment Musical no. 6, he talks of its "expressive potential" in terms of the "kinds of human situations" that "present themselves as congruous with its structure," and then suggests that the work "dramatizes the injection of a strange unsettling element into an otherwise peaceful situation."[12] Broadening the context he brings to the work, he suggests that the music can be heard as "a model of the effect of vice on a sensitive personality,"[13] and furthermore, if we think of the piece as an expression of Schubert's own emotional life, then we can relate it to Schubert's realization that he has syphilis and the "sense of desolation" that this realization engenders.[14] On this interpretation Schubert's piece does indeed express a particular cognitively complex emotional state (desolation about the fact that one has just learned one has syphilis) that is attributed to the composer or to his persona in the music. However, the interpretation rests heavily on the context that one particular listener has brought to the music. We need to find more adequate grounds for hearing musical gestures as the expression of particular emotional states in some musical persona.

One important contribution by Cone, which has been taken up and developed by Anthony Newcomb, is the idea that musical expressiveness depends on the development of a whole piece of music as it unfolds in time. In order to figure out the expressive meaning of a piece, we have to experience the music as an extended structure, and not concentrate just

[10] Cone, *The Composer's Voice*, p. 169.
[11] Ibid., p. 171.
[12] Edward T. Cone, "Schubert's Promissory Note," p. 239.
[13] Ibid., p. 240.
[14] Ibid., p. 241. Anthony Newcomb points out that Cone does not suggest that this is the only correct interpretation of the work, merely one possible one. See Newcomb, "Sound and Feeling," p. 628.

on isolated musical gestures in the way that Kivy, for example, does:[15] "Expressive interpretation must . . . concern itself with the way the piece presents itself to the listener as successiveness, as a temporal unfolding, as a large-scale process."[16] On Newcomb's view, musical expression is a function of the overall formal structure of a piece: "Formal processes themselves create expressive meaning."[17] Conversely, he also argues that expressive interpretation brings "the perceived structural patterns of a piece into relation with other patterns of the listener's experience" and may thereby "reveal new structural patterns in the music as well."[18] In other words, formal structure may in turn be a function of expressive structure. Thus in "Once More 'Between Absolute and Program Music': Schumann's Second Symphony," Newcomb explains puzzling features of the formal structure of Schumann's symphony by pointing out their expressive motivation. On Newcomb's view, then, expressive structure not only mirrors formal structure but provides the *motivation* for the formal structure: it shows *why* the piece develops formally in the way that it does. It may be the case, therefore, that formal and expressive structure are sometimes mutually dependent, expressive meaning both determining and determined by formal structure.

To some extent Newcomb echoes Langer: both believe that understanding musical expression involves experiencing the music as it unfolds in time. But Newcomb differs from Langer in his view that what an extended piece of music expresses can be a sequence of particular emotional states and not just the ebb and flow of unspecified inner feelings.[19]

---

[15] In a discussion of Kivy's views, Newcomb criticizes Kivy not only for concentrating on "such trivial distinctions as 'good humor' versus 'the darker emotions'" ("Sound and Feeling," p. 620) but also for "his almost exclusive reliance on detail, usually melodic detail" rather than overall musical structure (ibid., p. 626). In his reply to Newcomb in *Sound Sentiment* (Philadelphia: Temple University Press, 1989), chap. 14, Kivy argues that Newcomb's emphasis on the congruity between "expressive meaning" and large-scale musical structure is "entirely consistent with [his] contention [in *The Corded Shell*] that musical expressiveness results from the resemblance of musical structure to expressive behavior" (*Sound Sentiment*, p. 194). We think that Kivy is claiming too much for his theory of musical expressiveness as explained in *The Corded Shell*, for the kind of expressiveness that is functionally dependent on large-scale musical structure in the way suggested by Newcomb arises not just through the structure of a particular passage in a work but through the relationships between *different* passages in different parts of the work. Although Kivy suggests that one can understand large-scale structure by analogy to human expressive behavior, he gives no indication of how this is to be accomplished.

[16] Newcomb, "Sound and Feeling," p. 627.

[17] Newcomb, "Those Images That Yet Fresh Images Beget," *Journal of Musicology* 2 (1983): 232.

[18] Newcomb, "Sound and Feeling," p. 635.

[19] Newcomb adopts Nelson Goodman's view of expression as metaphorical exemplification of a quality, or, as Goodman prefers to say, of a "label," such as the label "sad," which applies to a quality. A musical passage that expresses sadness is one that is

Newcomb agrees with Cone that expression "results from intrinsic properties of an artwork but also from the metaphorical resonances these properties may have for the perceiver."[20] Like Cone, however, he has not directly broached the question of whether cognitively complex emotional states can be expressed by pure instrumental music.[21]

II

While musicians theorizing on expression have tended to be interested in how a full appreciation of a *particular musical piece* might require understanding what it expresses,[22] philosophers of music have been interested primarily in the more general and abstract question of what musical expression is, that is, what we mean when we say that a piece of music expresses something or other. Recently two interesting answers to this question have been proposed by Kendall Walton and Jerrold Levinson, which we think represent an important advance over the theories of Kivy and Langer.

In his book *Mimesis as Make-Believe*,[23] Walton proposes a theory of the representational arts in terms of the concepts of imagination and make-believe: a representation is, on his view, something whose function it is to be a prop in a game of make-believe. A representational picture, for example, is a prop in a visual game of make-believe. The representational content of a picture is given by what the picture prescribes that we imagine seeing when we look at it: in looking at a picture of a water mill

---

metaphorically sad and that "refers to" this quality of sadness, by which Goodman seems to mean that sadness is one of its aesthetically striking or noticeable qualities. See *Languages of Art* (Indianapolis: Bobbs-Merrill, 1968), chap. 2. Goodman does not discuss cognitively complex emotions in his account but restricts his attention to relatively simple expressive qualities such as "sad."

[20] Newcomb, "Sound and Feeling," p. 625.

[21] In an analysis of the dialogue between Mime and the Wanderer in act 1, scene 2, of Wagner's *Siegfried* he claims that the music accelerates in order to express "Mime's mounting pleasure, confidence, and finally joy at his success in answering the Wanderer's questions," but then "at the third question, the climax of the tempo process becomes a *sehr schnell* not of joy but of panic" (see Newcomb, "Those Images That Yet Fresh Images Beget," p. 244). Here Newcomb is indeed attributing to the music the expression of relatively complex emotional states, but his interpretation relies heavily on the words accompanying the music.

[22] For example, Newcomb on Schumann's Second Symphony; and Gregory Karl on Beethoven's *Appassionata* Sonata, Franck's Sonata for Violin and Piano, Rachmaninoff's Second Symphony, and Prokofiev's Sonata no. 1 for Violin and Piano, in his Ph.D. dissertation, "Music as Plot: A Study in Cyclic Forms" (University of Cincinnati, 1993).

[23] Kendall Walton, *Mimesis as Make-Believe* (Cambridge, Mass.: Harvard University Press, 1990).

we should imagine of our looking at the picture that it is a looking at a water mill. Walton has recently extended his make-believe theory to cover some kinds of musical expression. He argues that one important kind of musical expression consists in our *imagining* of our "actual introspective awareness of auditory sensations" as we listen to the music that "it is an experience of being aware of our own states of mind."[24] His idea is that in listening to expressive music, we hear it as an imaginary experience of our own emotional or other psychological states. For example, we imagine being introspectively aware of "an impression of or a feeling about" some instance of "returning or struggling or power,"[25] although it is usually quite indeterminate whether the specific instance of returning or struggle that one imagines is one's own or someone else's. The music simply induces the listener to imagine the experience of responding to a situation of a certain general kind.

No doubt we do sometimes imagine ourselves experiencing feelings that the music seems to be expressing. But we do not believe that we must always imagine ourselves feeling the emotions expressed. Sometimes we may simply imaginatively understand and sympathize with the feelings of some musical persona—either the composer's persona or that of some "character" in the music—but without having to imagine feeling these very feelings ourselves. In Cone's terminology we do not necessarily *identify* introspectively with the persona in the music; we may merely recognize or sympathize imaginatively with this persona. It may be that Walton does not want to distinguish between these two possibilities. He himself does not discuss the possibility of characters or personas in the music, nor does he seem to want to think of music as an expression of feeling in an authorial persona. We believe, though, that musical expression is often most usefully thought of as the expression of emotions or other psychological states in musical personas, as Cone suggests.

In an article called "Hope in *The Hebrides*" Jerrold Levinson develops a view much like that of Cone,[26] according to which we hear a piece or passage of music as an expression of some emotion or other psychological state in an imaginary musical persona. Informed listeners—those who are familiar in general with the style of the piece—will readily hear the passage as a special kind of behavioral manifestation of emotion in some imaginatively identified but indeterminate individual. Just as dancing, singing, gesturing, and posturing are all ways in which we can express

---

[24] Kendall Walton, "What Is Abstract about the Art of Music?" *Journal of Aesthetics and Art Criticism* 46 (1988): 359.

[25] Ibid., p. 360.

[26] Levinson does not refer to Cone's views and seems to have developed his own theory independently.

our feelings (and other psychological states), so music can be heard as "an alternate, audible ... mode of behaviorally manifesting psychological states" that is "imagined or felt as akin to" singing, dancing, and the like, but "not as equivalent to any of them."[27] *Why* we hear music in this way will be the result of analogies between the music and human expressive behaviors, conventional associations, and so on. Significantly, Levinson, like Cone and Newcomb, acknowledges the importance of considering more than just isolated phrases when one is trying to determine what a musical piece expresses, but he goes farther than any of the theorists we have so far discussed in that he explicitly claims that music can express cognitively complex emotions.

Levinson takes on Hanslick directly, arguing that music can express specific emotions, such as hope, which have a complex cognitive content. On his view, music accomplishes this without actually having to represent cognitive content, however, and without necessarily embodying all the distinctive noncognitive features of the emotion. All that matters is that the music regularly calls that emotion to mind in musically educated and experienced listeners. Levinson believes that very often music expresses a complex emotion merely by signifying or bringing to mind the noncognitive elements in an emotion, such as "qualitative feels, desires, and impulses, varieties of internal sensation, degrees of pleasure and pain, patterns of nervous tension and release, patterns of behavior (gestural, vocal, postural, kinetic)."[28] Occasionally music also manages at least to suggest the presence of cognitive content: Levinson claims that music is capable of conveying a general sense of "a psychological state's being intentional"[29] and may even "regularly call to mind in culturally backgrounded listeners certain thoughts, even ones of some complexity."[30]

We suspect that Levinson is too optimistic about the possibility of specifying the emotional expressiveness of music by reference to noncognitive features of the emotion in question.[31] Current evidence suggests that there are few reliable criteria for distinguishing emotions if one ignores their cognitive components; and in the few instances where empirical psychologists have found certain noncognitive distinguishing marks of particular emotions, they are not the sort of marks that are susceptible to

---

[27] Jerrold Levinson, "Hope in *The Hebrides*," in *Music, Art, and Metaphysics* (Ithaca: Cornell University Press, 1990), p. 338.
[28] Ibid., p. 344.
[29] Ibid., p. 347.
[30] Ibid., p. 346.
[31] We develop this and other criticisms of Levinson's position in "Levinson on Hope in *The Hebrides*," *Journal of Aesthetics and Art Criticism* 53, no. 2 (Spring 1995): 195–99.

musical expression.[32] In order to make a convincing case for his claim that music can express emotions by embodying their "qualitative feels," "varieties of internal sensation," or "patterns of nervous tension and release," Levinson must first demonstrate how these categories of noncognitive experience can individuate particular emotions, and second, explain more clearly how qualitative feels and the like can be embodied in and recovered from musical works.

On the other hand, we believe that Levinson is too pessimistic about the possibility of specifying the emotions expressed by music by means of their cognitive content. In his discussion of hope in the *Hebrides* Overture, Levinson refers to the way in which the melody takes leaps of a fourth and fifth, which he claims we hear as "reaching for something—for something higher," and which help to account for "a quality of aspiration."[33] He also suggests that the position of his focal passage "as general counterpoise to the worrisome tenor of the overture's first section" perhaps suggests "some of the pure conceptual content of hope—its favorable assessment of future in relation to present."[34] We think that Levinson should have developed further this idea that "our sense of a passage's expressiveness where it occurs . . . will be *contextually determined*," and that "in some complex way we refer a given passage's expressiveness to those of other ones, often under the postulate of a *shared persona*."[35] In the rest of this essay we will argue that if indeed we take into account the structure of an entire piece, it will sometimes be possible to detect the expression of cognitively complex emotions, and to detect them by identifying some significant part of their cognitive content. We will urge that the key to understanding how music can express such emotions is to consider not just the details of melody or mode but the overall musical context in which the expressive passage occurs.

Like Cone and Levinson, we think that musical expression can at least sometimes be analyzed as a kind of gestural expression of emotional or other psychological states in a musical persona, whether it be the composer's or that of some indeterminate character or characters in the music. We would go farther than Levinson, however, and argue that the expressive structure of some pieces of music can be interpreted as an unfolding of the psychological experience of the musical persona over time. As the

---

[32] The most reliable marks discovered have been patterns of autonomic nervous system activity and subtle changes in facial expression. See Paul Ekman, "Expression and the Nature of Emotion," in *Approaches to Emotion*, ed. Klaus Scherer and Paul Ekman (Hillsdale, N.J.: Lawrence Erlbaum Associates, 1984), pp. 319–43.

[33] Levinson, *Music, Art, and Metaphysics*, pp. 367–68.

[34] Ibid., p. 373.

[35] Ibid., p. 371.

listener experiences such a piece, she imagines of the musical gestures she hears that they are the expression of a series of psychological states in the musical persona, and may sometimes—as Walton suggests—imaginatively experience these states as her own. Furthermore, the formal coherence of the music often consists precisely in its embodying a coherent unfolding of psychological states in a musical persona.

We cannot hope to defend this thesis in detail here. Instead we will confine our attention to a particular piece of music which we think exemplifies our thesis. As we shall argue, Shostakovich's Tenth Symphony can be plausibly interpreted as a drama of feelings and impressions ascribed to the work's persona. We shall claim that within the work's expressive structure there is a passage expressive of the cognitively complex emotion of hope or hopefulness, and that if we consider the structure of the work as a whole we can attribute to the musical persona the complex cognitive states characteristic of hope.

III

What is the cognitive content of hope? In part, hope is an epistemic state: if I hope for something to occur, then necessarily I am uncertain whether it will occur. I cannot, for example, hope that I will meet Napoleon Bonaparte one day if I am absolutely certain that this is impossible.[36] By the same token, it is possible to hope for anything to occur, however wildly improbable, provided one is not certain that it cannot occur. I can hope that Napoleon has been reincarnated in my goldfish, given the relevant beliefs.[37] How *rational* a hope is depends partly on the degree of probability of the hoped-for event: hoping for a Napoleonic goldfish is not a very rational hope. Hoping that some event will occur also entails having a favorable conception of that event: I think of its occurrence as more pleasant than its nonoccurrence. Sometimes this involves merely hoping for the lesser of two evils. Hoping that something

---

[36] I can also hope for past and present events if I am uncertain of their outcome. Thus while reading a work of history, I can hope that Napoleon won the Battle of Waterloo, just as long as I don't know that he lost.

[37] J. P. Day claims that one of the truth conditions of "A hopes in some degree that P" is "A thinks that P is in some degree probable." This seems to us to be wrong, for I can quite well hope for things I believe to be utterly improbable. See J. P. Day, "Hope," *American Philosophical Quarterly* 6 (1969): 89–102. Ronald de Sousa takes a more extreme position than we do; he cites "irrational fear" and "theological hope" as examples of emotions that are not necessarily eradicated even when the agent knows that the object of the emotion does not exist. Ronald de Sousa, *The Rationality of Emotion* (Cambridge, Mass.: MIT Press, 1987), p. 115.

will occur entails *wishing* that it occur, and if what I hope for is the sort
of thing that I can help to bring about, then (other things being equal), I
will try to bring it about.[38] If I truly hope to win the race then I will do
what I can to ensure that I have a good chance of winning. Of course, I
may entertain hopes about which I can only be passive: if I hope that it
will rain tomorrow, there is not much I can do about it. If in addition I
know the odds are very high that what I hope for will not occur, then it
would seem that sometimes hoping is not very different from mere
wishing or wishful thinking.[39] One way in which hoping differs from mere
wishing, however, is that hope seems to involve the pleasurable focus of
attention on the hoped-for possibility.[40] This focus of attention is pleasant
in itself: filled with the pleasant vision of your being alive, my hope helps
to buoy me up even if I believe you to be dead. At the same time, where
what is hoped for is possible of achievement, the pleasurable conception
we have of the hoped-for event helps to motivate action to bring that
event about: we anticipate an increase in pleasure when the possibility
is actualized.[41] In general, then, if a person P hopes for some state
(event, etc.) S, then normally (1) P wishes for S; (2) P conceives of the
occurrence of S as a more pleasant outcome than its nonoccurrence; (3) P
is uncertain whether S will occur; (4) if P is able to, P will try to bring it
about that S; and (5) P's focus of attention on or contemplation of S is a
source of pleasure—or relief—to P. However, there can be great variation
in kinds of hope, particularly in how much one wishes for the desired
state, how pleasant one conceives it as being, how probable the hoped-for
event is thought to be, how much effort one puts out to try to bring it
about, and, finally, how much pleasure its contemplation currently
affords.

If we think of the hope expressed by a piece of music as belonging to
some persona or character in the music, then different *types* of hope will
be expressed by different types of persona in different musical contexts.
Levinson maintains that music can express a *type* of hope but never a par-

[38] I might have inconsistent wishes and hence inconsistent hopes. In such cases, trying to
bring about one wish may necessarily involve failing to bring about another.

[39] See Robert M. Gordon, *The Structure of Emotions* (Cambridge: Cambridge University
Press, 1987), p. 85.

[40] Day argues that hope is not really an emotion at all, but he does not seem to recognize
that hope, the epistemic state, becomes hope, the emotional state, when in addition to the
epistemic requirements we add that the agent derives pleasure from the contemplation of
the hoped-for state. Sometimes we will call the emotional state "hopefulness" rather than
"hope" to mark the fact that not all hope is emotional.

[41] "Aquinas observes . . . that Hope is an aid to action in two ways. First, because the
subject's awareness of the difficulty makes him concentrate his efforts on surmounting it;
and secondly, because Hope causes Delight, which makes for more effective operation"
(Day, "Hope," p. 94).

ticular *token* of hope. This is because a particular token or instance of hope always belongs to some particular person, is directed toward some particular object, and involves a particular assessment of that object; but on Levinson's view, music is incapable of picking out particular individuals, objects, or assessments. We agree that the musical persona cannot be characterized in as much detail as, say, a literary character; nor can the things such a person desires or hopes for be specified very clearly. It is unlikely that any music can express Anna Karenina's hope that she will see little Seryozha again, or her estimation of the probability of so doing. However, although music cannot express such specific instances of hope, it can give some general idea of the musical persona and what his or her hope revolves around and how likely it is to be realized. When hope is expressed by a piece of music, it is never some generic hope in the abstract but always a fairly specific *type* of hope. It is a fervent, childlike hope for something thought to be impossible, an exuberant, confident hope for something the agent fully intends to bring about, or a quiet, unassuming hope that the worst is now behind.

IV

The musical passage that on our view is an expression of hope is a section from the third movement of Shostakovich's Tenth Symphony. Although this is a largely pessimistic work, we argue that in our focal passage the musical persona looks forward to a future that he[42] conceives of as more pleasant than the prevailing grim and threatening situation. He is uncertain whether this more pleasant future will occur but nevertheless strives to achieve it, despite being surrounded by menaces from the past. Moreover, his contemplation of the anticipated future state provides a source of relief from these menaces. In short, the musical persona, though surrounded by gloom, feels, if only briefly, hopeful for the future. Our interpretation is no doubt controversial. Certainly we do not expect that a listener who encounters this piece for the first time will immediately spot the expression of hope in our focal passage. Our claim is, however, that the expression of hope can be detected if it is heard in the context of the symphony as a whole, which

[42] We say "he" even though the character in the music is not specifically gendered. In this music, at least, for various reasons, it is plausible to think of the musical persona as a musical persona of Shostakovich himself. The most obvious reason is that this symphony introduces a motive that Shostakovich used as a signature. It consists of D–E♭–C–B, corresponding to the German transliteration of his initials (D. Sch.). In German E♭ is represented by the syllable *es*, and H is used for B♮.

in turn needs to be heard in its historical context as an example of a particular genre.

Certain of the symphony's grossest formal features identify it with a genre of dramatic symphonic composition cultivated in the nineteenth and twentieth centuries that has its roots in the tradition of the Viennese *Grosse Sinfonie*.[43] The relevant features are its stormy first movement in the minor mode and overall progression to an exuberant finale in the major mode, with important themes developed or quoted from one movement to another. Works realizing this pattern have been commonly interpreted in quasi-narrative terms in relation to what Newcomb has called a plot archetype. Newcomb explains: "The conception of music as composed novel, as a psychologically true course of ideas, was and is an important avenue to the understanding of much nineteenth-century music: Beethoven's Fifth was so understood by at least some listeners from the outset. Thus we may find at the basis of some symphonies an evolving pattern of mental states, much as the Russian formalists and the structuralists find one of several plot archetypes as the basis of novels and tales."[44]

The plot archetype to which Shostakovich's Tenth Symphony conforms is conventionally interpreted as a progression from dark to light or struggle to victory (adversity to salvation, illness to health, etc.). In works following this pattern, the opening themes of the first movement and finale carry particular structural and expressive weight because these are the themes that most strongly define the diametrically opposed states or conditions that begin and end the overall psychological-dramatic evolution, thus justifying the conventional characterizations of dark and light respectively.

In making our case for the musical expression of hope, we first give a brief formal analysis of our focal passage, including its immediate context in the central section of the third movement and its motivic relationships with other parts of the symphony. Then we give an interpretation of the role of our focal passage within the expressive structure of the work. Finally, we argue that within this expressive structure our focal passage is indeed an expression of hope, and that it signifies hope chiefly by attributing to the musical persona the cognitive states that define this emotion.[45]

---

[43] Works in this genre include Beethoven's Fifth and Ninth, Schumann's Second and Fourth, Brahms's First, Franck's Symphony in D minor, Bruckner's Eighth, Tchaikovsky's Fourth and Fifth, Mahler's Fifth, and Rachmaninoff's Second and Third.

[44] Anthony Newcomb, "Once More 'Between Absolute and Program Music,'" p. 234.

[45] The interpretation of the symphony that follows is Gregory Karl's. For an elaboration of this interpretation, see his "Music as Plot: A Study in Cyclic Forms."

V

The central section of the third movement begins at rehearsal 114 with a horn call (marked H in example 7.1) which is to sound six more times throughout the section, and always at the same pitches. Its wholly diatonic character and motion by relatively large, consonant intervals (perfect fourths and fifths) are in sharp contrast to the pervasive chromaticism and predominantly stepwise motion of all the other themes of the symphony to this point. The first call, *forte*, is answered immediately by another, *piano*, the call and answer followed at rehearsal 115 by the only direct quotation in later movements of the symphony's opening theme. This time the theme is accompanied, however, rather than sounding in bare octaves as it did in the beginning of the first movement. At rehearsal 116 the horn call sounds again, now followed by a more subtle allusion to material of the first movement. Our focal passage, F, then follows at rehearsal 117. Here the fourth sounding of the horn call is heard against an allusion to the symphony's first gesture; the motive marked X in the first violins is the initial motive of the symphony's opening theme. The passage is harshly dissonant because the strings sound a B♭-minor triad (suggesting the key of B♭ minor) while the horn call sounds the unrelated pitches E and A, drawn from the foreign key of D major, which conflict sharply with the chord tones B♭ and F. Because of the way the music continues, the B♭-minor triad in the strings must ultimately be understood as a foreign element in a tonal sphere controlled by the pitch D, which proves to be the tonal center of the passage.[46] The final A of the horn call is sustained as a dissonance against the chords in the strings, becoming a consonant tone only when the progression resolves to D major at the beginning of the passage labeled T1.[47]

T1 begins on a sustained D-major triad at the most relaxed tempo to this point in the work. As shown in example 7.2, the melody in the flute and piccolo is derived from H. The portion labeled T1a contains a diminution of H (a version in shorter rhythmic values); T1b then inverts this diminution. The ascending fifth and semitone of T1b (marked Y in example 7.2) is the basis for a further series of transformations, T2 through T4, which are heard in the slow introduction to the finale. The last link in this chain of transformations, which we call the H complex, is the first allegro theme of the finale, labeled IV/1. Beginning at rehearsal 118, the horn call sounds three more times against allusions to the first movement

---

[46] In fact, the B♭-minor triad may be understood as the ♭VI chord in a ♭VI–iv⁷ progression in D minor.

[47] For the iv⁷ chord borrowed from D minor resolves to a D-major triad.

Example 7.1. Shostakovich, Symphony no. 10, third movement, rehearsal 114ff.

Example 7.2. H and its derivatives (the H complex)

played in hushed pizzicato; the retransition to the movement's opening theme follows soon after.

VI

So far, our account of our focal passage, F, has been from a purely formal point of view. We will now examine the same passage, focusing on its role within the expressive structure of the symphony as a whole. According to the theory of expression we have sketched, this means we must examine it as part of the coherent unfolding of the experience of the work's persona. Before we begin, however, it is important to make a few explanatory remarks.

Interpretations of expressive structure of the kind we are undertaking are characteristically the result of a complex interplay among a variety of different sorts of observations, including the recognition of formal relationships (such as the motivic connections illustrated in example 7.2), expressive contours and conventions (as discussed by Kivy), and plot archetypes (as described by Newcomb); observations of the relation between the forms of individual works and the formal conventions of traditional formal types and genres; and possibly even background information about the work's immediate historical context.[48] For many listeners, moreover, irrespective of their degree of musical training, an additional source of information often plays a significant role in the understanding of expressive structure. We refer to the listener's experience of the music "as a temporal unfolding, as a large-scale process,"[49] including especially the direct arousal of feeling.[50] Introspection by the listener of his or her emotional (and other) experience as the work unfolds may provide clues to the work's expressive structure, allowing a listener to construct imaginatively the experience of the persona in light of—or even in the image of—his or her own experience. Accordingly, we will include commentary on the role that the direct experience of the listener might play in arriving at an interpretation of the work's expressive structure.

[48] Shostakovich, for example, was required to produce works that embodied (or at least did not obviously subvert) the principles of "socialist realism," and this constraint had a demonstrable influence on his symphonies.

[49] See n. 16.

[50] For a discussion of the way the arousal of feeling in a listener contributes to musical expression, see Jenefer Robinson, "The Expression and Arousal of Emotion in Music," *Journal of Aesthetics and Art Criticism* 52 (1994): 13–22.

The horn call that opens the central section of the third movement marks a turning point in the experience of the persona. The initial clue is that it enters as a sudden and forceful interruption, calling a halt to the ominous and uncertain music that precedes it and with which it so starkly contrasts. Further, its slow unfolding implies patience on the part of the persona; its terseness and elemental power (a result of the horn's timbre and the leaps by perfect intervals) suggest decisiveness; and its holding to the same pitches in each of its seven soundings, despite considerable resistance, indicates steadfastness or resolve. All these expressive qualities suggest a force to be reckoned with, but it is the horn call's role in a much broader context that confirms it as a turning point.[51]

The horn call is answered at rehearsal 115 by a reprise of the symphony's opening theme—the persona's recollection of a grim past. This theme stands within the archetypal pattern of the symphony as the dark condition from which the work's progression toward the light proceeds. Now, I/1 is conventionally "dark" by virtue of its orchestration and its use of the minor mode; it is also unstable and chromatic. More important still, it carries expressive connotations from the antagonistic role it played with respect to the other themes of the first movement.[52] Each subsequent sounding of the horn call is either answered by or accompanied by similar impressions from the past. The horn call itself, on the other hand, looks toward the future. Through the series of transformations quoted in example 7.2, it ultimately generates the principal allegro theme of the finale, the embodiment of the goal state toward which the archetypal plot progresses. The significance of this turning point in the expressive structure is relatively straightforward: the horn call is the persona's resolution (vision? prayer?) for the future, its every statement answered by memories of a grim past representing that which must be

[51] It is likely that some listeners, without consciously registering any of the formal features that mark H as a turning point (discussed in our formal analysis), will nonetheless recognize that it represents an important new current in the expressive structure, merely on the basis of the feelings it arouses—feelings not unlike those it actually expresses. For a listener who recognizes the horn call as a conventional signaling gesture, an additional feeling, that of curiosity, may provide an impetus to interpretation. This is because signals, such as horn calls, when serving their conventional function, are never empty of meaning, and this expectation of meaning carries over into instrumental music. So, by having presented a gesture that sounds like a signal but whose meaning is left unspecified, Shostakovich has created an enigma for the listener to solve. As we shall see below, its solution yields a key to the work's expressive structure.

[52] Briefly, this theme continually intensifies its initial dark impression, sounding in self-sufficient motivic units and growing steadily in power and control, while the themes with which it interacts suffer in the exchange, subjected to fragmentation, forced into uncongenial expressive realms, and finally left in their most tentative forms at the end of the movement.

overcome before the resolution can be carried through. These recollections hold the threat that the travails of the past will recur, and perhaps the persona's fear that the drama will end in the darkness with which it began.[53]

At the beginning of our focal passage, at rehearsal 117, the horn call's look to the future directly confronts images of the past for the first time. As noted in the preceding, the strings at rehearsal 117 sound the first motive of the symphony's opening theme in what starts out to be B♭ minor. But when the horn enters in the second measure of this passage, it immediately begins to wrench the center of gravity away from the B♭ minor of the strings toward D. The strain is painfully audible in the harsh dissonances that result, but the persona maintains his resolve. The resistance in the harmony gives way, and H's final note, A, is welcomed as a consonant chord tone when the following passage (T1) begins. The persona's anguished strain is thus relieved, and his steadfastness in confronting a painful past is rewarded by T1, the first optimistic passage in the entire work.[54]

T1's sustained major-quality harmonies, relaxed tempo (the slowest so far in the work), and languid rate of harmonic change make it an oasis of calm, especially following the dissonant strain of the preceding passage. The euphonious string texture is a placid backdrop for the melody of the flute and piccolo. This line, derived directly from the horn call (see example 7.2), is light because of the pure timbre of the flute, its *pianissimo* dynamic level, and its high register, and buoyant because it employs scale degrees with strong ascending tendencies.[55] Most important, however, T1 contains the kernel of IV/1 and is therefore the movement's clearest anticipation of the lighter affect that is to come in the finale.

[53] Such a fear would seem to be well founded; the principal theme of the third movement, which plays a dominant role in the movement's opening and final sections, is derived from I/1, sounding like an uneasy backward glance at its source. Thus in the third movement, the past still holds sway over the present, and it is precisely this influence that is challenged by the resolve of the horn call.

[54] The listener who has not yet fully appreciated the horn call's role in the transformations of example 7.2 or the meaning of its juxtaposition with quotations from the first movement may simply feel nonspecific sensations of tension and discomfort followed by relief in this passage. But these simple sensations of tension and discomfort, feelings aroused directly by the passage's striking dissonances, may provide a crucial clue to the work's interpretation: they may bring the listener to recognize that the horn call and the allusions to the first movement with which its tones conflict stand in a relation of opposition in the work's expressive structure.

[55] Its opening emphasizes the sharped fourth and fifth scale degrees (G♯ and A in this case). The sharped fourth degree has a strong tendency to resolve upward to the fifth scale degree; whereas the fifth scale degree has a tendency to move upward to the tonic pitch D.

But T1's moment of relative serenity quickly passes. The rest of the central section is an unsettled combination of H and anxious recollections of material from the first movement. The return of the third movement's principal themes, which follows soon thereafter, provides no relief; the first theme is a furtive over-the-shoulder glance back to I/1 (from which it is derived), and the second is disturbingly grotesque. The coda juxtaposes all the movement's contrasting elements, the effect one of unstable equilibrium, like a number of incompatible or mutually exclusive alternatives weighed against one another. The atmosphere is thick with tension, and if this work slavishly followed the traditional plot line of the archetypal pattern, the tension would be swept away at the beginning of the finale. The finale, however, begins with a slow introduction lasting more than five minutes, during which transformations of T1 (see T2–T4 in example 7.2) ever more closely approximate the theme that is to embody the persona's goal state (IV/1, that is). As in the central section of the third movement, though, these anticipations are juxtaposed to allusions to the first movement. Finally, at rehearsal 153, the flute, clarinet, and strings burst forth into the exuberant IV/1 (arrived at by repeated transformations of T1, as shown in example 7.2), and the persona realizes the goal state first envisioned in our focal passage during T1.

The meaning of these events in the experience of the persona is fairly clear: the persona's doubts about the future persist until late in the work. The persona is unsure whether his envisioned future (IV/1 as anticipated by H and T1) will come to pass, or whether, on the other hand, some cataclysm like the climax of the first movement is in store as a final peripety.[56]

In summarizing the role our focal passage plays in the expressive structure of the work, we see that the various elements of the H complex anticipate IV/1, the embodiment of a future happy state, while at the same time being constantly juxtaposed with the dark, menacing material from I/1. While T1 is preceded and followed by passages in which its source

---

[56] Once again, the listener's emotional experience during these events may provide clues to constructing the experience of the persona, even when this experience has different emotional content. For example, a listener schooled in the epic symphonic tradition might expect that the tension of the third movement should be swept away at the beginning of the finale. (A listener with less experience or training may simply experience a nonspecific desire or expectation of change.) Upon finding this expectation frustrated, he or she may then feel tense, impatient, or bewildered. The music as an expression of the persona, on the other hand, may in fact be expressing a profound doubt about the approaching denouement of the psychological drama in which it is involved. The listener's feelings of impatience or frustration, while poorly mirroring the expressive structure of the work, may nonetheless provide the initial clues that something is amiss in the experience of the persona, providing an impetus to interpretation.

idea, the horn call H, is enmired in the disquieting residue of ideas from the first movement, it also embodies the lightest affect of any theme so far encountered, and it foreshadows the exuberant IV/1 theme of the finale. It seems an initially plausible hypothesis, then, to view T1 as embodying a single hopeful glance at the future from a time that is shrouded in uneasy contemplation of the past.[57]

VII

We will now look more closely at how F is an expression of hope. In the interest of clarity we will distinguish three different elements in the cognitive content of this particular instance of hope, and we will try to show how the music expresses each one. Obviously we are engaged in a process of abstraction: all these elements are interwoven with one another, and they also combine with expressive contours that mirror the behavioral and other aspects of hope.

First of all, F embodies a state of hopefulness in which the agent, whom we are assuming is the musical persona, *looks forward to a future state conceived of as more pleasant than the currently prevailing grim state of affairs.* F conveys this part of the cognitive content of hope, because it anticipates the future happy state represented by the lively theme, IV/1—the only remotely cheery theme in the whole work—while being itself surrounded by dark reminiscences of I/1.

Second, the musical persona of F both *wishes for* and *strives to bring about* this future state of affairs that is conceived of as more pleasant than the present. In attributing to the behavior and evolution of our focal material a desire to bring about change, we are making inferences in the same way that we do in ordinary life. If, for example, we see someone pounding on a door, then trying to open it by brute force, and still later attempting to open ground-floor windows, we infer that this person desires to be inside the building. We can further infer something about the intensity of this desire from a study of its behavioral manifestations. Among the criteria we might use are the amount of effort invested in achieving the goal, the persistence with which the goal is pursued, and the amount of suffering endured in the attempt. So, in supporting our interpretation that H and

---

[57] David Fanning has pointed out some of the hopeful expressive qualities of this passage but has failed to recognize it as the source for later transformations illustrated in our example 7.2. As a result, he mistakenly concludes that "what might have become an Ode to Hope peters out into the void." See *The Breath of the Symphonist: Shostakovich's Tenth*, Royal Music Association Monographs no. 4 (London: Royal Music Association, 1988), pp. 54ff.

its later transformations T1–T4 (the H complex) express a desire to achieve the condition embodied in IV/1, we might look for behavioral manifestations of effort, persistence, or suffering in the course of the evolution from H to its goal in IV/1.

The H complex conveys this part of the cognitive content of hope in several ways. First of all, the horn call H itself momentarily brings the uneasy, menacing music to a halt. Its confident perfect intervals sound a call to turn toward the future, and to break with the tragic past that is embodied in the return of I/1 at 115. The horn call has an open, vigorous quality quite different from its uneasy, threatening surroundings, and it also sounds resolute insofar as it always keeps to the same pitches, no matter what is going on in the accompaniment.

Not only does H itself express steadfastness but its development from its first to its fourth occurrence strongly suggests an expenditure of effort in generating T1, the movement's single optimistic passage. After sounding its call and receiving an answer from the distance, H is faced with a reprise of the work's opening theme. H3 is also cut off in this way. But H4 demands its resolution (in D major) in the face of direct resistance from its adversary, and the strong dissonance of the horn's E and A against the B♭-minor chord in the accompaniment makes the strain of H's effort audible. By standing fast, the horn call forces menacing material derived from the principal theme of the first movement to give way to T1, which provides a serene and pleasant interlude in the surrounding gloom and which also anticipates the future lively theme, IV/1.

Moreover, the way in which H transforms into T1, which in turn transforms into T2 and finally, after many transformations, becomes IV/1, exemplifies a process of persistent but tortuous groping toward a desired conclusion. The incremental changes accumulated over the five expectant minutes of introduction in the fourth movement certainly suggest perseverance or single-mindedness of purpose, just as in real life protracted incremental processes often indicate patient resolve on the part of the agents who undertake them. Effort or suffering is suggested by the juxtaposition of T4, the last intermediate transformation, with dark images from the past that are related to those that emerged in response to the first soundings of H. Clearly, even though the persona is groping toward the future—toward IV/1—he is still plagued with unease or doubt connected to events in the past; and the fact that he continues in the face of this resistance suggests a significant degree of motivation.

So far, we have tried to show that Shostakovich's musical persona desires to bring about a more pleasant future even while surrounded by menaces from the past. It is also important that this future state is *uncertain*: there is no assurance in the music that the hoped-for state will come about, and indeed there is so much delay and tentativeness, and the musical persona expends such effort and endures so much suffering, that until IV/1 actually arrives it seems as if a joyful conclusion is unlikely (despite what we expect, given the conventions of the epic symphonic form).[58]

The final element in the cognitive content of hopefulness that we have mentioned is the *pleasure* afforded by the agent's contemplation of an imagined future. Here we can point to the suddenly visionary quality of the music five bars after 117. It is as if the horn call were the persona's resolve to change, and T1 his vision of the future. With the arrival of T1 the mood of the music abruptly changes: it becomes languorous and dreamlike, and it lingers like a hopeful person lingering over the prospect of happiness. It is as if the persona momentarily forgets the dark past and lovingly contemplates a vision of hope.

VIII

Our analysis raises a number of questions that we have not directly addressed. We have, for example, explained musical expression in terms of the emotional states of musical personas, but we have not said much about how these personas are to be identified. Are they represented by musical themes? Motives? Instruments? Complexes of passages? We have not attempted to answer this question. Another question with which we have not directly engaged concerns the principles governing the kind of expressive interpretation that we give. We have sketched how the experience of the listener helps to provide clues to a work's expressiveness, but clearly much more needs to be said.

More fundamentally, perhaps: Is our "expressive" interpretation of Shostakovich's Tenth richer and more insightful than a purely formal interpretation? Why do we need to interpret this work in expressive terms at all? Isn't it enough to examine its "purely musical" structure of motives, harmonic progressions, and so on? Like Newcomb, we consider this dichotomy ill-conceived, because often the formal and expressive threads of a work's structure are so finely interwoven as to be inextricable. Thus in establishing our case for the musical expression of hope, we had to discuss not only the contours and conventional associations of our focal

---

[58] This raises a familiar hermeneutic problem: how do we know that this is an epic symphony? In general, the answer lies in the satisfactoriness of our overall interpretation after a number of listenings, given Shostakovich's own intentions and his place in the history of music. One of the corollaries of our analysis is that you cannot understand a complex work like Shostakovich's Tenth without hearing it more than once.

passage but also its role in patterns of thematic transformation and quotation spanning the entire symphony. To demonstrate that our focal passage expresses hope we had to engage in a *formal* analysis of the work as a whole. Conversely, we suggest that in a complexly integrated work like Shostakovich's Tenth, formal and expressive elements of musical structure are so thoroughly interdependent that the formal function of particular passages can often be accurately described only in *expressive* terms. Thus there is no "strictly formal" or purely musical explanation for why our focal passage unfolds as it does in the central section of the third movement; its formal function is simply to express the cognitively complex emotion of hope.

Epilogue

In establishing our case for the musical expression of hope in Shostakovich's Tenth we have told only half of the story; in this work Shostakovich stretches the bounds of the epic symphonic tradition—in fact, subverts this tradition—and the role of F in the musical and expressive structure proves to be more complex than our account thus far seems to suggest. Two further sources of information help fill in the picture. First is what the composer supposedly said about the symphony's meaning: "I wrote it right after Stalin's death, and no one has yet guessed what the Symphony is about. It's about Stalin and the Stalin years. The second part, the scherzo, is a musical portrait of Stalin, roughly speaking."[59] These statements accord well with our interpretation. If the work really deals with the Stalin years, we would expect that its leading idea, I/1, which generates most of the dark material of the first three movements, including the principal theme of the Stalin portrait, is meant to capture something fundamental about the experience and atmosphere of these times. Quotations and allusions to this idea surround our focal passage in the third movement, providing the brooding backdrop against which the single hopeful statement of T1 stands. The most obvious interpretation is that the backdrop evokes the oppressive pall of fear hanging over the Soviet Union during the Stalin era, whereas F expresses a hope for a brighter future following his death. The second, more direct, source of information, the fate of IV/1 in the last half of the finale, puts a new slant on this hopeful expression. The lively theme fails to retain its optimistic

---

[59] Dmitri Shostakovich, *Testimony: The Memoirs of Dmitri Shostakovich*, as related to and edited by Solomon Volkov, trans. Antonina W. Bouis (New York: Harper and Row, 1979), p. 141.

character; Shostakovich, ever mistrustful of happy endings, undercuts its optimistic qualities, transforming it gradually until it comes to resemble its antithesis, the theme of the Stalin portrait! The hope expressed by our focal passage proves, therefore, to be a token of a more specific type of hope than we had originally described: it proves to be false hope.

8

What Schubert's
Last Sonata Might Hold

CHARLES FISK

Musical commentators have often found, and continue to find, the trill at the end of the first phrase of Schubert's last sonata remarkable, even strange, in ways that call for interpretation. If, for example, the opening phrase of the sonata were to mean something, the strangeness of the trill might cast doubt on that meaning. If that phrase has a mood, then the trill abruptly, if quietly, alters it. From wherever the theme may come, the trill comes from somewhere else. Whoever sings the theme sings innocently, without anticipating the trill, without imagining the possibility of what the trill might intimate. The trill, accordingly, has to a marked degree a separate identity from the surrounding music. Instead of merely reinforcing an already participatory note or gesture the way most trills do, it brings a foreign tonal region—one centered in the chromatic G♭—into play, uncertainly yet emphatically revealing it, suggesting its presence through a tremulous whisper.

As a sonata composed just after Beethoven's death, the work whose opening this trill disturbs belongs to a tradition of serious pure instrumental music. As an exemplar of that tradition, this sonata serves no function and makes no explicit, or even implicit, reference to anything outside itself, except possibly to other music. It has become second nature, as Pierre Bourdieu might put it,[1] for listeners cultivated in this tradition

---

[1] Pierre Bourdieu, *The Field of Cultural Production* (New York: Columbia University Press, 1993), p. 5.

Schubert, Sonata in B♭ Major, D. 960

Diagram of First Movement (Molto moderato)

"Sonata Nomenclature"	Exposition			Development	Retransition	Recapitulation			Coda
	First group	Transition group k	Second group k			First group	Transition	Second group k	
Thematic Material	A_1 A_2 A_1	B_1	C_1 B_2	A_2 B_1 C_1 C_2	C_3 A_2 A_1 A_2	A_1 A_2 A_1	B_1	C_1 B_2	A_1
Principal Key Areas	B♭ (G♭) B♭	f♯ ⟿	F F	(c♯) continuous modulations (D♭) [E C a♭ b d]	d —— V/B♭	B♭ G♭ / B♭ (f♯)	(b) ⟿	B♭ B♭	B♭
Stage of Narrative	Opening chorus — Individuation of protagonist	Banishment of protagonist	Quest for reinclusion	Memory and reflection in exile	Way station; Entrance to hallowed place — WILDERNESS — No man's land; memory of beginning	Epiphany			

(1)* (2) (3) (4)

WILDERNESS

* (1) Departure from tonic
(2) Establishment of dominant
(3) Departure from dominant
(4) Reestablishment of tonic

to place special significance in instrumental music, but to hear that significance as emanating solely from musical sound and structure and not from any source outside music itself. According to the implicit laws of this tradition, as made partially explicit by various musicologists and aestheticians in what many consider the wake of Eduard Hanslick, such reference plays a role in musical understanding only when the composer has explicitly sanctioned it. When, by contrast, listeners or students of the music come to feel that it makes such a reference, their feeling remains only that: a personal association, of cognitive value only for their own self-analysis, and never as a contribution to musical understanding. Intellectually, this purist tradition has weakened in recent years: students of music have come to accept its contingency, its dependence on outside forces, and to articulate the ways it is embedded in culture. But the way this tradition has shaped our listening experience remains powerful. Indeed this kind of experience, when richest and most intense, seems to abandon conceptual thought and explicit reference altogether. One's mind and body become filled with the tones themselves, and one feels completely absorbed in a world of music. Such musical experience can even seem to become, ideally, a cathartic sublimation of oneself into music, a kind of musical absolution.

What, then, of the conceptual suggestiveness of Schubert's trill, giving rise to the speculations of my opening paragraph? The trill has this suggestiveness because it can seem quietly to disrupt, despite coming so near the beginning, the kind of musical continuity on which compositions of Schubert's time depend for their independence from conceptual thought. Because of its disjunctiveness with the phrase that precedes it, the trill calls for an account. And in their accounts, many listeners, including well-known writers, draw metaphorically on extramusical concepts, concepts as vague as my intimation or Charles Rosen's mystery, or as specific as my whispering or Tovey's distant thunder.[2] Among those who wish to account for the trill, however, there remain structuralists and other musical purists who refuse to admit such metaphor as a component of musical understanding. These investigators may search instead, in the music that follows, for later musical events in the piece that, through their relationship to the trill, make its significance as part of a *Grundgestalt* or a motive for *Auskomponierung* comprehensible in purely musical terms.

After describing some aspects of the trill and its context that make it seem strange to so many listeners, I shall begin by reviewing briefly this network of musical events to which the trill belongs. These events culmi-

---

[2] Charles Rosen, *Sonata Forms* (New York: Norton, 1980), p. 249. Donald Francis Tovey, "Franz Schubert," in *The Main Stream of Music and Other Essays*, ed. Hubert Foss (Cleveland: World Publishing, 1964), p. 119.

nate in the famous D-minor passage at the end of the development (examples 8.9–10) in which the trill returns, coming three times now, still low and hushed but far more integrated, both tonally and rhythmically, than at the beginning. To account for the trill, one must clearly account for this passage, in which the trill returns so prominently. Clearly too, however, this account must consider how the G♭, marked by the trill from the beginning, influences the course of tonal events throughout the movement before the trill returns; or how its motive, involving a chromatic upper neighbor to the dominant, is composed out. My discussion will ultimately focus on this D-minor passage, on the effect of its tonal stasis after so much tonal exploration, and on the resources a listener brings to hearing and understanding it.

I shall begin by exploring some kinds of understanding of that passage that one might gain from musical analysis alone. That is, I shall focus at first on relationships within the music rather than on relationships between the music and a listener's wider experience—except, to some extent, their musical experience. But I shall then argue that in order to experience music with any involvement, most listeners make use of their faculties for emotional engagement and for the configuration of actions in ways that cannot be separated from the supposedly pure perception of the parameters that musical analyses address. This argument does not reflect a belief that music represents real-life emotions or tells a story simulating real-life actions; I believe, rather, that what might have been certain real emotions or actions—or, more plausibly, the thought or memory of them—have sometimes instead become music.[3] Musical feelings and actions are thus feelings and actions that we have allowed music to appropriate, transforming them into music; they are not something outside music that it represents but rather something inside us that we vouchsafe to it. In becoming music, these feelings and actions never become articulated in just the ways they would in situations outside of music. But we can conjecture what they might otherwise have been or, for ourselves, what they could become. For the faculties on which musical emotions and actions draw must be the same faculties, at least to a degree, that we employ to feel emotions and configure actions generally, and that we develop, for the most part, outside of music. Even though music by itself tells no story, one powerful way to grasp one's own musical experience intellectually is to construct a kind of narrative overview, with

---

[3] I do not mean by this statement to imply the kind of reductionist view of the relationship of music to other experience that would construe everything in music as a transformation of something else. The ways in which musical materials come to generate their own implications are obviously much too complex to permit tracing all, or even most, of them to identifiable sources outside of music.

its emotional implications, closely following sequences of events in a piece of music and forging from them an envisionment of what they might have been had they not become music. To the extent that such a narrative can bring specific musical details and relationships into play without distorting them, it can bring to explicit awareness the kinds of meaning-generating faculties that music can engage in us. These remarks represent the basis on which I understand the work of Anthony Newcomb, Fred Everett Maus, and others investigating how theories of narrative, action, drama, and metaphor can help us to articulate musical understanding. Impelled by the trill to find a story in Schubert's last sonata, I gain an explicit understanding of what this music engages in me, what it consequently holds for me, but also a sense of the range and structure of what it might hold for someone else. But before I tell my story, I must describe the musical events it takes into account: first the trill, then the tonal web that the trill initiates, and finally the return of the trill.

The Trill

Of the distinguishing features of the trill (example 8.1)—its chromatic pitch, its low register, and its rhythmic placement—the least strange is its pitch. Even Mozart and Haydn made frequent use of the kind of modal mixture that the G♭ introduces, and by Schubert's time the use in the major of the sixth degree borrowed from the parallel minor had become perhaps

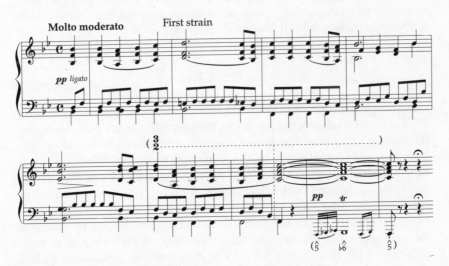

Example 8.1. Schubert, Sonata in B♭, D. 960, first movement, mm. 1–9

the most common of chromatic inflections. But Schubert's special way here of introducing this altered scale degree, through such a hushed, low trill, reinvests this chromatic inflection with strangeness and separateness.

Although most listeners will characterize the trill explicitly through its pitch, its register, its quietness, and perhaps its length, its rhythmic relation to its musical context—even if perceived only subliminally— probably contributes more to the effect of strangeness than any of these more apparent characteristics. The inner-voice motive, F–G–F, in m. 4 prepares for the chromatic variant of this motive, F–G♭–F, that the trill brings into focus in m. 8. The G♭, however, lasts four times as long as the G that it motivically echoes. Moreover, the second subphrase, to which the trill belongs, begins by reversing the pattern of rhythmic stress established in the first subphrase. It then continues by extending the following motion in quarter notes so that the melodic goal, C, arrives not on a downbeat, like the earlier long notes, but in midmeasure. The possibility of a metrical reinterpretation of these measures, whereby the six quarter notes become the first of two measures of 3/2, only corroborates the impression of a subtle disorientation in the musical scene into which the trill intrudes.

Through its relation to its context, then, as well as through its implicit reference to other music, to the operatic timpani roll that traditionally embodies an offstage disturbance, the trill seems quietly to imbue the lowered sixth degree with portent. What it might portend, at the beginning of a train of musical thought, is not merely further coloristic use of this degree but its active participation in the compositional process of the sonata. Even a simple description of the musical events that follow makes it apparent that such participation does in fact occur.

The Tonal Web

In most tonal compositions of the eighteenth and nineteenth centuries, the compositional process has as its framework a tonal plan involving movement away from the key of the tonic to that of the dominant, followed by an eventual return to and final confirmation of the tonic as tonal center. The sonata procedure, in particular, involves special articulation and thus dramatization of: (1) departure from the tonic key; (2) arrival in the dominant, and then its confirmation through strong cadential gestures; (3) ensuing departure from the dominant; and finally, (4) return to the tonic and its concluding cadential confirmation. Like most other compositions with this title, Schubert's B♭-major sonata articulates such a structure; but its way of articulating that structure involves quite marked and sudden emphasis of the minor key of the lowered sixth degree at both the departure from the tonic and the departure from the dominant.

At the end of the first thematic group, a moment that in most sonatas involves, either with or without a cadence in the tonic, the emergence of new material whose rhythms, textures, and harmonic progressions suggest instability and motion away from the tonic, Schubert produces neither cadence nor smooth transition to a new kind of motion (example 8.3). Instead, a cadence is prepared but then evaded through a B♮, and then replaced within three measures by a forceful cadential gesture in the wildly remote key of F♯ minor, immediately introducing a new theme in that key. But as many analysts of this movement have noted, F♯ minor is not as remote, or at least as unprepared, as it seems; for F♯ is the enharmonic equivalent of the G♭ of the first trill, and G♭ has by this time already been revisited as the key of what I shall call the second strain of the first group (example 8.2), the G♭-major version of the melody, making B♭ into scale degree 3̂, that has come, without modulatory preparation, in measure 20. Both G♭ major and F♯ minor arise, no doubt, through the composing out of the F–G♭–F motive of the trill, G♭ major quite directly, F♯ minor more indirectly. But the relationship of this F♯ minor to an underlying motive or *Grundgestalt*, without which its occurrence might seem simply incoherent, does not diminish its disjunctive, disorienting effect.

Once again, the motion away from the dominant key, F major, proceeds quite suddenly and without preparation to a remote key, C♯ minor (example 8.6). This key bears the same relation to F major as F♯ minor bears to B♭. The development begins with the quiet entrance of this key, echoing the last gesture of the exposition. The simplicity of the echo only throws into relief the strangeness of the new key—a strangeness prepared, to be sure, by the earlier dramatic appearance of F♯ minor, with the memory of which this C♯ minor resonates as the only other marked and sudden emphasis of a tonally remote minor key. For the next thirty measures, the music modulates continually, until a *fortissimo* arrival in D♭ major (example 8.8) introduces a seemingly new theme in that key.

Example 8.2. Schubert, Sonata in B♭, D. 960, first movement, mm. 18–21

Example 8.3. Schubert, Sonata in B♭, D. 960, first movement, mm. 42–53

The dramatic appearances of C♯ minor and D♭ major in the development thus parallel those of F♯ minor and G♭ major in the exposition, but also reverse their order and even their character in important ways. In the exposition (examples 8.2–3), G♭ major comes first, and quietly, followed at some distance by the forceful intrusion of its parallel minor, and a new theme in that key. In the development (examples 8.6 and 8), C♯ minor comes first, once again quietly. The exploratory passage that follows, reviewing all the themes of the exposition, culminates in the arrival of the parallel major, D♭, once again setting the stage for a new theme. Of course a listener does not necessarily, or even ordinarily, hear what these keys or their relationships are. Theorists of tonal music have good reason to

Example 8.4. Schubert, Sonata in B♭, D. 960, first movement, mm. 80–85 ("second theme")

Example 8.5. Schubert, Sonata in B♭, D. 960, first movement, mm. 99–101 ("closing theme")

Example 8.6. Schubert, Sonata in B♭, D. 960, first movement, mm. 116–21 (development)

Example 8.7. Schubert, Sonata in B♭, D. 960, first movement, mm. 126–31

Example 8.8. Schubert, Sonata in B♭, D. 960, first movement, mm. 149–54

emphasize the voice-leading from which these keys arise over the identity of the keys themselves. But the arrivals of these keys are texturally and thematically marked enough to stand out from their surroundings, and thus for their schematic pattern to take on significance. One must also remember that most music lovers, whether professional or amateur, who knew this sonata in the first century of its publication got to know it by reading the score rather than by hearing it performed. Their ways of hearing the music grew in part from seeing the relationships I am describing in the musical notation.

In listening to a performance of the movement, one feels the magic (or something like magic) of G♭ major, the shock of F♯ minor, the quiet but sudden darkness of C♯ minor, and the glowing affirmation (or something like affirmation) of D♭ major. Even without recognizing them as parallels, one may hear the G♭ major and F♯ minor, later the C♯ minor and D♭ major, as opposites, as dependent on each other for their effect, or, if one accepts such language, for their meaning. Seeing, in addition, the changes of key signature from two flats to three sharps, and later from two flats (although with only one in effect) to four sharps, only makes the listener who reads the music more inclined to relate these two pairs of parallel opposites to each other, to register the moments when F♯ minor and C♯ minor befall the music as closely related, as somehow interdependent in significance.

The new theme (example 8.8) stays in D♭ for only one four-measure phrase. A second phrase moves to E, a third to C, after which the latter part of the melody, in eighth-note slurs, breaks off, modulating sequentially to A♭ minor, then to B minor, and climaxing in D minor (example 8.9). In this key, the new thematic motive first heard in D♭ major comes again, its phrases now expanded to six measures. Instead of modulating further, the music remains in D minor now, and in this key the trill returns.

D minor is of course closely related to B♭ major, the home key. But this D minor arrives only as the last in the series of chromatic modulations just enumerated, in which no key is functionally related to the ones that precede and follow it. Even someone reading and recognizing this D minor will probably not hear it as close to home—in spite of the coherence of the voice-leading through which it comes about—but rather as lost, cut off from any tonal mooring, neither close to home nor recognizably far from it. To understand the return of the trill in this musical situation, one must take into account its failure to return sooner, in one of the keys associated with the G♭ of its first occurrence. Only after a full exploration of the tonal implications of the trill's pitch, it seems, can the trill itself return.

The Return of the Trill

D minor arrives as the culmination of the most agitated, thickly textured, tonally complex, and sustained buildup in the movement (example 8.9). The theme that this unique climax introduces carries the obvious memory, already mentioned, of the D♭-major theme marking the only distinctive point of arrival earlier in the development. But it also carries more subliminal memories from earlier in the movement, of events that originate in the first moment of agitated tonal disorientation (example 8.3), the

Example 8.9. Schubert, Sonata in B♭, D. 960, first movement, mm. 163–79

sudden deflection of the cadence of the first theme. The first measures of the ensuing F♯-minor melody are structured on a long-short-short rhythm, a half note and two quarters, that becomes more explicit in the left hand of the second theme (example 8.4), returns to its initial form in the closing group (example 8.5), and returns again to its explicit form in the sequen-

Example 8.10. Schubert, Sonata in B♭, D. 960, first movement, mm. 185–204

tial passage (beginning at the end of example 8.7), based on the second theme, that culminates in D♭ in the development. The bass of this sequential passage imparts a triadic melodic shape to the left-hand rhythm of the second theme and thus anticipates (examples 8.8–9) the D♭-major and D-minor melodies to follow. In phrase structure, this latest theme, the D-minor one, revisits the six-measure pattern (example 8.4), motivically three plus three, of the second theme. Harmonically, it shares with the F♯-minor theme (example 8.3), also the source of its rhythmic impulse, an ambiguous oscillation between a minor key and its relative major. Both themes withhold any unambiguous suggestion of the direction of their harmonic resolution until the moment of its actual occurrence. The F♯-minor theme finally cadences in A, its relative major, initiating a tonally indirect and vacillating transition to F major. But this D-minor theme remains in D, not responding to the pull of its penultimate chord to F. And when, in the echo of the first D-minor phrase, the cadential V of F falls back to a D-minor chord for the second time, the stage is set for yet another D-minor phrase (example 8.10). At this moment the trill returns, now on D, and hence confirming D as tonic through sheer reiteration.

Into this setting, following now upon the trill rather than preceding it, the sonata's opening theme returns. Intervallically, its melody is exactly that of the opening strain, but in beginning on the third degree of the scale it is closer in feeling to the second strain (example 8.2). Improvising a version of this passage in which the return of the theme begins instead with the tonic reveals at once how crucially the melodic emphasis on the third degree affects the feeling of this passage. The texture, too, is soloistic, like that of the second strain's first occurrence, and of the theme's return (also in minor and on the third degree) at the beginning of the development (example 8.6), only now accompanied by concentrated repeated chords rather than by fluid arpeggiations. The six-measure spans established through the first two D-minor phrases now incorporate both trill and theme. A second low trill on D ends in a descent to B♭, alluding to the home key without really going there, without changing the trill's E to E♭, and without a harmonically realized modulation. The *first* strain, the theme in its original form, its melody centering on the tonic, now returns; but in this context it, too, comes as a solo. The G♭ in its harmonization keeps it at an allusive distance from D minor. The conclusion of a third trill rolls the B♭ back up into the D, and the D-minor setting of the melody comes back to frame the first strain. Under its last note (m. 203), the expected D-minor chord gives its place to the V of B♭, at first only in inversion. Only through a chromatic descent to yet another trill, echoed by still another, just like the original one, does this harmony regain the bass note F, its root, that it needs in order to set the stage for recapitulation.

Here, then, are some of the musical parameters of this D-minor passage. Its stilled chordal accompaniment, its predominantly still or only chromatically stepwise bass, and its slowly unfurling succession of six-measure phrases in D minor all contribute to an impression of hushed expectancy. Its contrast with the constant exploratory harmonic motion and the more rhythmically and contrapuntally active textures of all the preceding music only deepens the stillness of this passage, or, rather, makes it intense. This stillness contrasts too markedly with all that has come before to be a restful stillness. It is, instead, a stillness in which something will be revealed, a place cleared (that is, a time hushed) for epiphany.

Some of the terms in the preceding paragraph, in particular "hushed expectancy" and "epiphany," do not typically figure in music-analytic discourse. I have described, in terms usually accepted as purely musical, some features of the passage that lead me to characterize it as hushed and expectant, and in a moment I shall attempt, once again in so-called musical terms, to justify the use of "epiphany."

An epiphany is a revelation, usually one made to an individual in solitude. The revelation comes in a time of quiet, if emotional, reflection—perhaps in a time of prayer—rather than in one of activity. The individual cannot actively seek or strive for this revelation but can only wait for it to occur, open to its possibility without ever fully expecting it to happen. Many moments in Schubert seem to me to have an epiphanic quality, to carry a sense of acceptance or enlightenment, granted from outside or above to one who simply waits, who has given up striving. The simplest passages of this kind are those in which music in the minor mode returns in the major, sounding transformed simply because it remains otherwise so much the same as before. Here, in the B♭ sonata, the events that seem to me to engender a sense of epiphany are more complex.

The first D-minor phrase and its echo already create an unprecedented stillness. The quiet refusal to follow the pull of the harmony to F major, to go the way the earlier F♯-minor theme did (example 8.3), deepens the stillness. Into this stillness comes the trill, clearly remembered yet remote enough in memory to be no longer expected. The theme, as it now follows, no longer initiates new melodic explorations, as it has before. Instead it holds itself within the shape of the original opening strain, renouncing further exploration and simply waiting. When the B♭-major first strain now returns, it returns in the schematic position that the G♭-major second strain once occupied. It sounds simultaneously near and far away: near because B♭ major is indeed tonally close to D minor, because what might have been the second strain has now assumed the shape of the first, because both now share the same texture, and because the first strain now incorporates the G♭, the pitch most closely associated with the second; yet remote because of the E♮ in the trill and the same G♭ in the harmonization, which keep B♭ major somewhat in abeyance, more like a memory than a true return of the opening phrase. This memory, however, makes possible the revelatory moment itself (m. 203), the moment when the home dominant takes the place of the D-minor chord at the end of the following phrase, bringing a yet quieter calm, and an actual return to the opening theme itself. For in the manner in which this memory occurs, a reversal of the tonally conferred roles of insider and outsider is suggested; and in this reversal, the outsider—the protagonist identified from the beginning with the second strain—regains a degree of access to the region represented by the sonata's opening phrase.

From Analysis to Narrative

It takes only a little imagination to construe how I adapt the terms "insider" and "outsider" to tonal music. Insiders are musical ideas presented in the tonic or in keys closely related to it, such as the dominant or the relative minor. Outsiders are, at least potentially, ideas in tonally remote keys, especially when so presented that one hears their tonal remoteness, as when, just after the sonata's first full cadence (example 8.2), a trill on B♭ and C♭ leads without modulation to a new phrase—the second strain—in G♭ major. Calling G♭ major an outside key is a neutral enough characterization to function in a structural analysis.

But I have also resorted to some other phrases—not only "epiphany" but the lost D minor, for example, or even the strange trill—that I cannot expect every listener to accept. I have sought through descriptions of musical detail to make the use of each of these terms seem plausible. The trill is unusual, for example, because of the ways it departs from the tonal, registral, and rhythmic norms of early nineteenth-century music; calling it strange is but a step away from calling it unusual. The D-minor passage toward the end of the development emerges from a series of chromatic modulations rather than from other tonal areas close to its own. These modulations do not clearly suggest a goal; indeed, in their rapidity and multiplicity, they suggest instead, at least in one way, a loss of direction. Once again, features of the music strongly support the characterization of this D-minor music as "lost," but they do not justify an attribution of "lostness" to the music itself. "Epiphany," finally, is clearly the hardest of these terms to justify; once again, I have argued for its use by describing musical events in ways that, I hope, make it plausible.

If one views musical meaning as representational, one cannot regard the strangeness of the trill, the lostness of D minor, or the epiphanic quality of the sudden arrival of the home dominant as part of the meaning of these musical events. Too many listeners will disagree with these characterizations for them to become, as Diana Raffman puts it, normative.[4] But is it fruitful to regard musical meaning as representational in this intersubjectively verifiable sense?

Representations usually identify their referents, and in doing so they affect our perceptions of what they represent, or our thoughts about it. What is represented stands outside or behind what represents it; the medium of representation is to some degree separate from and transparent to what it represents, and directed toward it. But it seems to me that music draws attention, ultimately, to itself, and away from whatever it

---

[4] Diana Raffman, *Language, Music, and Mind* (Cambridge, Mass.: MIT Press, 1993), p. 57.

could conceivably represent. As I said earlier, it transforms what it might have represented into itself. Musical experience, intense musical experience especially, thrives on the loss of meaning. Actions and emotions—or at least inner scenarios involving them—become themselves music in such experience. Indeed, when musical catharsis occurs, might it not depend, at least in part, on the loss of meaning through music?[5]

I speak impressionistically here, without precise definitions or close argumentation. But I wish to pursue my impressions just one step further. In order for a loss of meaning to have any psychic force, there has to be meaning to be lost. To engage a listener, it seems to me, music has to draw dynamically on a listener's emotional and other experience. Involved listening is not merely contemplation of a sound structure, followed, no matter how closely, by associative evocation of thoughts and feelings. Listeners use their capacities for feeling emotion and understanding action in order simply to open themselves to hearing the music. It makes no strong impression until these faculties are already engaged.

One can recover musical meaning—in the sense of something it might represent—only through conjecture, conjecture based on close attention to musical detail and structure. This conjecture must always grow out of personal engagement with the music, and its discoveries will represent, initially, only what the music holds for the one who conjectures. Analytic, stylistic, and historical understanding of the music—musical intertextuality especially—can help to validate the conjecture for oneself and make it plausible to others. But it always remains, to some extent, the conjecturer's own story.

I shall conclude by summarizing a story that encapsulates some of what this sonata holds for me as one of its very committed listeners and performers. In a sense, this story is little more than a naively poetic description of what happens in the music—one, to be sure, that has both incorporated and withstood the test of sustained harmonic and motivic analysis. In another, it is completely personal, a projection of states of mind from my own experience, albeit ones I believe I share with many others, into Schubert's music. It has always been a story about an outsider—in German, a *Fremdling*—who undertakes a quest for acceptance, or inclusion. Its experiential time span, like that of many such musical stories, is best measured in years rather than in hours or days. It is more like a life remembered in some important aspect, as illuminated through a particular mood and setting, than like the unfolding of an actual story. I venture to tell it publicly because it may apply to some of Schubert's

---

[5] That is, on forgetting what might have been meant while at the same time drawing energy from or even, in a sublimated way, resolving conflicts within, that lost or forgotten meaning.

other music, and because it may also represent a central preoccupation in his life, as in the lives of so many artists of his and subsequent generations.

Outline of a Narrative

The textural as well as tonal contrast between the two strains of the opening theme, as I am calling them, suggests a contrast between singing in a chorus in the first strain (example 8.1) and singing alone, as an individual, in the second (example 8.2). Perhaps the first phrase is more focused on its melody than most choral music, and the upper part of the left hand furnishes an ostinato rhythm that only an accompanying instrument would normally provide. But in their hymnlike character, the melody and supporting chordal texture strongly suggest the presence of a chorus in the opening strain, if only as the background for a principal singer. I speculated at the beginning of this essay that whoever sings the opening phrase sings innocently, without any awareness that the trill is about to occur. But this member of the chorus, in taking notice of the trill and responding to it, also does so, at first, innocently. The trill fascinates this singer, who initially has no understanding of its danger. This protagonist becomes individuated through the trill and hence is willing to explore where it will take him. (Because I make no claims for the universality of my narrative, and because I identify myself with the protagonist, I shall call this protagonist "he.") At first this exploration seems to bring him back together with the chorus, which he affirmingly rejoins.

But now that he has identified himself with the trill, the chorus cannot cadence as it ought with his participation (example 8.3). The anguished turn to F♯ minor exposes his hope of remaining with them as an illusion. The melodic line splits apart, the protagonist's melody falling to a lower register, and even within this register continuing at first to fall. In the ensuing transitional passage, individuals from the chorus reach out to him in an effort to draw him in again, so that he can dance with them in the new music (example 8.4) emerging from this transition. But dancing together is not singing together. Both this dance and the following, once again more choral, closing theme toward which it is directed (example 8.5) come close to losing their momentum, as if in doubt. The metric framework of the dance breaks down temporarily as the tonal center deflects toward D♭ (once again the lowered sixth degree) (mm. 92–96). The closing theme begins as an optimistic transformation of the protagonist's F♯-minor song of exclusion but immediately becomes hesitant again. The protagonist has not yet, in any full sense, regained membership in the chorus, and the closing theme eventually reverts to a soloistic texture. Indeed in the first ending of the exposition, the transition back to the beginning, the trill returns in a *fortissimo* explosion, fully revealing its threatening, as yet unassimilated power both to him and to them. If one hears the exposition again, one thus hears it in the aftershock of an event that brings the ontological insecurity of its main protagonist into radical focus.

With the second ending's C♯-minor echo of the last F-major gesture (example 8.6), the protagonist finds himself still an outsider, no longer actively seeking inclusion, but instead turning inward and becoming more reflective than in the F♯-minor moment of his banishment (example 8.3). In this C♯ minor he remembers, but only remembers, the opening melody: he can have this melody now only in minor, and only on the third degree rather than on the tonic. He uses its exploratory energy to bring his conflicting experiences together in memory, to link this melody with his F♯-minor melody and return then toward C♯. A deceptive cadence initiates further exploration (end of example 8.7), incorporating also the memory of the dancing second theme (example 8.4), and coming through a series of modulations to D♭ major (example 8.8). In the bass motive of the exploratory passage just finished he now finds the motive of a new melody, marking a way station on his psychological journey, as if he had come upon the entrance to a hallowed place. The tonal trajectory of which this melody marks the completion—from C♯ minor indirectly to D♭ major—is hopeful, especially in its reversal of the earlier movement from G♭ major to F♯ minor (examples 8.2–3) and in its incorporation of the major and its parallel minor into an experiential continuum. But as the protagonist turns toward this new place, emerging from contemplation, the environment becomes a wilderness through which he presses anxiously, abandoning the now familiar territory of his exile without knowing his next destination. The arrival in D minor (example 8.9) opens the way into a lonely clearing in this wilderness, a no man's land in which he treads quietly and vigilantly, searching for an indication of how to continue. His newest theme is poignant with memories of his banishment from the chorus, his quest to reunite with it, and of his reflections on that experience. Only now, after venturing outward again, does he rediscover the trill. Although now cognizant of its danger, he welcomes the opportunity to reengage its mysterious energy, to turn to it once again as a companion. He now lets his song turn around a single pitch, self-contained like the trill motive itself, and like the sonata's opening strain.

In the return of the first strain itself, more fully recalled for the first time only now, another voice from the chorus separates itself from it to bring this memory to the protagonist, to sing alone to him, its solo a response to his own solo singing, recognizing his lost feeling and his loneliness. Even though still poignantly at a distance, this voice grants him through this gesture of recognition an opportunity to reunite with the chorus. In keeping itself at a distance, an outsider to this clearing, this empathic voice allows the protagonist to take over its access to the tonic, and to feel the measure of serenity that this access entails.

To the extent that narratives rarely end with near-exact repetitions of their beginnings, movements in classical sonata forms abandon narrative paradigms in favor of purely musical ones. If, in any case, this music comes closer to emotionally charged recollection and reflection than to an actual series of events, then its formal repetitions pose no threat to an interpretation that, instead of mapping every musical event into a narrative equivalent, incorporates storylike sequences into an interior tableau of recollective meditation. To be sure, the second strain of the theme in the recapitulation does offer a moment of further integration (mm. 235–66), when G♭ major flows directly into F♯ minor, then to A major, bringing back the theme over a tonic rather than a dominant pedal. The protagonist now understands the implications of his fascination with the trill, and in taking them into account comes somewhat closer to full inclusion, but not close enough to alter the course of the remaining music. And the reflective coda (mm. 336ff.) once again integrates first F♯ and then G♭, now as simple chromatic inflections, assimilated memories of disturbance rather than full reenactments of it. The final choral refrain, in its three short subphrases, reiterates one last time the idea of a melodic strain beginning on the tonic framing one beginning on scale degree 3. But now the two strains share the same harmony and choral texture, as if able at least to imagine belonging fully together. And the trill does, indeed, seem integrated into the final cadence.

The remaining three movements of the sonata return to the G♭ and the F♯, and to the C♯ and D♭, as if to seek further integration of these foreign regions with the primary regions of tonic and dominant. They do not so much continue a story as focus on other aspects of the psychological world introduced and explored in the first movement. And the finale, with its stentorian opening G, asserts control over the G♭ through which the line passes again and again on its way from G to F.[6] Such a gesture suggests,

---

[6] This theme clearly derives, not only in its bass progression and harmony but also in melody and even in texture, from mm. 14–18 of the first movement, thus foregrounding one of the music's earliest responses to the G♭. It is extraordinary that this derivation has never been recognized, to my knowledge, in the Schubert literature. Indeed this finale theme is usually associated with the opening of the finale that takes the place of the *Grosse Fuge* in Beethoven's String Quartet in B♭, Op. 130, rather than with anything else in Schubert's own B♭ Sonata. But it seems that Schubert was, in this case at least, sufficiently grown up to depend on himself rather than on Beethoven for inspiration.

of course, that the G♭ resists assimilation and needs to be mastered. Indeed it seems to me that part of this sonata's enduring appeal is that it offers no simple, all-embracing resolution to its central conflict. Taken as an enactment in music of the psychological scenario I am proposing, it suggests ways of approaching the integration of its protagonist outsider with the inside that it posits, but offers no illusion that the protagonist's wish for inclusion can ever be entirely fulfilled.

Epilogue

It is easy to imagine that Schubert identified himself as an outsider. His family opposed his pursuit of a musical career. He never made a home for himself but instead boarded most of the time with friends. And if recent speculations about his homosexuality prove well founded, he may have felt himself, like the protagonist of his early song "Der Wanderer," a stranger everywhere, or at least almost everywhere.

Schubert's first published major instrumental work was the "Wanderer" Fantasy, incorporating the very same slow, sad stanza of the song that ends with the words "Ich bin ein Fremdling überall" into an extroverted, virtuosic environment to which it might well in many respects seem a stranger. As I have argued elsewhere, one can easily interpret the tonal events in the Fantasy as a presentation and working-through of the conflict between the C♯ minor of the song and the C major of the outer movements. The intrusion of the song's C♯-minor tonality upon what would have been the ending of the first movement resembles the wrenching away, in the B♭ Sonata, of the first full cadence into F♯ minor. Like the Fantasy, the sonata sets up a conflict between its tonic and a strongly articulated, at first unassimilated tonal region, whose exploration and eventual integration significantly determines the course of tonal events. It, too, suggests in this way the presence of a *Fremdling* in search of inclusion, but a presence that it articulates much more subtly, and with a much more lifelike complexity.

In moments like the introduction of C♯ minor into the Fantasy, the sudden turn to the F♯ minor of the contrasting episodes in the A♭-major Moment Musical, Op. 94, no. 2, or the G♭ trill at the end of the B♭-major Sonata's first phrase, Schubert presents foreign tonal material in ways that highlight its foreignness, so that remote tonal regions intrude as if they were outsiders. In this respect Schubert's chromaticisms contrast markedly with Beethoven's, which often seem so integrated into goal-directed motion as to engender a new form of diatonicism. Schubert thus embodies these outsiders in the striking, marked, even disjunctive appearances of what Edward T. Cone has called "promissory notes";[7] they return again and again after they first appear, seeking and eventually finding a home in the music, occasionally subverting tonal stability, as in the other A♭ Moment Musical, the one Cone writes about, but much more often closing the tonal rifts they initially open. It is tempting to think that Schubert identified alienated aspects of himself with these tonal *Fremdlinge* and that he sometimes took solace, at least unconsciously, in their eventual musical integration.

Thus in Schubert's music, remote tonal regions often seem to have a life of their own, in ways that lend the music not only color but pathos, but that can also make it seem diffuse and meandering to some listeners. But the ways this music can present tonal alternatives without initially suggesting their relative weight, or hover between tonal regions without seeming to decide on one or the other, or turn transition into song and song into transition, have always held meaning for me and thus charmed rather than disturbed me. The extraordinary prominence, exploration, and elaboration of the tonally marginal—in its potential for recognizing and emotionally enriching marginal positions in real life—is at the center of what Schubert's last sonata holds for me. Is it too fanciful to think that it might also have opened and enriched the possibility of such positions for him?

---

[7] Edward T. Cone, "Schubert's Promissory Note," in *Schubert: Critical and Analytical Studies*, ed. Walter Frisch (Lincoln: University of Nebraska Press, 1986), pp. 13–30.

9

Two Types of
Metaphoric Transference

MARION A. GUCK

When Milton Babbitt raised questions of "the nature and limits" of
musical discourse,[1] music theorists in the United States took his
assertion—that music theory must meet the same standards of cognitive
clarity or rigor as the sciences—as a restrictive endorsement of scientific-
style language. Though nothing that he said can be claimed to proscribe
any style of description so long as reasons can be given for assertions, the
theory community adopted scientific-appearing formulation as the standard for legitimate musical discourse. Thus certain styles of less formal
theoretic and descriptive discourse, such as metaphoric description, that
are of significant value in at least such practical contexts as teaching and
coaching performers, came to be dismissed.

In fact, however, even the legitimate technical vocabulary of Western
music is rooted in metaphor, and the metaphoric roots are often still in
evidence. For example, the notion of space is so pervasively and deeply
embedded in the language of musical discourse, and of musical thought,
that if we wish to speak of music, we must speak in spatial terms. Accord-

---

[1] Babbitt presents these ideas in "Past and Present Concepts of the Nature and Limits of
Music," *Congress Report of the International Musicological Society* (1961), reprinted in *Perspectives on Contemporary Music Theory*, ed. Benjamin Boretz and Edward T. Cone (New
York: Norton, 1972), pp. 3–9; "The Structure and Function of Musical Theory," *College
Music Symposium* 5 (1965), also reprinted in *Perspectives on Contemporary Music Theory*, pp.
10–21; and "Contemporary Music Composition and Music Theory as Contemporary Intellectual History," in *Perspectives in Musicology*, ed. Barry S. Brook, Edward O. D. Downes,
and Sherman Van Solkema (New York: Norton, 1971), pp. 151–84.

Example 9.1. Chopin, Prelude in B minor, Op. 28, no. 6

Example 9.1. (Continued)

ingly, in tonal music lines rise and fall in registral space, and the root identifies a chord with a pitch at the bottom of its third stack. Though these notions are thought literally true of music, their sources are metaphoric; and the remnants of those sources are still discernible: such technical terms are *music-literal*.

The notion of musical movement is almost equally pervasive. We resort to it, and to notions of change, to connect musical objects and to describe their succession. Thus pitch sequences are transformed into lines moving through the space defined by pitch location, responding to tendencies perceived as inherent in the pitch and chord relations. Some of these terms, too, are music-literal, but most retain an overtly metaphorical resonance, even in musical discourse.

It seems essential to consider how we do—in fact, how we must—resort to metaphoric language (and to analogical thinking) to describe music in order to discover what it contributes to musical discourse and to musical understanding.

To study the role of metaphoric and underlying analogical thinking in musical discourse, a circumscribed situation was developed—loosely speaking, an experiment—that attempted to duplicate some relatively informal contexts in which music is discussed principally in metaphoric terms, so that the contribution of such description would be exposed for examination. Three groups of musicians (students in an introductory tonal analysis class, students in composition, and graduate students in musicology) were asked to converse about Chopin's Prelude in B minor, Op. 28, no. 6, and, in particular, to focus their conversation on m. 11, beat 3, to m. 12, the beginning of beat 2 (see example 9.1). Initially, they were not provided with a score but were played a recording of Maurizio Pollini's performance of the passage, of the phrase that includes the passage (ending with the passage), and of the whole piece.[2]

---

[2] The recording is Deutsche Grammophon 2530, 550.

Though in the absence of scores even musicians rely less on technical description, conversants were asked to discuss the piece in nontechnical terms. Since common-language terminology for musical sounds (words like "loud") is very limited, the resulting conversation naturally turned to metaphor. In order to investigate the relation between metaphoric description and musical structure, conversants were, after a period of time, given scores, played the piece again, and asked what about the piece's structure had suggested the nontechnical descriptions they had proposed. These conversations were transcribed and analyzed.[3]

One of the graduate students in musicology proposed the metaphor of an arch to describe the general (in addition to the particular) shape of the melodic line over the course of the whole piece, with the passage cited seen as the top of the arch. The group's brief comments on the subject eventually suggested to me a detailed analysis of the prelude, which is presented here.

I imagine the prelude as two-measure arching melodies nested within phrase-length arches in turn nested within a single prelude-long arch. The relatively literal spatial notion of melodic arch shape leads me on to the movements of arching gestures and then, beyond those, to the rise and fall of mood and to a narrative curve. The interaction of image and musical structure at each level illuminates immediate and compelling features of the piece, and the interactions among the different arch interpretations and their analyses yield both a dynamic analysis of the prelude and a wealth of information about the imagery of musical description, which I will go on to examine.

As the prelude opens, the left-hand melody sweeps up through arpeggiating sixteenth notes to hover on D, drawn out by its lower neighbor in languorous quarter – dotted eighth – sixteenth. A lingering three-eighth note fall through the same arpeggio closes in sedate steps. The sheer registral span makes an arch of the melody's contour; and the progressive lengthening of sweep, hover, and lingering fall make it graceful. Dynamics, too, swell and shrink as the line rises and falls.

Melodic arching underlies each of the piece's two phrases as well. The first phrase rises as the sixteenth-note sweeps propel the line from D that touches the right-hand chords in m. 1, through the F♯ that intrudes on the chord space in m. 3, to G, the apex of the melody, in the midst of the right hand's chord space in m. 5. Each arpeggio broadens the line's span and

---

[3] A more detailed report of this study is found in my Ph.D. dissertation, "Metaphors in Musical Discourse: The Contribution of Imagery to Analysis" (University of Michigan, 1981). "Musical Images as Musical Thoughts: The Contribution of Metaphor to Analysis," *In Theory Only* 5 (1981): 29–43, interprets the analysis class's narrative about labored breathing.

increases the line's intensity. The simple, clear i–VI progression, opening diatonic tonal space and brightening from minor to major, inclines toward a rising mood.

As the phrase continues, sweeping ascents are complemented by a single, incrementally articulated decline (mm. 5–8). Sixteenth notes are forgotten in the falling quarter- and eighth-note steps. The mood falls as the music turns away from the diatonic G-major chord to chromatic diminished seventh sonorities. More tellingly, despite the greatly increased rate of chord succession, the progression stalls on vii and then V, entangled with frustratingly interstitial VI's and i's. Even the lift afforded by the soprano's escape upward to F$\sharp$ is obliterated by its sixteenth-note rush down to be captured in the cadence.

The left hand falls the final steps to regain the level of the opening (m. 9), but the rise of the new phrase is curtailed by elimination of the second B-minor arch. At the same time, the voice-leading rise is at first delayed by repeating m. 9's D in m. 11; then, it accelerates when E follows immediately and climbs directly to F$\natural$. The dotted eighth–sixteenth that impelled earlier lower neighbors forward is replaced by broad eighths that impede the rise of the line, drawing attention to the climaxing harmonic tritone. Its resolution in mid-arch to the sixth C$\natural$–E conclusively moves beyond G into the relatively remote tonal region of the Neapolitan. With resolution into the Neapolitan, the ascent of the phrase and of the piece conclude together. The apex and fall of the phrase are also the apex and decline of the piece.

At the apex the left hand plays through the expansiveness engendered by all the earlier upward sweeps when, having dropped to C (m. 13), it wells up through its broadest arpeggio twice without an intervening descent (more later). But the repeated surging upward to E begins to call for further decisive progressive movement, and the arpeggios seem to have forgotten how to continue the melodic line. When they fail (m. 14), the climax is revealed to contain the seeds of its own destruction. E continues to hover, now requiring resolution; the right-hand soprano reverses mm. 11–12's B–C to C–B; and the chord dissolves. The descent of the arch has already begun.

The decline of the piece (and second phrase) exaggerates the downward mood swing of the first phrase. A slow step up and rushing stepwise fall, heard earlier when the right hand's melodic escape was forestalled in m. 7, now replaces the left-hand sweeps (m. 15). The lowering mood recurs with the diminished seventh chords, and irresolution is enhanced by waffling between the dominant and tonic that stretches out through the repeated melodic figure. The right hand no longer ascends from B but alternates restlessly with A$\sharp$ below it. The music is stuck, aimlessly retracing familiar ground until the sixteenths fall further to the cadence (m. 18). But it is deceptive, and the soprano delays the chord at that, so it all has to be done again.

Instead of "decisive progressive movement," the piece meanders about the dominant, dissipating the energy of the first half's sweeps. It declines to a dimly recalled echo (mm. 22–26) of the opening measures, the accompanying chords stripped down to an increasingly feeble third. The promise of the piece's rise is undermined, and, thwarted, the piece withers away.

In the prelude, arch shape—abstracted from the material features of arches as a line ascending to curve toward a focus of structural tensions and curving again to descend—models the pitch aspect of the left hand's two-measure melodic arches as a linear contour. It is most convincing over this short span, because the music can be taken in as a single continuous event and converted into a single continuous object, almost as if it were not presented over a span of time at all but in a single instant, the moment required to take in the shape of a real arch. Because arch shape depends on music-literal ascent and descent, it is possible to describe pitch relatively precisely and objectively by claiming that a given melody is an arch. Because arches are typically symmetrical, the claim points as well to the temporal symmetries and dynamic complementation perceived in this piece; but already this suggests that there is more to a melodic arch than what meets the metaphoric eye.

Arching shape can also be glimpsed in the emphasis on repeatedly ascending or descending lines over longer spans and on middleground voice-leading arcs. However, because the former do not form a continuous line but rather generalize a directional emphasis, and because the latter is a slow, intermittent, gentle curve, a greater imaginative effort must be made to convert them into an arch shape: if they are heard as archlike, it is under the influence of the foreground arches. Something else must make vivid the continuity of line, and something more must be made of the piece than a projection of pitch contour alone.

Of course, "something more" is already there in the prelude, and it is the guide to "something else." From the beginning, I described the lines rising and falling; just above, I described how an arch's line ascends, focuses, and curves. *Movement* infuses both at the moment I try to describe them. It might be like the movement of a ball thrown in the air, or the movement of an observing eye or of the arm that threw the ball. Consider the gesture of the arm.

To hear arching movement, one most likely recalls, subliminally, memories that incorporate the fine, continuous adjustments in muscle tensions needed to produce the smooth gesture: the initial impetus that increasingly opposes gravity as the arm rises, stretching to the point of fullest extension, then decreasing tension as the arm yields to gravity. In the gesture, rise and fall are also converted into increase and decrease of effort and tension. In fact, the notion of increase and decrease has already been introduced through the melodic arch's swelling dynamics. The conversion superimposes a metaphorical reinterpretation on the music-literal, and the resulting description is more deeply metaphoric.

The notion of gesture is most clearly discernible in the phrase-length arches. Though music-literal ascent and descent are still evident in the phrase's melodic contour, its line is not brief enough to convert into an instantaneously perceived shape, like the left-hand melodic arches. The time span of the phrase is more appropriate to sensing movement through the shape as it unfolds through the mediation of the foreground figures.

This sense is not conveyed just by the interpretation of conventional pitch relations. Sweeping ascent and lingering fall are conveyed through durations, through the gradual widening of arpeggios contrasted with laborious steps and through the breadth of a slow, brightening diatonic harmonic rhythm opposed to a relatively fast chromaticism. Thus the phrase's arch retains vestiges of its origin in shape, while it incorporates the movement and tension *qualities* of gesture.

However, these notions of sweeping and subsiding do not yet capture all the senses in which we might care to hear the phrase expand and contract. The opposition between broad, clear chord progression and constrained, entangled alternation suggests expansive, rising *moods* in opposition to exhausted, falling moods. The tensions and sensations of physical acts can be extended to the realm of feeling. Increases and decreases can be of emotional tension, and ups and downs can be of mood.

On the model of the phrase and melodic arches, the whole prelude can be heard as a single arch. It, too, emphasizes ascent followed by descent, but this alone is an inadequate explanation. In addition to music-literal shape the single arch draws on the figurative senses of movement and tension embodied in gesture and on their further figurative interpretation as mood, incorporating all in a depiction of human (inter-)actions: the piece's arch is a *narrative curve* (a notion that is figurative even in its home domain). A narrative curve is usually thought of as the presentation of a situation that, through some exploration, development, or complication, rises to a confrontation, culmination, or climax. This crisis initiates the untangling, resolution, or simplification that leads to closure.[4]

---

[4] This outline of narrative curve is similar to that more carefully elaborated in Tzvetan Todorov, *The Poetics of Prose* (Ithaca: Cornell University Press, 1977), pp. 108–19.

The prelude initiates a registral expansion in a primarily diatonic framework that turns into an inexplicable chromatic contraction; when expansion arises a second time, it continues on to climax at the furthest tonal remove;[5] but the climax fails, and its intensity drains aimlessly away until it arrives at a wasted form of its initial state. In this way the prelude can be heard as a narrative curve framed in terms of its own particular logic of aural interactions.

An arch is a plain, even dull, image; but once suggested, notions of arches worked their way into my hearing of the prelude and began to proliferate and direct my attention to more and more refined details of the music, while gathering those details into their conceptual nets. This is, of course, because the notion of an arch was just a starting point; denuded of its physical properties, it took on many forms and moved progressively deeper into figurative territory.

The role of the perceiver-promoter of a visual image like the arch shape is that of the observer of an external object. Directly observable features of the image are correlated with directly observable features of the musical work. Each feature may undergo metaphoric reinterpretation as even music-literal terms do, but each is directly perceivable in both domains.

A gestural arch unites the external, visible movement with internal, therefore private, physical experience. The visible movement incorporates arch shape and thus arch shape's musical correlates. It also incorporates directly observable aspects of the sound, like duration, that correlate with such features as rate of movement. However, these and other audible features also suggest how it feels to move through a particular gesture: whether muscles feel tight, whether great exertion is required. For example, at the top of the mm. 11–12 line, greater exertion is conveyed in part by eighth notes inching up a step and then a half step beyond the arpeggio's top note. Thus gesture depends on both correlations between directly perceivable features and interpretation of the perceivable as quality of movement.

Apprehension of rising and falling moods requires an even more subtle interpretation of the directly observable features of the sound. There is no directly perceivable arch in this case, and even in its home domain the notion of rise and fall is figurative. Scruton describes this process by analogy with our ability to interpret mental states in other people.[6] External, physical gestures are taken in; and the perceiver, remembering what that complex of gestures feels like and what it means when he or she per-

---

[5] See Alexandra Pierce, "Climax in Music—Structure and Phrase (Part III)," *In Theory Only* 7 (1983): 3–30, for a detailed discussion of climax as a point of structural extremity.
[6] Roger Scruton, "Understanding Music," in *The Aesthetic Understanding* (London: Methuen, 1983), pp. 77–100.

forms it, identifies the mood and reconstructs its progress from the physical symptoms. Similarly, one can take in the gestural interplay in a piece's sounds and correlate them with physical gestures, interpreting those gestures as if they were symptomatic of real moods in an individual. To clarify this last point, let me explore another image.

One of the musicology graduate students discussing the prelude made the claim that "what's so interesting about [m. 13] is that same harmony through the whole measure, and yet the urgency and the speeding up nonetheless, because of the repeated sixteenth thing, is really striking to the ear." Urgency describes a situation that evokes strong feeling. Response to it typically takes the form of agitated activity that nevertheless feels like it gets one nowhere. This conflict can cause anxiety, disorientation, and both intense focus of attention and a failure of concentration. The music conveys the response to urgency.

In m. 13 the pattern of melodic arches breaks when two ascending arpeggios immediately succeed each other. The pace is quickened by the occurrence of two sixteenth clusters without an intervening neighbor and descent (without, as the speaker noted, "working out [the] momentum"). Exacerbating the faster pace is disorientation resulting from temporarily cutting 3/4 to 2/4. E is left hanging twice, melodically unfinished by a neighbor or fall of a third. But, contradicting this flurry of activity, the Neapolitan, introduced early (in the middle of a two-measure arch), stretches on for too long, stalling the harmonic progress.

Metaphorically, music-structural features exemplify the qualities of frantic movement associated with urgency: a faster rate of events, a disorienting metric shift: an unfinished line, yet unchanging harmony.[7] In this way musical features are assimilated to qualities of human behavior. As one might read the signals projected by an individual tearing around heedlessly while talking on and on about getting nothing done and, entering into those movements, recall how one has felt, one can recognize the urgency behind the individual's activities. Similarly, by entering into their metaphoric portrayal in this piece, one thereby recognizes the urgency of the piece's activities. Thus the passage can be interpreted as metaphoric movement or action interpreted as symptomatic of metaphoric emotion; the metaphoric emotion is thereby at a level of greater figurative remove than the symptomatic metaphoric movements. The speaker was so convinced that the piece possessed such qualities that she did not say "urgency" is descriptive of the passage; she said the passage *is* urgent. Nor would she have been likely to recognize her description as

---

[7] On exemplification, see Nelson Goodman, *Languages of Art* (Indianapolis: Bobbs-Merrill, 1968), esp. pp. 52–57.

metaphoric: it was true of the passage for her. I might even claim that she dealt with the piece as if it were a human being whose actions she was interpreting.[8]

Often *ascriptions* like urgency arise apparently acontextually in response to a complicated or striking point in a piece. However, as with urgency, such a claim can be interpreted only in light of its precise musical context: events can seem fast only in contrast with slower events; meter can be upset only if first set; a pattern can be left unfinished only if the finished version is known; and a harmonic rhythm that seems to stop suddenly requires an earlier, faster pace. While such metaphors focus attention on a single point, they are highly interactive in their structural sources.

Urgency, and metaphors like urgency, are more context-dependent than metaphors like arch shape. Their virtue is the strength of their bond to a specific context. They distinguish precisely how the music's qualities are interacting at a particular point.

This difference in degree of context dependency partially distinguishes comparative from ascriptive metaphors. Roughly, a *comparative metaphor*, like arch shape, seems more straightforward, more like a technical term, in delimiting the relevant features of an analogy and therefore implying, relatively clearly, its extension. The features so correlated are directly perceivable, even if they undergo metaphoric transformation in the process. An *ascriptive metaphor*, like urgency, is more evocative, less clearly limited. It promises a greater wealth of transference; however, the transference is not feature by feature but more like urgency's complex of interactive symptoms united in a single effect and requiring an imaginative leap to conjoin the image and the music. The heart of ascription is found in the fact that it is not the perceivable features themselves but what they allude to that is transferred.

Ascriptives need not be novel. Tension is a conventional ascriptive that, despite its ubiquitous use, has never achieved technical status in musical discourse. The inability to become literal (even music-literal) also seems indicative of the nature of ascription. As with urgency, criteria for invoking tension cannot be generalized: its assertion depends on the particular way things proceed at a particular point in the progress of a piece—that is, it depends absolutely on interpretation of contextual particularities. If one takes the three types of arch as representative of three increasingly figurative levels of metaphor, progressing from shape through gesture to

---

[8] In addition to Scruton, see Edward T. Cone, *The Composer's Voice* (Berkeley and Los Angeles: University of California Press, 1974), and Fred Everett Maus, "Music as Drama," in this volume, both of which elaborate theories of musical works as evocations of human beings.

psychological state, then ascriptives seem to be characteristic of the most figurative level.[9]

To the extent that "arch" is a theoretical (or technical) term, it is because what is specified is clearly specified—the shape seen frontally—and what is omitted is equally clear. In this guise it is a comparative metaphor that can be applied without significant change of interpretation in many contexts. At the same time, it is not an ideal theoretical term, because it can have the unhappy tendency to undergo metaphoric transformation dependent on its context; and each transformation—based on interpretation of a complex of features that suggest a symmetry of increase and decrease, expansion and contraction, or some such "shape"—endows it with new properties. In such circumstances it is an ascriptive metaphor, and the proliferation of interpretation cannot be controlled.

As a result, it inhabits the borders of technical discourse: sometimes it is legitimately based on music-literal spatial notions and is music-literal itself under those conditions; but it is not trustworthy, because it is able to take on metaphoric connotations and change its character for every piece it encounters. So its chameleonlike nature is both a source of appeal that grants room for imaginative reconstruction in the presence of a particular piece, and a source of distrust, since its particular appearance—its extension—cannot be depended on.

Perhaps there is another source of appeal as well. The capacity for the notion of arch shape to transform itself into almost any dynamic process that waxes and wanes over what we might care to perceive as equivalent time spans makes it archetypical, not only of music's temporal structure but also of temporal structures and experience in general. Arch forms are universally evident and connect any entity that can be so described to the archetype. But to make the description of sound palpable, they must cease to be merely arches. The arch skeleton must be fleshed out in precise and vivid terms in order to depict convincingly a particular musical context: if anything, it must be much more thoroughly figurative in order to describe, exactly, the structure of a particular musical work.

A piece's sounds do not drift inertly in air. Just as they literally vibrate, I think they become vibrant. Every minute aspect of the sound is directed toward projecting an entity that transcends its individual features. Each moment's experienced qualities are achieved through active interpretation of the particular ways in which the sound at that point is shaped with

[9] Glenn Guhr, in a seminar at Washington University, spring 1988, posited a yet more figurative level that detaches itself from linguistic elaboration almost immediately. For example, Kendall Walton once reported that Pablo Casals, in a master class, encouraged a student to play a passage "like a rainbow." Beyond some sense of playing a particularly glorious arc, it is difficult to know precisely what to say in further explanation.

its variously prominent and recessive features. The experienced qualities are equally shaped by the shades of their particular relations to other moments, both immediately successive and recalled distant moments.

To really engage these compelling qualities of a piece, I embroil myself with imagery that is at least as figurative as gesture and, more likely, with images comparable in figurative complexity to emotional and intellectual states. They encapsulate the creative act of listening that greedily encompasses the manifold sounds and, by an imaginative leap, reifies their qualities as they influence and are influenced by the larger context. They distinguish each separate facet of the sound while assimilating all to the specific qualities of the whole. They are attuned to each event's intensity to compel attention, to its magnitude and weight, and to each moment's temporal focus, its degree of absorption in the present, its straining backward or its impulsion forward. They constantly direct me back to the piece. This is the point of drawing on metaphoric description—to facilitate an endlessly closer, more profound hearing of each musical work.

III

EXPERIENCING MUSIC
EMOTIONALLY

10

Music and Negative Emotion

Jerrold Levinson

A grown man, of sound mind and body, manipulates the controls of an electronic apparatus. He settles into an easy chair, full of expectancy. Then it begins. For the next hour or so this man is subjected to an unyielding bombardment of stimuli, producing in him a number of states that prima facie are extremely unpleasant and that one would normally go to some lengths to avoid. He appears upset and pained; occasionally a small sigh or a shudder passes through his body. Yet at the end of this ordeal our subject seems pleased. He avers that the past hour and a half has been a highly rewarding one, and he declares his intention to repeat this sort of experience in the near future.

What has our man been doing, and, more interesting, why has he been doing it? He has been listening to music—just that. It turns out that his fare on this occasion was the *Marcia funebre* of Beethoven's *Eroica* Symphony, the Scriabin Etude Op. 42, no. 5, the third movement of Brahms's Third Symphony, Mozart's Adagio and Fugue in C minor, K. 546, and the opening of Mahler's Second Symphony, all neatly assembled, with suitable pauses, on a reel of recording tape. What he experienced can be described—at least provisionally—as intense grief, unrequited passion, sobbing melancholy, tragic resolve, and angry despair. But why would anyone in effect torture himself in this manner? What could induce a sane person to purposely arrange for himself occasions of ostensibly painful experience?

My object in this essay is to give a comprehensive answer to this query. The general question can be formulated thus: Why do many sensitive

people find the experience of negative emotion through music a rewarding or valuable one, and—what is especially paradoxical—rewarding or
valuable partly in itself? Not only do appreciators of music appear to
regard such experiences as instrumentally good or worthwhile—which
itself needs much explaining—but they standardly seek them out and
relish them for their own sakes, enjoying them or pleasuring in them, if
truth be told.

At this point many readers will have ready some favorite wand for dissolving this paradox with a wave of the hand. But I do not intend to
encourage them. While admitting that my initial description of the phenomenon will need to be modified somewhat, I maintain that even when
all niceties on the aesthetic and psychological fronts have been attended
to, the phenomenon, in essence, remains.

I

In its general form, of course, the problem of the value and desirability
of the negative or unpleasant in art is one of the hoariest in aesthetics. It
is the problem Aristotle raises for the appreciation of tragedy, evocative
of pity and terror, and that he answers with the doctrine of catharsis. It
is the problem of the sublime in eighteenth- and nineteenth-century
thought, the "delightful horror" analyzed among others by Burke and
Schopenhauer, which a spectator feels face to face with some threatening
aspect of life as embodied in a work of art. But in the case of music the
problem is generated in the absence of any representational content, and
so answers to it must be framed accordingly.

We see in the following more recent writers a concern with the specific
paradox of enjoyment of emotionally distressing music. It is interesting to
note the virtual consensus of these writers that negative emotion is not
actually evoked in the attuned listener by even the most intense of musical
works.

> If to hear the intense grief of the fugal passages of the *Eroica* required real
> tears and adrenal secretions, then an anomalous if not impossible psycho-
> logical state would have to prevail. The gorgeous clash of dissonant minor
> seconds which brings the tremendous but short fugue to an incomplete
> close—several measures of almost unbearable anguish—has been a source
> of supreme delight to countless lovers of music. How can a listener be at
> once pleased and pained?[1]

[1] Carroll C. Pratt, introduction to *The Meaning of Music* (New York: McGraw-Hill, 1970),
pp. 3–4.

Why should I ever wish to hear . . . [sad music]? Sad experiences, such as suffering personal bereavement or keen disappointment, are not the kind of thing we wish to repeat or prolong. Yet sad music does not affect us in this way; it may bring relief, pleasure, even happiness. Strange kind of sadness that brings pleasure![2]

The most unpleasant emotions imaginable are perceived in music; and if that meant our *feeling* these emotions, it would be utterly inexplicable why anyone would willfully submit himself to the music. *Tristan und Isolde* is full of music expressive of deep anguish. None, I would think, except the masochists among us, would listen to such music if indeed it were anguish-producing.[3]

I agree with these writers, on the bottom line, that full-fledged emotions of the paradigm sort fail to be aroused by music in the course of aesthetically respectable auditionings. But I want to stress that this failure in many cases is only a marginal one, and thus that the paradox of desirable-though-unpleasant experience in music remains despite this admission. Something *very much like* the arousal of negative emotions is accomplished by some music, and so there is indeed something to explain in our avidity for such experience.

Before essaying explanations of my own, it will help to review a number of responses to the problem that attempt to solve it, roughly, by dissolving it. This will occupy me for the next several sections. These responses in effect deny the phenomenon while introducing in its stead harmless replacements. Such moves are inadequate, however, to resolve the paradox of musical masochism limned in the opening illustration.

It is best to forestall at the outset a possible misunderstanding. In defending the reality and importance of emotional response to music I imply no position on the proper analysis of emotional expressiveness in music. The three writers quoted in the preceding are all concerned to undercut the equation of expression in music with evocation by music. In that they are certainly right. What a passage expresses and what it standardly evokes are, for an assortment of reasons, rarely (if ever) quite identical. But while I reject an evocation theory of expression, I am unwilling to see emotional response to music, particularly of a "dark" sort, exorcised so completely in the name of it. One can reject the evocation theory without regarding every instance of negative emotional response to music—whatever the work and whatever the conditions of listening—as

---

[2] John Hospers, "The Concept of Artistic Expression," in *Introductory Readings in Aesthetics*, ed. J. Hospers (New York: Free Press, 1969), p. 152.
[3] Peter Kivy, *The Corded Shell* (Princeton: Princeton University Press, 1980), p. 3.

either illusory or aesthetically inapropos. It seems to me that there are indeed compositions that can, when listened to in certain appreciatively admissible frames of mind, produce in one real feelings of both the positive and negative variety.

It is our attitude toward the latter that seems puzzling. One can be on the musical rack—one can hear the screws turn, so to speak—and yet like it. This is what we must explain.

II

One hypothesis concerning the effect of music would, if accepted, neatly defuse the paradox that concerns us. This hypothesis, less popular today than at some earlier times, is that of a special "aesthetic emotion," totally different from the emotions of life and occasioned only by the perception of works of art. This view is identified with Clive Bell in its general form, but its foremost exponent with specific application to music is the English psychologist Edmund Gurney.[4] According to Gurney, there is a unique, sui generis "musical emotion" that is raised in listeners by all pieces of "impressive" (i.e., beautiful) music, and only by such. This unvarying effect of impressive music is either a kind of pleasure itself, or else something the experience of which is pleasurable. Clearly, if the chief result of music that was both impressive and, say, anguished was the arousal of such a "musical emotion," there would be little difficulty in understanding how such music could be enjoyable.

There is, however, little else to be said for the view that appreciative response to music consists of but one type of emotion, a music-specific, invariably pleasant one. The effects of different sorts of music are too different from one another, and too reminiscent of life emotions, for this view to carry much plausibility. Our manifest interest in a multiplicity of musical works and experiences begins to seem puzzling if the primary benefit to be derived from any or all of them is this selfsame "musical emotion." It just is not the case that all good or impressive music induces a single positive emotion in listeners.

This is not to say that there could not be something specifically musical, and perhaps unduplicatable, in the experience of a particular piece of music. The total experience—perceptual, emotional, cognitive—of listening to a given work may indeed be unique to it, and this fact is not without aesthetic relevance.[5] But one can maintain that without adopting the

---

[4] Gurney's chief work, *The Power of Sound*, was published in 1880.
[5] See, on this, my "Aesthetic Uniqueness," in *Music, Art, and Metaphysics* (Ithaca: Cornell University Press, 1990), especially p. 132, n. 25.

hypothesis of an invariant and specifically musical emotional element in each such experience.

III

Another approach to our paradox is implicit in some reflections on music by the composer Paul Hindemith. Hindemith denies that music has an emotional effect on listeners, properly speaking. One of his main reasons for this denial seems to be the rapidity with which the typical musical composition changes its emotional character, coupled with a reasonable assumption of emotional inertia on the part of human beings. Hindemith believes that because a person cannot change emotional states as quickly as music changes its expression, it is implausible to think the music is evocative of real emotion in him.

> There is no doubt that listeners, performers, and composers alike can be profoundly moved by perceiving, performing, or imagining music, and consequently music must touch on something in their emotional life that brings them into this state of excitation. But if these mental reactions were feelings, they could not change as rapidly as they do, and they would not begin and end with the musical stimulus that aroused them. . . . Real feelings need a certain interval of time to develop, to reach a climax, and to fade out again; but reactions to music may change as fast as musical phrases do, they may spring up in full intensity at any given moment and disappear entirely when the musical pattern that provokes them ends or changes.[6]

Instead of emotions themselves, Hindemith claims that musical passages evoke in the listener merely memories or images of emotions that the listener has experienced in the past. It follows that there can be no emotional reaction to music that is not strongly rooted in emotional experience in life. On Hindemith's view listening to music becomes an occasion for a selective tour of one's gallery of emotional remembrances, with some sonata or symphony functioning as guide.

The musicologist Deryck Cooke offered two replies to Hindemith's remarks that are worth recalling.[7] The first is that even admitting a certain inertia in the average person's emotional responsiveness, the rapid changes of character from passage to passage in a musical work do not

[6] Paul Hindemith, *A Composer's World* (New York: Doubleday, 1961), pp. 44–45.
[7] Deryck Cooke, *The Language of Music* (London: Oxford University Press, 1959), chap. 1.

themselves ensure that no emotions are raised in the course of it, for we need not assume that such reactions come abruptly to an end when the passages that stimulate them are over. According to Cooke, the response elicited by a passage will often linger and develop after the passage is no longer heard, instead of being entirely obliterated or erased by succeeding passages or completion of the piece.

Second, Cooke very plausibly maintains that our reactions to music cannot all consist of memory images of prior experiences, since it appears that music (some music) has the power to make us feel in ways that we simply have not felt before. The feeling raised in me by certain hearings of the finale of Schumann's Piano Concerto was distinct from any I had encountered in ordinary life before those hearings. It may have been related in complex ways to particular prior experiences of mine, but it was clearly not equivalent to a memory replay of them either singly or collectively.

Furthermore, if what we can neutrally call a *sadness reaction* to sad music typically consisted of some memory image of a particular earlier sadness, it seems we would generally be conscious while listening of the particulars of that occasion—the time, place, object, and reasons of it. But we are not. Listeners' capacities for feeling sadness from music will be exercised and deepened by their experiences of sadness in life, to be sure, but there is little reason to think either that listeners could not possibly be saddened by music if they had not been saddened outside of music or, more important, that their sadness reactions could only be the recollection of particular experiences of sadness in their pasts.

Two other observations on Hindemith's remarks are in order with respect to the problem of negative emotional response in music. First, if it is doubtful whether the listener's response to varied, swiftly changing musical works can be a coherently emotional one, we can focus attention instead on extended parts or sections thereof which are emotionally relatively homogeneous. There is certainly enough time in the course of the *Eroica's* sustained *Marcia funebre* to build up a substantial feeling of grief leavened with little else. Our paradox remains even if only a small number of compositions have sufficient continuity and depth to elicit properly these ostensibly undesirable affects.

Second, even were Hindemith right that emotional response to music is simply a matter of the reviving of old emotions in memory, this would not really dispel the paradox of why we should desire to hear music that revives memories that are of negative emotional experiences. If it is puzzling that one should want to be *made* sad, it is only a little less puzzling that one should want to *remember* particular occasions of having been sad. For memories of sad occasions are often sad themselves; that is to say, summoning them up often reawakens the sadness they encode. Memories are not only records, but repositories as well: to revive a memory of sadness is often in part to relive that sadness. As has been observed, experiential memories standardly preserve and transmit the affective tone of the original experience.[8]

Thus we will no more find a solution to our puzzle in Hindemith's hypothesis than in Gurney's.

IV

In order to discuss certain other approaches to our problem we must pursue the analysis of emotion somewhat further. It is by now orthodoxy among philosophers of mind that emotions are more than simply states of inner feeling.[9] Although there is not absolute accord on what all the components of an emotion are, and on which, if any, are essential to the emotion, most writers agree at least that emotions contain a *cognitive* component in addition to an *affective* one. This may be expressed in the form of a belief, attitude, desire, or evaluation, focused on and identifying the *object* of the emotion. Thus if one is afraid, one feels a certain (rather unpleasant) way, and feels that way *toward* some object that one believes to be dangerous and wants to avoid. If one hopes, one feels a certain (rather more pleasant) way, and feels that way *about* some situation that one believes may possibly obtain, and that one desires to obtain. The presence of an intentional object on which thought and feeling are directed, then, is taken as central to the paradigm of an emotion.

In addition to affective and cognitive components, a case can be made that emotions have *behavioral* and *physiological* components as well. Being afraid may typically involve cowering, shaking, or the like, and perhaps necessarily a tendency or disposition to flee in the presence of the feared object. Being afraid may require, in addition to anything one is subjectively experiencing, a certain state of the endocrine or circulatory systems.

[8] See Richard Wollheim, "On Persons and Their Lives," in *Explaining Emotions*, ed. Amélie O. Rorty (Berkeley and Los Angeles: University of California Press, 1980), pp. 299–321.

[9] See the discussions in William Alston, "Emotion and Feeling," in *The Encyclopedia of Philosophy*, ed. Paul Edwards (New York: Macmillan, 1967); Georges Rey, "Functionalism and the Emotions," in *Explaining Emotions*; Moreland Perkins, "Emotion and Feeling," *Philosophical Review* 75 (1966); Patricia S. Greenspan, "Ambivalence and the Logic of Emotion," in *Explaining Emotions*; and Malcolm Budd, "The Repudiation of Emotion: Hanslick on Music," *British Journal of Aesthetics* 20 (1980). The first two essays include extended analysis of the concept of an emotion, and I am particularly indebted to them for some distinctions employed in this essay.

Concerning the *affective* component—that part of an emotion which consists in what one *feels* in a narrow sense—there is some question as to how this should be conceived. On one view, the affective component of emotion consists in a certain overall coloring of consciousness, a certain quality of inner feeling, of which pleasurable/painful is an important, though not the only, dimension. On another view, the affective component is simply a set of internal sensations of bodily changes—for example, sensations of lumps in the throat, goosebumps on the skin, churnings in the stomach, and tension across muscles of the head. I am inclined to think that the feeling component of emotion is best understood as involving both sorts of things. I will accordingly refer to these, respectively, as the *phenomenological* and the *sensational* aspects of the affective, or feeling, component of an emotion.

It is time to say clearly that the standard emotional response to a musical work—for example, what I have called a sadness reaction—is not in truth a case of *full-fledged* emotion. This is mainly because music neither supplies an appropriate object for an emotion to be directed on nor generates the associated beliefs, desires, or attitudes regarding an object that are essential to an emotion being what it is. When a symphonic adagio "saddens" me, I am not sad at or about the music, nor do I regard the adagio as something I would wish to be otherwise. Furthermore, this weakening of the cognitive component in emotional response to music generally results in the inhibition of most characteristic behaviors and in the significant lessening of behavioral tendencies.

Yet the purely physiological and, more important, affective components are occasionally, it seems, retained in something like full force. If music inevitably fails to induce by itself a proper, contextually embedded *emotion* of sadness, still, some music appears fully capable of inducing at least the characteristic *feeling* of sadness.[10] This is enough, I take it, for the problem of negative emotional response to music to resist complete solution by any of the proposals shortly to be considered. I shall have occasion to distinguish between *emotions* (including cognitive elements) and associated *feelings* (lacking cognitive elements) in what follows. And when I speak subsequently of "emotional response" to music, this should be understood as an experience produced in a listener which is *at least* the

[10] It is helpful to keep in mind here a distinction between the *inducing* and the *reviving* of emotions. Music does not by itself normally induce full-fledged emotions, but it can sometimes revive ones had earlier so that they are reexperienced—beliefs, desires, feelings, and all. (More often it will simply *recall* such emotions, i.e., revive the memory of them.) But the objects and cognitive contents of revived emotions will have been supplied on earlier, usually nonmusical, occasions.

characteristic feeling of some emotion, but which is short of a complete emotion per se.

I am going to assume for the purposes of this essay that the majority of common emotions have affective components (comprising both phenom-enological and sensational aspects) that are more or less distinctive of them, apart from the cognitive components that are perhaps logically distinctive of them. That is to say, I will assume that there are introspectible differences between common emotions. Some evidence for this is provided by cases in which persons suddenly realize that they are sad, happy, depressed, anxious, in love, and so on, without recognizing explicitly that they harbor certain beliefs, desires, or evaluations, and thus apparently on the basis of quality of feeling. Granted, there is psychological research that appears to suggest that common emotions are not much differentiated in inner feeling or affect, but that research strikes me as inconclusive, as well as somewhat questionable in method.[11] In any event, it is undeniable that negative affect is integrally involved in a number of emotional conditions, and that there is at least some range of qualitative difference in affect across the spectrum of negative emotions. The persistence of our problem and the viability of certain answers to it that we shall entertain actually require nothing more than that.

V

Those who are skeptical of the claim that music often induces familiar emotions in listeners sometimes maintain that what is induced is neither one special aesthetic emotion nor memory images of past emotions but instead musical *analogs* of the familiar emotions of life. There are two questions that arise here. One is the respects in which these music-emotions differ from ordinary emotions. The second is the respects in which they are the same and which presumably justify calling them by a common name.

John Hospers, in a well-known essay on expression in art, suggests that the emotional response to sad music is indeed not real sadness but only music sadness. Here is Hospers's explication of this phenomenon:

---

[11] I have in mind the well-known paper by S. Schacter and J. E. Singer, "Cognitive, Social and Physiological Determinants of Emotional State," *Psychological Review* 69 (1962). Schacter and Singer's paper barely recognizes the possibility of an affective component in emotional states distinct from that of purely physiological arousal and, further, is mainly concerned to establish the necessity of cognitive components in emotion, rather than their sufficiency.

Sadness expressed in music is a very different thing from sadness in life; it is only by a kind of analogy that we use the same word for both. . . . Sadness in music is depersonalized; it is taken out of or abstracted from, the particular personal situation in which we ordinarily feel it, such as the death of a loved one or the shattering of one's hopes. In music we get what is sometimes called the "essence" of sadness without all the accompanying accidents, or causal conditions which usually bring it into being. In view of this, it is said, we can continue to say that music expresses sadness, but we should distinguish the *music-sadness*, which is a happy experience, from *life-sadness*, which is not.[12]

We may interpret Hospers as saying that music sadness feels (narrow sense) like life sadness but (1) lacks an object or situational context, and (2) lacks the usual causal conditions of sadness. What it has in common with life sadness, then, is presumably a certain mode of feeling, possibly lessened in intensity, and certain underlying physiological disturbances.

It is not obvious that the invocation of music emotions—muted, objectless analogs of life emotions—is of itself any help in understanding why negative emotional response in music should be so sought after. The prick of a needle hurts less than the stab of a knife, but it is not for that reason to be desired. One would not go out of one's way to have it administered, even if all consciousness of perpetrating agent, physical environment, and lasting effect were eliminated. The appeal to weaker, cognitively impoverished forms of the normal negative emotions faces the following dilemma: If music αness involves the same mode of inner feeling as life αness, however muted in strength, then its prima facie unpleasantness would seem to make it something to avoid. On the other hand, if music αness and life αness involve different modes of inner feeling, then it becomes unclear what connection there is between them at all, and unconvincing that emotional response in music consists in something so wholly unrelated to the ordinary emotion by which we are disposed to denominate it. In short, if there is such a thing as music sadness, resembling life sadness and evoked by sad music, it has not yet been shown how this can be a "happy experience."

Another suggestion worth considering here is that when we are "saddened" by music we are not made really sad but only make-believedly so.[13] That is to say, music raises certain states of feeling in us, which we

[12] Hospers, "The Concept of Artistic Expression," p. 152. In this paragraph Hospers is considering evocation theories of expression, and so the assumption that expression equals evocation is in effect.

[13] A suggestion like this might be drawn from Kendall Walton, "Fearing Fictions," *Journal of Philosophy* 75 (1978): 5–27.

then make-believe to be emotions in the full sense, by supplying ourselves the requisite cognitive filling out.

Our response to the previous suggestion would seem to apply here as well. If the feeling component of, say, make-believe anger were the same as that of real anger, then given its unpleasant tone, it is unclear why make-believe anger should be any more pursued than real anger. Why should make-believing that I am angry, given an appropriate state of inner agitation, provide me with satisfaction? Furthermore, to the extent that the make-believe is effective, the more distressed I would seem to become, imagining not only that I felt (narrowly) a certain unpleasant way but that all the undesirable life consequences and accompaniments of being truly angry were also in the offing.

Furthermore, I am skeptical that in the cases we are interested in, those of deep emotional response to music, we in fact standardly make-believe that we are truly possessed of various emotions, at least if this requires our doing so in an explicit and determinate manner. Our imaginative responses to music, it seems, are typically not so definite as that. When we are "saddened" by sad music, or "frightened" by fearful music, we generally do not make-believe that there is a particular object, with particular characteristics, for us to be sad about or frightened of. Nor do we make-believe that we have certain attitudes or desires toward such determinate intentional objects.

In other words, emotional response to music does not have the same degree of cognitive structure as emotional response to well-delineated entities of fictional worlds. To maintain otherwise is to exaggerate the extent to which listeners intellectually augment their basic affective responses to music. On the other hand, this is not to deny that a listener may, in a less concrete way, imaginatively assume an emotional state in virtue of identifying with music that is engaging him. I shall return to this point in section VIII.

VI

Another possible way around the question of emotional response to music, and thus around the problem of negative emotion in music, is to claim that the appearance of emotional response is simply a well buttressed illusion, founded on a confusion between perceiving and feeling. The proper aesthetic response to music, it will be said, is a purely *cognitive* one, consisting in, among other things, the recognition and appreciation of emotional qualities in music. What occasionally seems to us to be the experiencing of something like sorrow, while listening in anything like a correct manner, is in fact always only the vivid grasping of sorrowfulness in music.

I regard this line as highly implausible. Of course, the exclusively cognitive response to expression in music is a possible mode of aesthetic involvement—the detached, critical mode of the auditory connoisseur. To be sure, one can detect expression without being moved, and one can come to understand a work's moods without necessarily mirroring them. But the detached mode of involvement is just one mode among several that can be adopted, and is hardly the only aesthetically recommendable one. Its aesthetic superiority over a more open and inclusive mode of involvement—in which one both registers *and* reacts to emotion in music—is at least questionable.

Responding emotionally to music is clearly consistent with perceiving emotional qualities in it. But what is more, these activities may be subtly interdependent ones. What we seem to perceive influences what we feel, and what we feel influences what we say we perceive. On the one hand, part of what inclines us to describe a quality of music with a given emotional term is a sense of what emotion the music tends to evoke in us; but on the other hand, part of the reason we have an emotional reaction to music is perception of a corresponding emotional quality in it, provisionally identified on the basis of physiognomic resemblance—analogy to expressive behavior—or conventional associations. We are saddened in part by perception of a quality in a passage that we construe as sadness, but we in part denominate that quality "sadness," or confirm such denomination of it, in virtue of being saddened by the music or sensing its capacity to sadden us under somewhat different conditions. Recognizing emotion in music and experiencing emotion from music may not be as separable in principle as one might have liked. If this is so, the suggestion that in aesthetic appreciation of music we simply cognize emotional attributes without feeling anything corresponding to them may be conceptually problematic as well as empirically incredible.

VII

Nelson Goodman, certainly, does not make the error of representing the perception of expression in music as an emotionless undertaking. On the contrary, he emphasizes the role of feeling as an essential aid in determining what expressive properties a work actually has. In his now familiar words, "In aesthetic experience the emotions function cognitively."[14]

---

[14] Nelson Goodman, *Languages of Art* (Indianapolis: Bobbs-Merrill, 1968), p. 248.

Their chief role is to inform us about the character of the works we are involved with.

But can this by itself explain the attraction that negative music has for us? Goodman tells us that "in aesthetic experience, emotion positive or negative is a mode of sensitivity to a work."[15] The value of despairing or sorrowing response to music, then, is that it is requisite to our correctly discerning the emotional qualities of the music. So by this account we let ourselves in for often considerable distress solely in order to learn accurately the characteristics of the object that is tormenting us. What seems puzzling is why we should be so committed to ascertaining the properties of works of art that put us in unpleasant states. Do we have a duty to all artistic objects to discern their characters correctly, whatever the cost? Surely not. Does the cognitive reward we derive from perceiving rightly that a movement is, say, anguished outweigh the anguish we may feel in the course of that perception? It would not seem so. Getting to know a work's dark qualities may be a partial justification for suffering from it, but it cannot be the whole story. Two things in particular seem insufficiently explained. One is the depth to which we often want to feel negative emotion in music, beyond what could plausibly be required as an assist to cognitive assessment; the other is the fact that the Goodmanian observation, as far as it goes, accounts more for the instrumental value than for the peculiar desirability of negative emotion from music.

VIII

In this section I shall describe more fully what I take the typical strong emotional response to music to consist in. Sketching the outline of this experience in greater detail will aid us in determining what value it has that has not been adequately explained on any of the perspectives canvassed in the preceding section. I begin by stating the conditions of listening that conduce to a response of this kind. For clearly not every hearing of an emotionally powerful work will affect a listener in that way, nor would one want it to. The first condition would seem to be that a work be in a familiar style, and that the work itself be rather familiar to the listener, so that its specific flow and character have been registered internally, but not so familiar that there is any measurable boredom in hearing it unfold on the given occasion. This occurs when a piece is well known

[15] Ibid., p. 250.

though not tiresome, when expectations are firmly aroused in the course of it but denouements remain uncertain.[16]

The second condition is generally taken to be central to the "aesthetic attitude" on any defensible account of that frame of mind. And that is a mode of attention closely focused on the music, its structure, progression, and emergent character, with a consequent inattention to, or reduced consciousness of, the extramusical world and one's present situation in it.

A third condition is one of emotional openness to the content of music, as opposed to distant contemplation of the same. One must be willing to identify with music, to put oneself in its shoes. One must allow oneself to be moved in a receptive manner by the emotion one hears, as opposed to merely noting or even marveling at it.

Such a listener is not, however, moved straight into a slough of feelings and as a result into oblivion of the music itself. On the contrary, deep emotional response to music typically arises as a product of the most intense musical perception. It is generally in virtue of the *recognition* of emotions expressed in music, or of emotion-laden gestures embodied in musical movement, that an emotional reaction occurs.[17] Usually what happens is of an *empathetic*, or *mirroring*, nature. When we identify with music that we are perceiving—or perhaps better, with the person whom we imagine owns the emotions or emotional gestures we hear in the music—we share in and adopt those emotions as our own, for the course of the audition.[18] And so we end up feeling as, in imagination, the music does. The point to note here about this phenomenon is that cognition is central to it. If I

---

[16] An interesting account of the point of "optimum appreciation" for a musical work, from an information-theoretical perspective, can be found in Leonard Meyer, "On Rehearing Music," in *Music, the Arts, and Ideas* (Chicago: University of Chicago Press, 1967), pp. 42–53.

[17] Here I leave out of account, for simplicity, the extent to which identification of emotional expression in music and evocation of feeling by music may be mutually dependent (this was touched on in section VI).

[18] Of course, it is possible to have an emotional response to music that is not *empathetic* but rather *reactive* in nature. Instead of identifying with music, we may just react directly to a quality the music is literally possessed of, or we may imaginatively regard music as an other and react to it from the outside, instead of equating ourselves with it emotionally. Examples of the former sort would be amusement at humorous music, indignation at plagiaristic music, annoyance at badly constructed music. In such response the music serves not only as the cause but as the proper object of the emotion aroused. Examples of the latter sort would be a fearful response to a threatening passage imaginatively taken to be a threatening individual, or a pitying response to an agonized passage that one imaginatively regards as a person in agony. To deal further with reactive emotional responses to music would take us too far afield. It should be obvious, however, that some of these responses pose the same problem of negative emotion in music as empathetic ones when they are ostensibly unpleasant in feeling tone.

don't perceive what emotions are in the music by attending to it intently, I have nothing to properly identify and empathize with.[19]

Now, what I am maintaining is simply that when the three conditions I have listed are fulfilled, then for certain musical compositions there is often an empathetic emotional response that consists in something very like experience of the emotion expressed in the music. As noted earlier, this experience includes at its core the characteristic physiological disturbances of the emotion and its characteristic inner affect. The crucial falling-off from bona fide emotion occurs in the cognitive dimension; music emotions lack objects and associated thoughts about them.

This is not to say, however, that emotional responses to music have *no* cognitive (or thoughtlike) component. They do, but it is etiolated by comparison to that of real-life emotion. Say the emotion expressed in the music is sadness. Then in an empathetic response, in addition to physiological and affective elements, there is, in the first place, the general *idea* of sadness. Because a listener is standardly made sad by apprehending and then identifying with sadness in the music, the thought of that emotion will generally be present to the mind concurrent with whatever is felt. In the second place, identifying with the music involves initially the cognitive act of imagining that the music either is *itself* a sad individual or else is the *audible expression* of somebody's sadness. In the third place, such identification involves subsequently a cognitive act of imagining that one, too, is sad—that it is *one's own* sadness the music expresses—and thus, however amorphously, that one has something to be sad about.

Let us look at this last phase more closely. When one hears sad music, begins to feel sad, and imagines that one is actually sad, one must, according to the logic of the concept, be imagining that there is an object for one's sadness and that one holds certain evaluative beliefs or attitudes regarding it. The point, though, is that this latter imagining generally remains *indeterminate*. That is to say, one does not actually imagine a particular object for one's sadness and does not imaginarily hold beliefs about it. In imagining that I have actually become sad in virtue of hearing some music I allow only that my feeling has *some* focus, but without going on to specify this any further. In other words, the object of an empathetic sadness response to music is a largely formal one. When through identification with music I am saddened by the *Poco allegretto* of Brahms's

---

[19] There is, naturally, much more that could be said to fill in the basic picture of how affective response to music is generated. For a description of the mirroring response to emotional characteristics in music, see Stephen Davies, "The Expression of Emotion in Music," *Mind* 89 (1980): 67–86. On the mechanism of identifying with music, see the discussion in R. K. Elliott, "Aesthetic Theory and the Experience of Art," in *Aesthetics*, ed. H. Osborne (Oxford: Oxford University Press, 1972), pp. 145–57.

Third Symphony, my "sadness" is not directed on the music, or on any real-life situation of concern to me, but instead on some featureless object posited vaguely by my imagination.[20]

Summing up, then, empathetic emotional responses to music of the sort we are interested in—the sort that our anecdotal hero underwent at the beginning of this essay—typically comprise the following: physiological and affective components of the emotion that is embodied in the music; the idea or thought of this emotion; and the imagination, through identification with the music, of oneself as actually experiencing this emotion, though without the usual determinateness of focus.

IX

We are now, I think, in a fair position to offer explanations of the appeal of negative emotional response to music, the nature of which I have been trying to make clear. I begin by acknowledging two contributions to a complete answer that emerge from views mentioned earlier. The first is the Goodmanian observation that emotional response facilitates our grasp, assessment, and description of the expression in a musical work. This is doubtless true, and even if it can hardly account totally for our willingness to suffer negative emotion from a sonata, neither should it be ignored.

The second is the Aristotelian element of catharsis. Surely in some circumstances the virtue of, say, a grief response to music is that it allows one to bleed off in a controlled manner a certain amount of harmful emotion with which one is afflicted. One "grieves" while listening, in a pure and limited way, thus purging oneself to some extent of real grief that one has either been consciously yielding to, in typical unruly fashion, or else has been suppressing in the oubliettes of the unconscious. From a cathartic perspective, negative emotional response to music is desirable because it conduces to mental health, improving the listener's future self by administering momentarily painful doses of emotional medicine in the present. There seems no denying that dark music can be therapeutic in this way; the thing to notice, though, is that the cathartic explanation applies strictly to listeners currently in the grip of unhealthy emotions, whether on a conscious or unconscious level. Yet it seems that negative emotional response has appeal for, and offers rewards to, listeners for

---

[20] It might be suggested that the imagined object of my sadness is just whatever is the object of the sadness of the sad person "in the music" with whom I am identifying. I think this may sometimes be so, but it does not really affect the matter of indeterminacy I am addressing, for this object, too, remains completely unspecified or only formally indicated.

whom this is not the case. I may seek out and relish grief, longing, and anguish from music when I am neither overwrought by these emotions nor occupied by them in subterranean fashion. Furthermore, just the raising of such emotions seems to provide satisfaction prior to any siphoning off that may ultimately ensue. Cathartic benefits, while occasionally very real, seem too indirect and prudential to be the whole or even the largest part of why we crave the experience of negative emotion from music.

X

The first point to be noted in arriving at the more comprehensive solution we seek is that emotional response to music and emotion in ordinary life differ in one crucial and obvious respect, connected to the attenuation of cognitive content in the former. Emotional responses to music typically *have no life implications*, in contrast to their real counterparts. The "sadness" one may be made to feel by sympathetically attending to music has no basis in one's extramusical life, signals no enduring state of negative affect, indicates no problem requiring action, calls forth no persisting pattern of behavior, and in general bodes no ill for one's future. One does not really believe—though one may intermittently imagine—that one's sadness response is objectively apt, that some situation exists in one's life that is to be bemoaned. On the other hand, if one is truly sad one must believe this, and will, accordingly, both expect one's feeling to persist until objective conditions are changed and be disposed to take action to remedy one's unhappy state. The person having a sadness response to music is generally free, however, from this expectation and disposition. The experience of sadness from music consists primarily of a feeling under a conception, but bracketed from and unfettered by the demands and involvements of the corresponding emotion in life.

Because negative emotional response to music is devoid of the contextual implications of emotions such as sadness, grief, and anger, we are able to focus more fully on just the feeling involved in these emotions. This opens the way for three benefits that we may reap by allowing ourselves to mirror darkly emotional music. These are benefits of enjoyment, of understanding, and of self-assurance.

To make out the first requires a somewhat startling claim, but it is one without which we cannot, I think, wholly resolve the paradox we have been addressing. This claim is that emotive affect itself, divorced from all psychological and behavioral consequences, is in virtually all cases something that we are capable of taking satisfaction in. That is to say, the pure feeling component of just about any emotion, providing it is not too violent or intense, is something we can, on balance, enjoy experiencing.

When feelings are made available to us isolated, backgroundless, and inherently limited in duration—as they are through music—we can approach them as if we were wine tasters, sampling the delights of various vintages, or like Des Esseintes, the hero of Huysmans's *À rebours*, reveling in the flavors conveyed by a mouth organ fitted with a variety of liqueurs. We become cognoscenti of feeling, savoring the qualitative aspect of emotional life for its own sake.

This is not to say that the pure feeling has nothing unpleasant about it. If in itself it did not possess a negative tone it could hardly count as the feeling of some negative emotion. But in the detached context of musical response, it becomes possible for us to savor the feeling for its special character, since we are for once spared the additional distress that accompanies its occurrence in the context of life. The characteristic feeling at the core of, say, grief or despair has an irreducibly painful aspect, to be sure, but the distastefulness and undesirability of the emotion as a whole springs at least as much from the beliefs involved in it regarding the real existence of an evil and the consequent persistence of negative affect. An uncomfortable state that we know will not last and that testifies to no fault in our world does not pain us as it would if we had no such assurance. It is not so much the resulting feeling that we mind in grief or despair as the *significance* of that feeling, which is carried by the associated beliefs or attitudes. When these are absent, as in emotional response to music, we find ourselves able to a large extent to appreciate feelings, even negatively toned feelings, for themselves. We relish the particular qualities of such feelings to a degree sufficient to compensate us for the element of painfulness they still contain. The undistracted experience of affects of just about any sort, when free of practical consequence, appears to have intrinsic appeal for many of us. I will label this the reward of savoring feeling.

The second reward attaching to negative emotional response to music in virtue of its contextual freedom is that of greater understanding of the condition of feeling involved in some recognized emotion. It is notoriously difficult to say what the knowledge of how an emotion feels consists in, but I think it is clear that such knowledge, whatever it amounts to, can be augmented by emotional experiences during or after occasions of music listening. At such times we have an opportunity to introspectively scrutinize and ponder the inner affective dimension of an emotion—say, anguish—whose idea is before the mind, in a manner not open to the individual who is caught in the throes of real anguish. We can attain insight into what the feeling of anguish is *like*, not in the sense that we learn what it resembles, but in the sense that we perceive and register it more clearly. This in turn cashes out in an improved ability to recognize and to recollectively contemplate this feeling in the future. One can deepen or reinforce one's image of what it is to feel melancholy by experiencing the *Poco allegretto* of Brahms's Third, or of what it is to feel hopeless passion by responding to Scriabin's C♯-minor Etude. Note, finally, that the cognitive reward attested to here, that of understanding feeling, is distinct from, though not unrelated to, the Goodmanian one mentioned earlier, that of apprehending expression.

The third of these rewards relates directly to a person's self-respect or sense of dignity as a human being. Central to most people's ideal image of themselves is the capacity to feel deeply a range of emotions. We like to think of ourselves as able to be stirred profoundly, and in various ways, by appropriate occurrences. The individual whose emotional faculty is inactive, shallow, or one-dimensional seems to us less of a person. Because music has the power to put us into the feeling state of a negative emotion without its unwanted life consequences, it allows us to partly reassure ourselves in a nondestructive manner of the depth and breadth of our ability to feel. Having a negative emotional response to music is like giving our emotional engines a "dry run." If there is something amiss with the plane it is better to find this out on the runway than in the air. Although one would not opt to try on real grief just to see if one were capable of it, confirmation of this of a sort can perhaps be had less riskily by involvement with music. Whether such confirmation can legitimately be had in this way is not clearly to the point; for even if it is epistemically flawed, its psychological effect is real enough. Furthermore, in exercising our feeling capacities on music we might be said to tone them up, or get them into shape, thus readying ourselves for intenser and more focused reactions to situations in life. It is worth noting that this reward of emotional response to music is more naturally associated with negative than with positive emotions. It is usually not emotions like joy, amusement, or excitement that we have a need of proving ourselves equal to and prepared for feeling, and it is generally not the ability to feel those emotions that has the most weight in the common idea of an emotionally developed individual. Call this the reward of emotional assurance.

XI

So far we have reckoned up certain rewards of negative emotional response to music that accrue to it regarded as an experience of pure feeling concurrent with the mere idea of a corresponding emotion. We must now turn to the rewards of imagining, through identification, that one is in the full emotional condition, while knowing throughout that one is not.

These are collectively as important as the rewards already considered. There seem to be at least three of them, which I will address in turn. The first is of special relevance to the paradox we have been concerned with, because it, unlike the other rewards, attaches most transparently to negative, as opposed to positive, emotional response to music.[21]

If I empathetically experience feelings of despair or anguish from a despairing or anguished piece of music and also regard the music as the unfolding expression of someone's despair or anguish, then I may begin to identify with that someone and consequently to imagine, in a fashion described earlier, that I myself am in actual despair or anguish. I may even have the impression that I am generating the music de profundis as an expression of the despair or anguish that I imagine I am now experiencing. In any case, because my imagined emotion is one with that of the music's persona, it will partake in the destiny and vicissitudes of that emotion as conveyed by the development of the music.

Because I have identified my emotional state with that expressed in the music, I can feel that what seems to happen to that emotion in the course of the music is happening to me as well. And this, because of the way in which emotional content is carried by musical structure, is often a source of satisfaction, especially where unpleasant or difficult emotions are involved.

Emotions presented in and imaginatively experienced through music, unlike those encountered in real life, have a character of inevitability, purposiveness, and finality about them. This is undoubtedly because they seem so intimately connected with the progress of musical substance itself as to be inseparable from it. Thus what primarily or initially characterizes musical movement or development comes to seem, as well, an attribute of the emotional content it underpins. Emotion in a musical composition, because of its construction, so often strikes us as having been resolved, transformed, transfigured, or triumphed over when the music is done.

When the first, C-minor section of Brahms's *Poco allegretto* gives way smoothly to a trio in A♭ major, we can imagine our sobbing melancholy melting into a mood of hesitant gaiety. When the main material of Beethoven's *Marcia funebre* breaks at midpoint into a stately fugue on the

---

[21] I would in fact claim that a variant of this reward may attach, though less straightforwardly, to emotional responses to expressive progressions in a piece of music of various sorts, not only those in which negative emotions are satisfyingly worked through. But for obvious reasons, it is cases of the latter sort that are most germane to our puzzle.

same themes, we can imagine our bottomless grief as metamorphosed, diffracted into shining fragments of a more easily borne pathos. And when the extended musical logic of the finale of Dvořák's Seventh Symphony eventuates in a dissonant though shortly resolved brass-dominated yawp in the final measures, one can share in its experience of stern tragedy culminating in hard-won, reluctant resignation.

By imaginatively identifying our state with that of the music, we derive from a suitably constructed composition a sense of mastery and control over—or at least accommodation to—emotions that in the extramusical setting are thoroughly upsetting, and over which we hope to be victorious, when and if the time comes. And emotional response, it should be emphasized, seems necessary to reap this benefit. Unless one actually feels something as the music is heard, and projects oneself into its condition, one will not be entitled to think, "That was my emotion, that is how I dealt with it, that is what became of it." This clearly helps compensate us for whatever additional distress derives from allowing in imagination that we are melancholy, despairing, grieving, or the like. Call this the reward of emotional resolution.

The second reward of identifying with music to the point of imagining oneself possessed of real negative emotion is simpler than and in a sense prior to that just discussed. If one begins to regard music as the expression of one's own current emotional state, it will begin to seem as if it issues from oneself, as if it pours forth from one's innermost being.[22] It is then very natural for one to receive an impression of expressive power, of freedom and ease in externalizing and embodying what one feels. The sense one has of the richness and spontaneity with which one's inner life is unfolding itself, even where the feelings involved are of the negative kind, is a source of undeniable joy. The unpleasant aspect of certain emotions we imagine ourselves to experience through music is balanced by the adequacy, grace, and splendor of the exposition we feel ourselves to be according that emotion. Of course we do not really have such expressive ability; that which we seem to ourselves to have while identifying with music is obviously founded in the musical abilities of the composer. But we are not actually deceiving ourselves. We do not literally believe we are creators of music. The composer's musical genius makes possible the imaginative experience described in the preceding, and we can remain aware of that throughout, but this does not take away the resulting satisfaction. The coat may be borrowed, but it is just as warm. Call this the reward of expressive potency.

---

[22] See Elliott, "Aesthetic Theory and the Experience of Art," on the experience of hearing music "from within."

The last reward of imagining negative emotion I will discuss arises most clearly when a listener is willing to entertain what I call the expressionist assumption concerning the emotional content of what he is hearing. According to the expression theory of music, espoused by Tolstoy and Cooke among others, emotion heard in a sonata is always emotion experienced by the composer on an earlier occasion, which has now been transmuted into music. The sonata is a vehicle for conveying a particular sort of emotional experience from one person to another. Now, it seems that without subscribing to the obviously inadequate expression theory itself, we may sometimes as listeners adopt the expressionist assumption—that the emotion expressed in a particular piece belongs to its composer's biography—while imagining ourselves to be possessed of the full emotion whose feeling has been aroused within us. If we do so we are in effect imagining that we are sharing in the precise emotional experience of another human being, the man or woman responsible for the music we hear. This, as Tolstoy so well appreciated, carries with it a decided reward—the reward of intimacy—which accrues whether the emotion is positive or negative in tone. The sense of intimate contact with the mind or soul of another, the sense that one is clearly not alone in the emotional universe, goes some way toward counterbalancing the possibly distressing aspect of the grief, sorrow, or anger one imagines oneself to have. The emotional separateness and alienation that are a common phenomenon of daily life are here miraculously swept aside in imaginative identification with the composer whose feelings are—given that the expressionist assumption is in force—plainly revealed for the listener to hear and to mirror. Call this the reward of emotional communion.[23]

XII

In this section I address a charge sometimes levied against concern with evocation of emotion by music.[24] It has been said that an interest in music for the emotional experiences it can induce cannot be an aesthetic interest. For to have an aesthetic interest in music is to be interested in it for its own sake, in all its concrete and particular detail, and not as an instrument to some further end. One must be interested in a musical composition *itself*, so that no other object, musical or nonmusical, would serve as

---

[23] The eight rewards identified are thus these: (1) apprehending expression, (2) emotional catharsis, (3) savoring feeling, (4) understanding feeling, (5) emotional assurance, (6) emotional resolution, (7) expressive potency, and (8) emotional communion.

[24] This is particularly well formulated in Malcolm Budd, "The Repudiation of Emotion," pp. 39–41.

well, even though it induced the very same emotional state. Otherwise put, the specific composition must be *integral* to aesthetic appreciation of it, and not in principle replaceable by anything that provided approximately the same effects.

I have some doubt whether this position as to the necessary character of aesthetic interest is ultimately defensible. But that aside, I want to consider to what extent an interest in music for the negative emotional response it can occasion can be construed so as to qualify as aesthetic by these lights—so that, in particular, the specific piece of music involved can be seen to have an ineliminable role in the resulting experience.

If we consider the eight rewards of negative emotional response I have detailed, we may note first that three of them—apprehending expression, emotional resolution, and expressive potency—inherently involve attention to specific musical substance concurrently with any feelings that are aroused. For it is manifest that one cannot categorize the emotion in a passage, hear one's emotion transmuted in the course of a development section, or glory in the power and richness of one's expression of emotion in sound without attending explicitly to the musical matter of what is before one's ears. The music is not just a means to an end that can be understood apart from it but is integrally involved in that end.

But even with respect to the other five rewards it may be possible for appreciation of emotional response to music to be aesthetic in virtue of the way such response is tied to perception of individual musical form. In we review the total experience of emotion in a musical work we typically find something like this: (1) perception of individual musical form; (2) apprehension of embodied expression; (3) empathetic feeling response to embodied expression; (4) imagination of real emotion on the basis of (3); and last, (5) awareness of how (2), (3), and (4) are rooted in (1). The perceptual part of this experience is irreplaceable; not only is it causally responsible for the affective part, but the relation between them is an object of awareness in its own right. Now, because musical works are perceptually distinct from one another, no other work can have associated with it the same comprehensive experience—the same fusion of evoked emotion with apprehension of musical form and quality, together with awareness of their relation. Thus if this total experience is what we are after, if what we are primarily seeking is emotion embedded in a particular complicated perceptual activity that generates it, then regardless of what further rewards attach to such emotion, our appreciation remains recognizably aesthetic, focused on individual compositions and involving them essentially.

In maintaining an aesthetic interest in music, the apparent extrinsicality of certain of the rewards we derive from evoked feeling is modified if our concern is specifically with those feelings *as communicated by a particular musical structure*. Deriving satisfaction from an emotional reaction seems legitimately aesthetic if one attends to the particular musical entity responsible for it and if appreciation is basically directed on an emotional state as founded in and intertwined with an intricate aural perception. In the aesthetic mode we properly value the specific—though not necessarily unique[25]—shade of feeling a passage evokes through apprehension of its wholly individual note-to-note form, and not just that shade of feeling *simpliciter*, however produced.

The question, though, is how plausible it is to maintain, with respect to the remaining five rewards, that the appreciative focus is this complex I will call the *music-qualified* feeling or emotion—that is, the feeling or (imagined) emotion *as induced by and experienced with* these particular notes—as opposed to the feeling or emotion by itself, apart from that musical environment. The answer, I think, is that it is more plausible for some of our rewards and less so for others.

If I am savoring a bit of objectless sorrowful feeling aroused in me by Albinoni's famous Adagio for Organ and Strings, it may be that I am savoring especially that feeling as emerging from the Adagio's unique strains. And if I commune in imagination with Schubert's psyche by way of the stern determination raised in me by some passages of his late C-minor Piano Sonata, D. 958, it may be that the state I imagine us to share is specifically such determination *as felt in* the sounding of those very measures. So I might, for those rewards, be valuing particularly the music-qualified feeling rather than the feeling in the abstract. And if so, then Albinoni's and Schubert's works are essentially involved in the satisfactions I extract from them; the experience I am specifically valuing is not detachable from the music that provides it.

On the other hand, when it comes to appreciating or valuing feeling evoked by music because of the occasion it offers for either eliminative catharsis, or deeper understanding of what it is like, or increased conviction of one's emotional range, then it appears unlikely that the focus of appreciation or value would be the music-qualified feeling rather than the feeling *simpliciter*. What I want to know better, assure myself about, or purge myself of is just the ordinary feeling, not a perceptually qualified relative of it.

Thus we can reclaim most, though not all, of the rewards of negative emotional response to music from the anteroom of the aesthetic. Whether the others could be redeemed would depend on rethinking or broaden-

---

[25] I do not assume that the emotional content of a musical structure, or the emotional response it induces as a result, must necessarily belong to it alone, for reasons explored in my "Aesthetic Uniqueness."

ing what may properly be included in aesthetic, or at least artistically appropriate, intercourse with works of art. But what should not be lost sight of is that even if some of these rewards are ultimately adjudged non-aesthetic, that would not affect their relevance to the basic problem of this essay, namely, to explain how negative emotional response in the course of normal, if not unadulteratedly aesthetic, interaction with musical works can be valued and desired by listeners.

XIII

Have we now succeeded in rescuing the occupant of the musical "electric chair" with which we began? I think so. We have suggested, first, that although this person is actually registering the feelings of some negative emotions this may, in the circumstances, itself afford a certain satisfaction, and second, that there are a number of more indirect rewards deriving from those feelings and the imagined emotions erected upon them that more than compensate for what disagreeableness we may be inclined to ascribe to the conditions assumed in the course of listening. Those works of Beethoven, Mozart, Brahms, Scriabin, and Mahler do not constitute for aesthetic appreciation a bed of hot coals, to be sure, but neither do they present themselves as merely a display case of mineral specimens, mounted and remote. I hope in this essay to have avoided the errors of both images and to have presented a more balanced picture. Little short of the story I have told, I think, can fully account for why we often seek negative emotion from the art of sound rather than remain content with mere perception, at arm's length, of its musical embodiment.

Postscript, 1996

A. Peter Kivy, in the course of a general attack on music's power to engage the ordinary emotions, holds up "Music and Negative Emotion" at the end to show that he has not been beating a dead horse (*Music Alone* [Ithaca: Cornell University Press, 1990], chap. 8, "How Music Moves"). His main target is the claim that music can, in nonpathological individuals, arouse full-fledged emotions of the ordinary variety. With this, of course, I agree, as Kivy acknowledges. Where we differ, apparently, is on whether anything *like* those emotions—for instance, the feelings characteristic of them—might be raised by music, or whether music's emotional effect on us is exclusively of a different and sui generis order. Kivy maintains the latter; he says that music can move us—by its beauty, perfection, craftsmanship, or even the excellence of its expressiveness—but that this emotion is unrelated to the ordinary emotions that such music might embody.

Now, I am happy to allow that there is a distinctive reaction to the beauty and other artistic virtues of a piece of music, that this kind of reaction is central to aesthetic appreciation of the music, and that, being of the nature of admiration or even exaltation, it can well be qualified as emotional. But I am unwilling to allow that that is *all* there ever is, on the emotional side. Identifying a kind of feeling called "being moved" does nothing to show that *other*, more specific feelings, ones characteristic of the ordinary life emotions, are not sometimes present as well. I have tried, in my essay, to show how those might reasonably come about; via the listener's vivid *imagining* of the emotions in question, courtesy of the music embodying them, and not by the listener's actually *having* those emotions, for the music or anything else. And whereas that latter would be irrational, there is nothing irrational about imagining, say, a real sadness belonging to the music's persona—and then, by extension, to oneself— given the rewards one is then, if I am right, in a position to reap.

Kivy has published, in another place, a full-scale critique of my essay (*Sound Sentiment* [Philadelphia: Temple University Press, 1989], chap. 16, "Formalism and Feeling"); I cannot, however, respond to that critique in this space.

B. Since I have found that "Music and Negative Emotion" has given some readers the impression that I am endorsing an *evocation* (or *arousal*) account of expression, despite my explicit disclaimer to this effect in section I, I think it worth restating my position with respect to music's evocative capacity. One is *saddened* by sad music, let us say, if one is made or led to *feel* a certain way—a way I claim is fairly distinctive of sadness, though that is not the issue at present—and to *imagine*, on that basis, that one is sad or is experiencing sadness. This typically occurs, recall, through an act of empathetic emotional identification with the perceived persona of the music. It was, then, a claim of my essay that listeners are *sometimes* saddened by sad music, and that the state of being saddened is *somewhat like*, and particularly internally, the state of being sad. But it was not my intent to intimate (1) that listeners are *always*, or even usually, saddened by sad music, (2) that music's expressing sadness *consists*, even partly, in its evoking sadness, or (3) that music's expressing sadness is even a matter of its evocative *power*.

C. Much work on emotions relevant to the issues in this essay has appeared since it was written. I would call attention especially to two papers by Stephen Leighton that are sympathetic to and argue for the idea that the standard emotions involve *differing characteristic feelings*: "A New

View of Emotion," *American Philosophical Quarterly* 22 (1985): 133–41, and "On Feeling Angry and Elated," *Journal of Philosophy* 85 (1988): 253–64.

It is a matter of contention, and hard to settle introspectively, whether the different higher, or more complex, emotions—ones such as hope or shame or despair or jealousy, as opposed to, say, sadness, joy, or anger—have distinctive affective (i.e., sensational or phenomenological) components. But I believe it would be rash to say it is unlikely they do. For first, we should take care to consider feelings occurring at the most characteristic, or most intense, phases of such emotions, lest we be too easily convinced that all emotions involve, at one time or another, more or less the same feelings. And second, we should remind ourselves that the fact that, in the main, complex emotions are logically individuated by their cognitive components hardly entails, and doesn't even give good reason for thinking, that their noncognitive components are virtually interchangeable, or of only two or three broad types.

The place of desires or wishes or concerns—what we might call *conative* elements—in a complete account of emotion was insufficiently acknowledged in my essay. It has, however, been rightly emphasized of late by others. (See, e.g., Jenefer Robinson, "Emotion, Judgment and Desire," *Journal of Philosophy* 80 [1983]: 731–41; Ronald de Sousa, *The Rationality of Emotion* [Cambridge, Mass.: MIT Press, 1987]; and Patricia Greenspan, *Emotions and Reasons* [London: Routledge and Kegan Paul, 1988].) I don't believe my conclusions regarding the rewards of negative emotion in music are materially affected by this oversight, but I grant that a fuller picture of what one is imagining about oneself when one is empathetically saddened by sad music would need to recognize more explicitly the conative aspect of emotional states.

D. I have developed further my thoughts on music and emotion in "Hope in *The Hebrides*," in *Music, Art, and Metaphysics* (Ithaca: Cornell University Press, 1990); "Musical Expressiveness," in *The Pleasures of Aesthetics* (Ithaca: Cornell University Press, 1996); and "Emotion in Response to Art: A Survey of the Terrain," in *Emotion and the Arts*, ed. M. Hjort and S. Laver (Oxford: Oxford University Press, 1996). See also Gregory Karl and Jenefer Robinson, "Levinson on Hope in *The Hebrides*," *Journal of Aesthetics and Art Criticism* 53 (1995): 195–99, and my response, "Still Hopeful: Reply to Karl and Robinson," ibid., pp. 199–201.

11

Why Listen to Sad Music
If It Makes One Feel Sad?

Stephen Davies

Why listen to sad music if it makes one feel sad? Let me begin with some assumptions for which I will not argue, though some of them might be regarded as controversial. (1) Some purely instrumental music expresses emotions. (2) These usually are of a rather general character. (3) Music's expressiveness does not consist in its power to move the listener; that is, the expressive qualities of music are distinct from its effect on the listener. (4) Some listeners sometimes are moved, nevertheless, to feel emotions that mirror the expressive character of the music; that is, happy music sometimes induces happiness in the listener, and music expressive of sadness sometimes leads the listener to feel sad.

Now, the problem to be discussed can be stated: if it is sadness that sad music makes people feel, why would they bother to listen to sad music? To put what I take to be a related point: why would one value being made to feel sad?

The Dilemma Posed by the Sad Response

It seems that one is trapped on the horns of a dilemma. If we enjoy the sadness that we claim to feel, then it is not plainly sadness that we are talking of, because sadness is not an enjoyable experience. On the other hand, if the sadness is unpleasant, we would not seek out, as we do, artworks leading us to feel sad. Each horn has been addressed. I review the two sets of arguments in what follows.

How might one argue that the sadness evoked by music is, if not pleasant, then less unpleasant than ordinary, emotional object–directed sadness? It is common to reply that the "negative" response to music is not a full-blown instance of the emotion and, to the extent that it is not full-blown, is not so unpleasant as usually would be the case.[1] Such responses lack "life implications"; they do not involve, for example, the desires or the need to act that would normally be their accompaniments. Much of the unpleasantness attaching to such emotions might usually reside in the actions to which they lead. Jerrold Levinson goes so far as to suggest that their absence might make it possible for us to savor the unpleasant character of our responses; Colin Radford describes music as an "especially inviting" way to experience the somber, indeed tragic aspects of life.[2] A traditional view of aesthetic experience regards it as "distanced," and this distancing is identified as a feature arising from the lack of life implications in the responses aroused. Marcia Eaton identifies another element in aesthetic experience—that of control—as ameliorating negative aspects of emotional responses to artworks.[3] In responding to artworks we are usually in command of our situation, and that provides a security counteracting the unpleasant aspects of our experiences. In ordinary contexts, where so often we lack control of the events with which we are faced, we cannot calm our emotions in the same way. Among the eight reasons offered by Levinson for our acceptance of negative emotions are three appealing to the element of control provided by our imaginative involvement in the work. First, we can imagine the musical expression as that of an anonymous agent and, in doing so, can follow its course and final resolution. This gives us a sense of mastery over, or accommodation with, powerful emotions. Second, we can imagine that the emotions expressed in the music are our own and thereby come to a sense of our possessing the power to express and control emotions. Or third, we can imagine that the emotions expressed in the music are the composer's and thereby achieve a feeling of communion with the emotions of another.[4]

---

[1] For example, Jerrold Levinson accepts that the emotional response is not one of real sadness; he sees the issue as one about whether something like real sadness is experienced. See "Music and Negative Emotion," in this volume.

[2] Colin Radford, "Muddy Waters," *Journal of Aesthetics and Art Criticism* 49 (1991): 247–52.

[3] Marcia M. Eaton, "A Strange Kind of Sadness," *Journal of Aesthetics and Art Criticism* 41 (1982): 51–63.

[4] In these cases, Levinson appears to be talking about our apprehension of the music's expressiveness rather than our own feelings. He does note, however, that there is a problem not only about the negativity of our own response but also in explaining why we should be interested in expressions of negative emotions. These three suggestions seem to be offered as an answer to that second problem rather than to the first.

The detail of these claims deserves critical comment. As Eaton notes, distance might transform an unpleasant experience into a pleasurable one—for example, a fire might seem beautiful rather than terrifying—but it cannot explain away the unpleasantness of a sad response to an artwork, except by showing that the response is not one of sadness at all. But Eaton's own theory, appealing to the notion of control, also looks suspect. As the reader of a novel or member of an audience at a concert, one does not control the course of the artwork. A person's mastery of the situation amounts to the possibility that he might always put down the book or walk out of the concert hall. If he continues to read or listen, though, it seems he does not exercise control of a type that could mute the force of a sad response. The response he feels might not be under his control. Moreover, Eaton's view faces a further problem in seeming to entail the false idea that a person's experience of art would be the more enjoyable if he *could* suppress always the inclination toward negative responses.[5] Finally, Levinson's appeal to self-empowerment through imaginative engagement with the musical work might be queried also. Peter Kivy finds Levinson's approach "fantastic."[6] If we indulge in such imaginings then we are not concentrating on the music (as we should). Levinson anticipates this objection and replies: the problem of negative reactions is posed as much by nonaesthetic as by aesthetically proper reactions. He also questions whether such imaginings are, anyway, aesthetically improper, because the imagination is directed by the work's character. Levinson does not, however, anticipate this objection raised by Kivy: in the cases described by Levinson, the satisfaction comes from the negative emotion's being vanquished during the work and from the sense of power going with that; yet, says Kivy, we do not experience a surge of satisfaction or relief when the work attains its happy conclusion. Thus our experience of responding to music does not fit the model proposed by Levinson. To this I add: not every sad piece ends happily. The problem of explaining why we are interested in works such as Tchaikovsky's Symphony no. 6 or Berg's *Wozzeck* remains.

Despite these reservations about the arguments directed at the first horn of the dilemma, the observation that responses to artworks lack life implications is successful to some extent in showing, if not that the sadness of the response is pleasant, that the sadness is less drastic or dire in its unpleasantness than often is the case for sadness experienced in nonaesthetic situations. Success of this sort must be partial, however. The artistic context of appreciation might strip the emotional response of some of

[5] See Gary Iseminger, "How Strange a Sadness?" *Journal of Aesthetics and Art Criticism* 42 (1983): 81–82.

[6] Peter Kivy, *Sound Sentiment* (Philadelphia: Temple University Press, 1989), pp. 238–54.

its aspects—desires and the need to act on them, the vitality of the feeling tone of the experience, and so on—but it cannot remove altogether the unpleasantness that is in part constitutive of negative emotions. If the baby is not to be thrown out with the bath water, the emotional experience cannot be characterized as a pleasant one, though it might be argued that its unpleasantness is muted by features of the aesthetic context in which the response occurs.

A standard approach to the second horn of the dilemma—why would we bother with artworks if they make us feel sad?—involves arguing that there are benefits to be gained from tolerating negative emotional responses to artworks, and that these benefits outweigh or compensate for that unpleasantness. A first version of the line might be put this way: artworks are a source of knowledge and deep enjoyment, so if they happen also to make us feel sad sometimes, that is a price we might pay willingly for the sake of other values. The obvious difficulty with this version is that it treats the emotional response as incidental, in that the work's value is not described as depending on its expressive character. It implies that the work would be better for its not leading us to feel sad, for the benefits as described do not depend on our feeling sad. Moreover, given the number of worthwhile artworks, the view implies also that we might always pursue the benefits of an interest in art while conscientiously avoiding those works that might make us feel sad. For such reasons this reply to the dilemma's second horn is feeble.

A stronger counter would concede that the value that leads us to seek out artworks making us feel sad depends to some extent on their affecting us in that way, despite the unpleasantness of the response. In Aristotle's view, negative responses to artworks have value through their cathartic effects; they purge our emotions. On the face of it, this view is not attractive. It implies that the value of experiencing such emotions is the relief we feel when the work comes to an end. No doubt the torturer's victim feels enormous, wonderful relief when the torture is ended, but one would hardly regard that as a reason for undergoing torture for its therapeutic consequences. Even if the negative emotions experienced in connection with artworks are muted in their character, it remains unclear why one would seek them out for the sake of catharsis. The answer to criticisms of this sort no doubt depends on the elaboration of the notion of catharsis, so that it is shown to involve more than mere relief from suffering. It may be, for example, that catharsis provides a knowledge not obtainable in any other way. Or it may be that dispositions of a kind that are only rarely exhibited need the outlet art offers. Because such responses arise in a context in which belief and the desires and need to act depending on belief are absent, it is possible to take a reflective attitude toward one's response and thereby to come to a better understanding than otherwise of the general nature of the emotions involved (again, appeal is made here to the lack of "life implications" in the experience). Moreover, the knowledge acquired might have a special significance when gained at first hand; it might have a heuristic value not conveyed by merely "propositional" knowledge. Levinson suggests that negative emotional responses to artworks reassure us of our emotional sensitivity and humanity. Another practical value of such knowledge, perhaps, is that it builds character, or makes us better able to handle emotions in a mature way in other contexts.

Kivy is skeptical of arguments such as these. He doubts, and I agree, that there is much evidence to suggest that those who interest themselves in artworks expressive of sadness, and who claim to respond to such works by feeling sad, have a deeper understanding of emotions than do others, or that they are better able to cope with life's tragedies as a result of their experiences. Accepting (for the sake of the argument) that some people are moved to sadness by sad music, Kivy allows that such experiences might be tolerated for the sake of other benefits, or for the sake of benefits depending in practice on the production of the unpleasant experience itself, but he holds that, though such claims are not thoroughly implausible, they fail to answer the problem adequately. His point, I take it, is one about degrees of plausibility. At best, such arguments explain why one might *resign* oneself to such experiences. That account is inadequate to the phenomenon in question, because people show no more reluctance in the face of tragic than other good artworks. Indeed, they avidly seek out all artworks, including tragic ones. One might resign oneself to going to the dentist, but few people adopt to that experience the attitude commonly taken to artworks, which, after all, are not usually forced upon one by others or by the circumstances of life. Just as the considerations offered against the first horn of the dilemma remove some of its edge without disposing of it, so the arguments offered against its second horn, to the extent that they work, are finally unconvincing.

Understanding Art

Neither horn of the dilemma is vanquished. At this stage I recommend a new approach, one that calls into question the formulation of the problem. I suggest in this section that one should ask not, Why do people concern themselves with music that makes them feel sad? but instead, Why do people concern themselves with music? Part of the puzzle, I suggest, arises from too narrow a focus.

The problem posed by negative responses to artworks frequently seems to be presented as one concerning our interest in a subset of artworks. Radford says, "If there is a problem about sad music making people sad, because why then should they want to listen to it, there is no corresponding problem about why people would and would want to listen to happy music."[7] But there is a problem, as I see it, concerning happy music, though I admit the difficulty is less obvious. Much happy music is trite and boring. That a musical work expresses happiness is not, just like that, a good reason for wanting to listen to it, and if a person is addicted to such music his or her commitment might be no less puzzling than is that of the person who willingly listens to sad music. To see the puzzle as arising only in connection with a subset of artworks is to misconceive the problem and to do so in a way making it difficult to answer.

Whereas there are many motivations for an interest in music, to be interested in music "aesthetically," "for its own sake," is to aim at understanding a work, such as Beethoven's Symphony no. 5, for the piece it is. Those of us who have this concern have it because we derive pleasure from music in understanding it. Not every work affords pleasure when it is understood, though. To the contrary, it is just because some works are appreciated that they are avoided, for they are revealed to be overblown, lifeless, and mechanical in their predictability, or whatever. My point is a general one: much music presents a content such that the deeper one's understanding, the more enjoyable is the experience, and we value as great those works providing such enjoyment.

Now, if it is true that (many) people concern themselves with music for the sake of the enjoyment that comes with understanding it, and if it also is true that works dealing with "negative" emotions are no less worth understanding than those dealing with "positive" feelings, the listener should be as interested in the one kind of work as the other. And in either case, if the listener aims at understanding and appreciating the music, and if the emotional response is an aspect of the understanding she gains, then it is to be welcomed. If one desires comprehension, and if a response of sadness can indicate an appreciation of the nature of the given situation, just because it is appropriate to that situation, then the response, despite being negative, allows the satisfaction that goes with understanding. The response is not merely a by-product of the process of understanding; it is not merely a pleasant bonus or an irritant to be accepted with resignation. The response is not an incidental accompaniment but rather something integral to the understanding achieved. It is not something with which one puts up for the sake of understanding; it is an element in that under-

---

[7] Radford, "Muddy Waters," p. 249.

standing. If negative responses are no less an aspect of artistic appreciation than are positive responses, and if the concern lies with artistic understanding rather than, say, emotional titillation, and if understanding
requires effort and commitment, whatever emotions might arise in connection with it, then the question to be asked cannot narrow the focus to
the negative emotions without losing touch with the wider context in
which the explanation should be sought. Many people engage with
music for the enjoyment of understanding and appreciating it, or at least
in anticipation of its meriting these in an enjoyable way. Understanding
sometimes leads to responses, some of which are pleasant and some of
which are unpleasant. The enjoyment of appreciating art is not reducible
to the enjoyment of responding to it with pleasant emotions, no more
than it is inhibited by a negative emotional response; the enjoyment of
understanding is no less consistent with the one response than the other.

We pursue artworks that are liable to give rise to negative emotional
responses no less avidly than those likely to produce positive emotional
responses because what motivates our interest is a concern with locating
those artworks that merit understanding, and these are as likely to be
works causing negative responses as those causing positive ones. The
works to avoid are those that are unlikely to repay the effort of appreciation—works that are clichéd, banal, boring. Some works might generate
pleasant reactions to their expressive character, others unpleasant
ones, but the latter works are neither more nor less to be avoided than
the former if one is motivated to seek the pleasure that goes with
understanding rather than with mere titillation.

Personally, I avoid many films and books depicting gore and violence.
Equally, though, there are books and films I avoid no less assiduously
because I believe them to be happy in a trite, overly sentimental fashion.
Also, there are books and films I seek out though I know in advance that
they are gory or violent. The issue for me in these cases is neither that of
whether "negative" emotions are dealt with nor that of whether the work
might make me feel sad or depressed; it is, instead, whether I predict that
the work presents a content worth appreciating and understanding. The
distinction rests on my anticipated judgment of the work's artistic merits.
If it strikes me as worth the effort, I accept that what I understand, through
its very comprehension, might generate experiences that are not in themselves enjoyable. My attitude is not one of resignation, because I do want
to understand works that richly reward the effort involved.[8]

---

[8] I am not always so high-minded. Sometimes I choose mindless entertainment over the
artistically demanding (I have nothing against the pursuit of titillation as such). When I
do, I prefer those entertainments that I expect to amuse me or make me feel happy over
those I expect to make me sad. In the case of art, I doubt that its powerful attraction can
be explained merely as a mindless pursuit of emotional *frissons*.

Some individuals are not much interested in any art, and many of those who are interested in some kind of art are not much interested in all forms of art. But to love music from, say, the late eighteenth century is to be interested in understanding all such music if it rewards the effort required. For some (good) artworks, negative emotions come with the understanding we seek. These are not enjoyable emotions, but they are, for some people at least, an inevitable aspect of the understanding and appreciation they seek from art. The response would not be better for lacking this aspect because the response would, for the works and people concerned, not then be an understanding, appreciative one.

The view for which I have been arguing bears affinities with that presented by Nelson Goodman, though the brevity of Goodman's observations on the topic makes difficult their interpretation.[9] Goodman rejects as unacceptable any crude distinction between the emotional and the cognitive; emotions centrally involve propositional attitudes, usually beliefs, and are not reducible to raw feelings. Accordingly, an emotional response can provide evidence of a person's understanding (of a situation, say) no less clearly than would his or her descriptions. Negative responses to artworks—for example, the horror and revulsion we feel at Macbeth's murder of Duncan—are no less indicative of understanding than is a dispassionate account of the work. "In aesthetic experience, emotion positive or negative is a mode of sensitivity to a work. The problem of tragedy and the paradox of ugliness evaporates."[10]

Levinson acknowledges Goodman's argument but thinks it falls short of explaining why one should take the trouble to ascertain the properties of works that lead to negative emotions. But I think that Levinson does not give due weight here to Goodman's point that negative responses are no more problematic than positive ones, because both kinds of responses arise equally from an understanding engagement with the work. Goodman appears to reject, as I have, the approach that frames the problem as one arising peculiarly with respect to an interest taken in only some artworks, those liable to arouse negative responses. I read him as suggesting that the problem really is to be understood as one about why people concern themselves with art at all.

Life and Suffering

I have argued that the issue is not so much why we concern ourselves with a subset of artworks that lead us to feel sad as why we take pleasure in understanding art that might involve a negative response to some of

[9] Nelson Goodman, *Languages of Art* (New York: Bobbs-Merrill, 1968), pp. 248–51.
[10] Ibid., p. 250.

the properties of the given work. Someone might take the point but claim that it shifts, rather than answers, the problem with which we began. My earlier answer to the problem was that art is enjoyable through the understanding of it. Now, though, the problem is revived in this form: why should we find *that* enjoyable? Why do we enjoy understanding art, given that an aspect of that understanding sometimes can be unpleasant; and, more generally, given that an appreciation of art can require hard work and practice; and, finally, given that the understanding often does not serve obvious, practical goals? The answer to such a grand question lies beyond the scope both of my subject and my powers, but I cannot resist pursuing it a short distance.

Many people watch or listen to the daily news broadcasts (and do so knowing that much of the news will be depressing). Why? Presumably because they would rather know what is happening than not; they would rather know the worst than live in blissful ignorance. Much of what is reported in the news deals with events that do not touch one directly— accidents on freeways in foreign countries and the like—but one attends to the news despite this obvious fact. We are interested in understanding the actions of people and the complex products of human society not always for the sake of the benefits flowing to us from doing so, though there may be many such, but because such things have an abiding interest. Given the importance of information, it is not surprising that curiosity has considerable motivating power. Curiosity motivates us, I believe, even when it is not regarded as a means to some particular end. We are curious on occasions when no obvious, immediate, practical value derives from being so.

Our interest in art, I have suggested elsewhere, is a spin-off, activated by curiosity.[11] We are creatures concerned (up to a point) with understanding and appreciation for their own sakes, in the sense that not all the things that concern us are tied directly to specifiable, practical goals. An interest in art in general may have many practical consequences of value (as a source of knowledge, heightened moral sensibility, character development, and so on), and perhaps the arts would not be regarded as a good thing were this not so, but to be interested in art usually is to be interested in works approached not for the sake of their typicality but for that of their individuality. We are capable of finding enjoyment in attempting to comprehend such works in their particularity; to the extent that the identity of works is relative to context, an interest in their individuality involves a concern with the piece as of a genre, of an oeuvre, of a style, of a school, of an artistic period.

[11] Stephen Davies, *Definitions of Art* (Ithaca: Cornell University Press, 1990), pp. 57–62.

In reply to the question, Why do we enjoy art (and the news for that matter) if the experience sometimes is constituted in part by features leading, through our grasp of their character, to negative responses? I have said, "We just are like that." One way of elaborating that answer would be by explaining why we find interest in human action and the complex products of human agency. In turn, this would involve an account of human nature and psychology in terms of evolutionary theory, the demands of social life, and whatever else might be relevant. Rather than taking that course, I settle for emphasizing how much and how often we "just are like that." If the puzzle is one about the meaning of life (not merely about the importance of both art and the broadcast news), I might hope to be excused from answering it.

Loss, deprivation, suffering, pain, struggle, and discomfort—all are part of life. Sometimes these things are avoidable; sensible navigators on the ocean of existence give rocky outcrops a wide berth. But also, such things are, as it were, inherent to the medium of life rather than merely a part of its content that one might try to skirt. They come unavoidably with life itself, so the living of a life includes one's dealing with such things as an inescapable part of existence. (So it is that prudence, courage, fortitude, stalwartness, endurance, and commitment are numbered among the moral virtues, or are the stuff from which virtuous actions might be forged, and their opposites are counted as vices. If the world yielded without resistance to our every whim and desire, the virtues as we understand them could have no social significance, for there would be no occasion for the exhibition of the qualities of character they involve.) In this world, to choose life is also to choose loss, pain, and the like. And we do choose life, even at an age when we know what that choice includes. The evidence of attempted suicides suggests that pain, loneliness, grief, humiliation, and the like can be so acute that death is to be preferred to life. But suicide is far from the most common form of death overall. Suffering and discomfort are by no means always worse than death or unconsciousness. Sometimes they are preferable to sensory deprivation, or to being ignored, as is apparent from the behavior of children who, if they cannot attract attention to themselves in any other way, do so by being naughty, even knowing that their actions will lead to penalties.

Negative emotions and feelings are not unavoidably a part of life merely as the price of admission, as an unpleasant extra tolerated so long as it does not prevent our participation in the games that give us pleasure. They are more intimately elements in the activities giving our lives meaning and importance than this view suggests. Some of the projects providing the greatest fulfillment demand fearful risks and known costs. Yet people commit themselves cheerfully to intellectually and physically demanding professions, to intense personal relationships, to birthing and raising children, and so on—and they do so not entirely in ignorance of what the future holds in store. Often the hard work, pain, anxiety, and stress are so much a part of the project that it would no longer be the same project were their possibility removed. One expects to bring up children, not angels, so one expects all the difficulties and disappointments, as well as all the rewards, that go with trying to teach slowly maturing human beings how to become adults who might respect themselves and deserve the respect and affection of others. There is no gain without pain, as they say. The deepest satisfactions depend sometimes not just on what was gained but on how hard it was to attain.

These observations cannot be dismissed as covering merely the serious side of life. People race in cars at speed, crawl through mud and water in narrow tunnels in the bowels of the earth, wrestle with the intellectual problems posed by chess, crosswords, and the like, throw themselves off bridges with bits of elastic tied to their ankles, attempt time and again to improve their ability to hit a small ball into a slightly larger hole a quarter of a mile away, and so on and on. They do such things not always for money, or esteem, or fame, or glory, or because they have a duty to engage in such activities, or for the sake of their health and character development (though they may be mindful of such matters sometimes) but also, and mainly, out of love of the activity. These activities are engaged in for fun! Many involve unpleasantness in one way or another, if only as hard work directed to no obvious payout beyond what is found in the activity itself.

In some cases the unpleasant aspects might be regarded merely as inconveniences that must be tolerated, but in others the unpleasant side of the activity is integral to it—integral not in the sense that, masochistically, the unpleasantness is to be enjoyed for its own sake but, rather, in the sense that the activity found enjoyable would no longer be what it is if that unpleasantness (or the risk of it) were absent. For example, the danger faced by the mountaineer is not tolerated merely for the sake of the view from the top; if it were, the person would opt for a safe helicopter ride if she had the choice. The dedicated mountaineer's enjoyment is taken in the activity of climbing mountains. Now, to ask if climbing would be the more enjoyable if the climb were always without danger is to ask a strange question. Climbing on mountains is inherently dangerous, so it is not clear how to make sense of the question. And to ask if climbing would be more enjoyable for the person if she were always without fear is also to ask a far from straightforward question. If the enjoyment derived from climbing comes from meeting the demands of the activity, then the climber must display the requisite skills, and these include a proper assessment of the dangers posed by the mountain and, in view of this, the adoption of methods making the climb as safe as it can be, given the route, and so on. It is far from clear how someone could recognize the danger for what it is while never feeling fear, though the person might display the courage or nerve required to overcome that fear calmly. The fear comes from understanding the conditions of climbing, and it is that very same understanding that is the key to enjoying the exercise of the skills required in climbing (one among many of which is that of controlling one's own anxieties). The climber takes pleasure in mountaineering—in its challenge and so forth—and, if the activity were such that it might be climbing-in-a-context-in-which-fear-could-not-naturally-arise, then it would no longer be the climbing she enjoys; climbing of that kind just is not mountaineering, it might be said. To understand why the mountaineer takes on a scary sport is to understand how she can find enjoyment in a complex activity including among its elements the possibility of ever-present fear.

Why do people climb mountains for fun? For the same sort of reason they take an interest in the appreciation of music, or marry, or work at carpentry as a hobby. Because they choose the enjoyment that comes with taking charge of their own lives, even if that means taking on the negative as well as the positive constituents making life what it is. One's own life is what one does, and what happens to one, and what one makes of what happens to one, in the time between one's birth and death. A person who rehearsed too hard or waited too long for the right moment would find not that he was prepared for life but that the life he had lived was the life that consisted in preparing for something else, not the life he took himself to be preparing for. And a person who tried always to shun confrontation with pain and suffering would miss out on everything normally judged to make life worth living, while condemning himself to the sadness of realizing that the wait was in vain. At least some of the pleasure life can give comes from one's attempting with a degree of success to deal with one's situation and circumstances—controlling what can be controlled, accepting with grace and equanimity the unavoidable. If the appreciation of art is specially important in this process, it is so not because it is a training or a substitute for life (as sometimes is held) but because it is a celebration of the ways people engage with each other and the world in giving significance to their existence.

Index

Abbate, Carolyn, 50–53, 119n

Absolute music, 1–2, 13–14, 57–58, 155

Action, 75–76, 221; and character, 58, 62–72, 75–76, 118–25, 133–34, 137–50, 174–76; and cognitive content, 174–75; and composer, 121; and experience, 182–83; and imagination, 63–64, 121–22; and individuation, 122–23; and intention, 124–25; interpretation of, 119–21; music as, 182, 195; as occurring in present, 121; patterns of, 134, 142. *See also* Agency; Character; Musical attributes; Representation

Action-force, 140–41, 152. *See also* Agency

Affect. *See* Emotion; Expression

Agawu, Kofi: *Playing with Signs: A Semiotic Interpretation of Classic Music,* 28–32, 41–42

Agency, 7, 9; and action, 119–20, 125–26; and explanation, 119–20; external, 141; and imagination, 121–22; as indeterminate, 11–12, 67–68, 122–23, 125–28, 134, 136, 149–50, 229–30; and individuation, 122–23; and instrumentation, 115, 118, 122–23; as intermittent, 12, 133; and interpretation, 13, 135; and listener, 135–36; nineteenth-century view of, 132–33; and protagonist, 141; and succession of events, 131, 135, 137–39,

157–58, 162–63, 170, 174–75; and voice, 133. *See also* Action; Character; Musical attributes; Representation

Albinoni, Tomaso: Adagio for Organ and Strings, 238

Alfie, 24–25n

Allenbrook, Wye Jameson, 43n

Alperson, Philip, 23n

Alston, William, 221n

Analysis, 2–3, 8, 11, 45, 107; and anthropomorphism, 10–11, 114–19, 123–24, 129n, 130; as autonomous, 111; and criticism, 10–11, 105–6; and description, 106, 108–11, 114–16; and explanation, 116, 119–20; and expression, 176–77; feminist, 3; limitations of, 105–6; mathematical models, 2–3. *See also* Anthropomorphism; Theory

Animism. *See* Anthropomorphism

Anscombe, G. E. M., 119n

Anthropomorphism, 7, 10–11, 114, 119, 123, 210; in analysis, 10–11, 114–19, 123–24, 129n, 130; and dramatic structure, 128–30; and exemplification, 36–40; and expression, 63–66, 162–63, 170–73; and metaphor, 206–12; and musical attributes, 137–38, 195–96. *See also* Agency; Analysis; Hope; Nostalgia; Sadness